*A*

# Short History

*Of*

# Scotland

Andrew Lang

Merchant Books

1911

# CONTENTS

## CHAPTER XVIII.

## CHAPTER XIX.

## CHAPTER XX.

## CHAPTER XXI.

## CHAPTER XXII.

## CHAPTER XXIII.

## CHAPTER XXIV.

## CHAPTER XXV.

# CHAPTER I

# Scotland *and the* Romans

If we could see in a magic mirror the country now called Scotland as it was when the Romans under Agricola (81 A.D.) crossed the Border, we should recognise little but the familiar hills and mountains. The rivers, in the plains, overflowed their present banks; dense forests of oak and pine, haunted by great red deer, elks, and boars, covered land that has long been arable. There were lakes and lagoons where for centuries there have been fields of corn. On the oldest sites of our towns were groups of huts made of clay and wattle, and dominated, perhaps, by the large stockaded house of the tribal prince. In the lochs, natural islands, or artificial islets made of piles (crannogs), afforded standing-ground and protection to villages, if indeed these lake-dwellings are earlier in Scotland than the age of war that followed the withdrawal of the Romans.

The natives were far beyond the savage stage of culture. They lived in an age of iron tools and weapons and of wheeled vehicles; and were in what is called the Late Celtic condition of art and culture, familiar to us from beautiful objects in bronze work, more commonly found in Ireland than in Scotland, and from the oldest Irish romances and poems.

In these "epics" the manners much resemble those described by Homer. Like his heroes, the men in the Cuchullain sagas fight from light chariots, drawn by two ponies, and we know that so fought the tribes in Scotland encountered by Agricola the Roman General (81-85 A.D.) It is even said in the Irish epics that Cuchullain learned his chariotry in *Alba*—that is, in our Scotland.[1] The warriors had "mighty limbs and flaming hair," says Tacitus. Their weapons were heavy iron swords, in bronze sheaths beautifully decorated, and iron-headed

---

[1] A good example of these Celtic romances is 'The Tain Bo Cualgne.'

spears; they had large round bronze-studded shields, and battle-axes. The dress consisted of two upper garments: first, the smock, of linen or other fabric—in battle, often of tanned hides of animals,—and the mantle, or plaid, with its brooch. Golden torques and heavy gold bracelets were worn by the chiefs; the women had bronze ornaments with brightly coloured enamelled decoration.

Agriculture was practised, and corn was ground in the circular querns of stone, of which the use so long survived. The women span and wove the gay smocks and darker cloaks of the warriors.

Of the religion, we only know that it was a form of polytheism; that sacrifices were made, and that Druids existed; they were soothsayers, magicians, perhaps priests, and were attendant on kings.

Such were the people in Alba whom we can dimly descry around Agricola's fortified frontier between the firths of Forth and Clyde, about 81-82 A.D. When Agricola pushed north of the Forth and Tay he still met men who had considerable knowledge of the art of war. In his battle at Mons Graupius (perhaps at the junction of Isla and Tay), his cavalry had the better of the native chariotry in the plain; and the native infantry, descending from their position on the heights, were attacked by his horsemen in their attempt to assail his rear. But they were swift of foot, the woods sheltered and the hills defended them. He made no more effectual pursuit than Cumberland did at Culloden.

Agricola was recalled by Domitian after seven years' warfare, and his garrisons did not long hold their forts on his lines or frontier, which stretched across the country from Forth to Clyde; roughly speaking, from Graham's Dyke, east of Borrowstounnis on the Firth of Forth, to Old Kilpatrick on Clyde. The region is now full of coal-mines, foundries, and villages; but excavations at Bar Hill, Castlecary, and Roughcastle disclose traces of Agricola's works, with their earthen ramparts. The Roman station at Camelon, north-west of Falkirk, was connected with the southern passes of the Highland hills by a road with a chain of forts. The remains of Roman pottery at Camelon are of the first century.

Two generations after Agricola, about 140-145, the Roman Governor, Lollius Urbicus, refortified the line of Forth to Clyde with a wall of sods and a ditch, and forts much larger than those constructed by Agricola. His line, "the Antonine Vallum," had its works on commanding ridges; and fire-signals, in case of attack by the natives, flashed the news "from one sea to the other sea," while the troops of occupation could be provisioned from the Roman fleet. Judging by the coins found by the excavators, the line was abandoned about 190, and the forts were wrecked and dismantled, perhaps by the retreating Romans.

After the retreat from the Antonine Vallum, about 190, we hear of the vigorous "unrest" of the Meatæ and Caledonians; the latter people are said, on very poor authority, to have been little better than savages. Against them Severus (208) made an expedition indefinitely far to the north, but the enemy shunned a general engagement, cut off small detachments, and caused the Romans terrible losses in this march to a non-existent Moscow.

Not till 306 do we hear of the Picts, about whom there is infinite learning but little knowledge. They must have spoken Gaelic by Severus's time (208), whatever their original language; and were long recognised in Galloway, where the hill and river names are Gaelic.

The later years of the Romans, who abandoned Britain in 410, were perturbed by attacks of the Scoti (Scots) from Ireland, and it is to a settlement in Argyll of "Dalriadic" Scots from Ireland about 500 A.D. that our country owes the name of Scotland.

Rome has left traces of her presence on Scottish soil—vestiges of the forts and vallum wall between the firths; a station rich in antiquities under the Eildons at Newstead; another, Ardoch, near Sheriffmuir; a third near Solway Moss (Birrenswark); and others less extensive, with some roads extending towards the Moray Firth; and a villa at Musselburgh, found in the reign of James VI.[2]

---

[2] The best account of Roman military life in Scotland, from the time of Agricola to the invasion by Lollius Urbicus (140-158 A.D.), may be studied in Mr Curie's 'A Roman Frontier Post and Its People' (Maclehose, Glasgow, 1911). The relics, weapons, arms, pottery, and armour of Roman men, and the ornaments of the native women, are here beautifully reproduced. Dr Macdonald's excellent work, 'The Roman Wall in Scotland' (Maclehose, 1911), is also most interesting and instructive.

# CHAPTER II

# Christianity—The Rival Kingdoms

To the Scots, through St Columba, who, about 563, settled in Iona, and converted the Picts as far north as Inverness, we owe the introduction of Christianity, for though the Roman Church of St Ninian (397), at Whithern in Galloway, left embers of the faith not extinct near Glasgow, St Kentigern's country, till Columba's time, the rites of Christian Scotland were partly of the Celtic Irish type, even after St Wilfrid's victory at the Synod of Whitby (664).

St Columba himself was of the royal line in Ulster, was learned, as learning was then reckoned, and, if he had previously been turbulent, he now desired to spread the Gospel. With twelve companions he settled in Iona, established his cloister of cells, and journeyed to Inverness, the capital of Pictland. Here his miracles overcame the magic of the King's druids; and his Majesty, Brude, came into the fold, his people following him. Columba was no less of a diplomatist than of an evangelist. In a crystal he saw revealed the name of the rightful king of the Dalriad Scots in Argyll—namely, Aidan—and in 575, at Drumceat in North Ireland, he procured the recognition of Aidan, and brought the King of the Picts also to confess Aidan's independent royalty.

In the 'Life of Columba,' by Adamnan, we get a clear and complete view of everyday existence in the Highlands during that age. We are among the red deer, and the salmon, and the cattle in the hills, among the second-sighted men, too, of whom Columba was far the foremost. We see the saint's inkpot upset by a clumsy but enthusiastic convert; we even make acquaintance with the old white pony of the monastery, who mourned when St Columba was dying; while among secular men we observe the differences in rank, measured by degrees of wealth in cattle. Many centuries elapse before, in Froissart, we find a picture of Scotland so distinct as that painted by Adamnan.

The discipline of St Columba was of the monastic model. There were settlements of clerics in fortified villages; the clerics were a kind of monks, with more regard for abbots than for their many bishops, and with peculiar tonsures, and a peculiar way of reckoning the date of Easter. Each missionary was popularly called a Saint, and the *Kil*, or cell, of many a Celtic missionary survives in hundreds of place-names.

The salt-water Loch Leven in Argyll was on the west the south frontier of "Pictland," which, on the east, included all the country north of the Firth of Forth. From Loch Leven south to Kintyre, a large cantle, including the isles, was the land of the Scots from Ireland, the Dalriadic kingdom. The south-west, from Dumbarton, including our modern Cumberland and Westmorland, was named Strathclyde, and was peopled by British folk, speaking an ancient form of Welsh. On the east, from Ettrick forest into Lothian, the land was part of the early English kingdom of Bernicia; here the invading Angles were already settled—though river-names here remain Gaelic, and hill-names are often either Gaelic or Welsh. The great Northern Pictland was divided into seven provinces, or sub-kingdoms, while there was an over-King, or Ardrigh, with his capital at Inverness and, later, in Angus or Forfarshire. The country about Edinburgh was partly English, partly Cymric or Welsh. The south-west corner, Galloway, was called Pictish, and was peopled by Gaelic-speaking tribes.

In the course of time and events the dynasty of the Argyll Scoti from Ireland gave its name to Scotland, while the English element gave its language to the Lowlands; it was adopted by the Celtic kings of the whole country and became dominant, while the Celtic speech withdrew into the hills of the north and northwest.

The nation was thus evolved out of alien and hostile elements, Irish, Pictish, Gaelic, Cymric, English, and on the northern and western shores, Scandinavian.

# CHAPTER III

# Early Wars *of* Races

In a work of this scope, it is impossible to describe all the wars between the petty kingdoms peopled by races of various languages, which occupied Scotland. In 603, in the wild moors at Degsastane, between the Liddel burn and the passes of the Upper Tyne, the English Aethelfrith of Deira, with an army of the still pagan ancestors of the Borderers, utterly defeated Aidan, King of Argyll, with the Christian converted Scots. Henceforth, for more than a century, the English between Forth and Humber feared neither Scot of the west nor Pict of the north.

On the death of Aethelfrith (617), the Christian west and north exercised their influences; one of Aethelfrith's exiled sons married a Pictish princess, and became father of a Pictish king, another, Oswald, was baptised at Iona; and the new king of the northern English of Lothian, Edwin, was converted by Paullinus (627), and held Edinburgh as his capital. Later, after an age of war and ruin, Oswald, the convert of Iona, restored Christianity in northern England; and, after his fall, his brother, Oswiu, consolidated the north English. In 685 Oswiu's son Egfrith crossed the Forth and invaded Pictland with a Northumbrian army, but was routed with great loss, and was slain at Nectan's Mere, in Forfarshire. Thenceforth, till 761, the Picts were dominant, as against Scots and north English, Angus MacFergus being then their leader (731-761).

Now the invaders and settlers from Scandinavia, the Northmen on the west coast, ravaged the Christian Scots of the west, and burned Iona: finally, in 844-860, Kenneth MacAlpine of Kintyre, a Scot of Dalriada on the paternal, a Pict on the mother's side, defeated the Picts and obtained their throne. By Pictish law the crown descended in the maternal line, which probably facilitated the coronation of Kenneth. To the Scots and "to all Europe" he was a Scot; to the Picts, as son of a royal Pictish mother, he was a Pict. With him, at all events, Scots and Picts were interfused, and there began the *Scottish* dynasty, supplanting the Pictish, though it is only in popular tales that the Picts were exterminated.

Owing to pressure from the Northmen sea-rovers in the west, the capital and the seat of the chief bishop, under Kenneth MacAlpine (844-860), were moved eastwards from Iona to Scone, near Perth, and after an interval at Dunkeld, to St Andrews in Fife.

The line of Kenneth MacAlpine, though disturbed by quarrels over the succession, and by Northmen in the west, north, and east, none the less in some way "held a good grip o' the gear" against Vikings, English of Lothian, and Welsh of Strathclyde. In consequence of a marriage with a Welsh princess of Strathclyde, or Cumberland, a Scottish prince, Donald, brother of Constantine II, became king of that realm (908), and his branch of the family of MacAlpin held Cumbria for a century.

## English Claims Over Scotland

In 924 the first claim by an English king, Edward, to the over-lordship of Scotland appears in the Anglo-Saxon Chronicle. The entry contains a manifest error, and the topic causes war between modern historians, English and Scottish. In fact, there are several such entries of Scottish acceptance of English suzerainty under Constantine II, and later, but they all end in the statement, "this held not long." The "submission" of Malcolm I to Edmund (945) is not a submission but an alliance; the old English word for "fellow-worker," or "ally," designates Malcolm as fellow-worker with Edward of England.

This word (midwyrhta) was translated *fidelis* (one who gives fealty) in the Latin of English chroniclers two centuries later, but Malcolm I held Cumberland as an ally, not as a subject prince of England. In 1092 an English chronicle represents Malcolm III as holding Cumberland "by conquest."

The main fact is that out of these and similar dim transactions arose the claims of Edward I to the over-lordship of Scotland,—claims that were urged by Queen Elizabeth's minister, Cecil, in 1568, and were boldly denied by Maitland of Lethington. From these misty pretensions came the centuries of war that made the hardy character of the folk of Scotland.[3]

# The Scottish Acquisition *of* Lothian

We cannot pretend within our scope to follow chronologically "the fightings and flockings of kites and crows," in "a wolf-age, a war-age," when the Northmen from all Scandinavian lands, and the Danes, who had acquired much of Ireland, were flying at the throat of England and hanging on the flanks of Scotland; while the Britons of Strathclyde struck in, and the Scottish kings again and again raided or sought to occupy the fertile region of Lothian between Forth and Tweed. If the dynasty of MacAlpin could win rich Lothian, with its English-speaking folk, they were "made men," they held the granary of the North. By degrees and by methods not clearly defined they did win the Castle of the Maidens, the acropolis of Dunedin, Edinburgh; and fifty years later, in some way, apparently by the sword, at the battle of Carham (1018), in which a Scottish king of Cumberland fought by his side, Malcolm II took possession of Lothian, the whole south-east region, by this time entirely anglified, and this was the greatest step in the making of Scotland. The Celtic dynasty now held the most fertile district between Forth and Tweed, a district already English in blood and speech, the centre and focus of the English civilisation accepted by the Celtic kings. Under this Malcolm, too, his grandson, Duncan, became ruler of Strathclyde—that is, practically, of Cumberland.

Malcolm is said to have been murdered at haunted Glamis, in Forfarshire, in 1034; the room where he died is pointed out by legend in the ancient castle. His rightful heir, by the strange system of the Scots, should have been, not his own grandson, Duncan, but the grandson of Kenneth III. The rule was that the crown went alternately to a descendant of the House of Constantine (863-877), son of Kenneth MacAlpine, and to a descendant of Constantine's brother, Aodh (877-888). These alternations went on till the crowning of Malcolm II (1005-1034), and then ceased, for Malcolm II had slain the unnamed male heir of the House of Aodh, a son of Boedhe, in order to open the succession to his own grandson, "the gracious Duncan."

---

[3] For the Claims of Supremacy see Appendix C. to vol. i. of my 'History of Scotland,' pp. 496-499.

Boedhe had left a daughter, Gruach; she had by the Mormaor, or under-king of the province of Murray, a son, Lulach. On the death of the Mormaor she married Macbeth, and when Macbeth slew Duncan (1040), he was removing a usurper—as he understood it—and he ruled in the name of his stepson, Lulach. The power of Duncan had been weakened by repeated defeats at the hands of the Northmen under Thorfinn. In 1057 Macbeth was slain in battle at Lumphanan, in Aberdeenshire, and Malcolm Canmore, son of Duncan, after returning from England, whither he had fled from Macbeth, succeeded to the throne. But he and his descendants for long were opposed by the House of Murray, descendants of Lulach, who himself had died in 1058.

The world will always believe Shakespeare's version of these events, and suppose the gracious Duncan to have been a venerable old man, and Macbeth an ambitious Thane, with a bloodthirsty wife, he himself being urged on by the predictions of witches. He was, in fact, Mormaor of Murray, and upheld the claims of his stepson Lulach, who was son of a daughter of the wrongfully extruded House of Aodh.

Malcolm Canmore, Duncan's grandson, on the other hand, represented the European custom of direct lineal succession against the ancient Scots' mode.

CHAPTER IV

# Malcolm Canmore–Norman Conquest

he reign of Malcolm Canmore (1057-1093) brought Scotland into closer connection with western Europe and western Christianity. The Norman Conquest (1066) increased the tendency of the English-speaking people of Lothian to acquiesce in the rule of a Celtic king, rather than in that of the adventurers who followed William of Normandy. Norman operations did not at first reach Cumberland, which Malcolm held; and, on the death of his Norse wife, the widow of Duncan's foe, Thorfinn (she left a son, Duncan), Malcolm allied himself with the English Royal House by marrying Margaret, sister of Eadgar Ætheling, then engaged in the hopeless effort to rescue northern England from the Normans. The dates are confused: Malcolm may have won the beautiful sister of Edgar, rightful king of England, in 1068, or at the time (1070) of his raid, said to have been of savage ferocity, into Northumberland, and his yet more cruel reprisals for Gospatric's harrying of Cumberland. In either case, St Margaret's biographer, who had lived at her Court, whether or not he was her Confessor, Turgot, represents the Saint as subduing the savagery of Malcolm, who passed wakeful nights in weeping for his sins. A lover of books, which Malcolm could not read, an expert in "the delicate, and gracious, and bright works of women," Margaret brought her own gentleness and courtesy among a rude people, built the abbey church of Dunfermline, and presented the churches with many beautiful golden reliquaries and fine sacramental plate.

In 1072, to avenge a raid of Malcolm (1070), the Conqueror, with an army and a fleet, came to Abernethy on Tay, where Malcolm, in exchange for English manors, "became his man" *for them*, and handed over his son Duncan as a hostage for peace. The English view is that Malcolm became William's "man for all that he had"—or for all south of Tay.

After various raidings of northern England, and after the death of the Conqueror, Malcolm renewed, in Lothian, the treaty of Abernethy, being secured in his twelve English manors (1091). William Rufus then took and fortified Carlisle, seized part of Malcolm's lands in Cumberland, and summoned him to Gloucester, where the two Kings, after all, quarrelled and did not meet. No sooner had Malcolm returned home than he led an army into Northumberland, where he was defeated and slain, near Alnwick (Nov. 13, 1093). His son Edward fell with him, and his wife, St Margaret, died in Edinburgh Castle: her body, under cloud of night, was carried through the host of rebel Celts and buried at Dunfermline.

Margaret, a beautiful and saintly Englishwoman, had been the ruling spirit of the reign in domestic and ecclesiastical affairs. She had civilised the Court, in matters of costume at least; she had read books to the devoted Malcolm, who could not read; and he had been her interpreter in her discussions with the Celtic-speaking clergy, whose ideas of ritual differed from her own. The famous Culdees, originally ascetic hermits, had before this day united in groups living under canonical rules, and, according to English observers, had ceased to be bachelors. Masses are said to have been celebrated by them in some "barbarous rite"; Saturday was Sabbath; on Sunday men worked. Lent began, not on Ash Wednesday, but on the Monday following. We have no clearer account of the Culdee peculiarities that St Margaret reformed. The hereditary tenure of benefices by lay protectors she did not reform, but she restored the ruined cells of Iona, and established *hospitia* for pilgrims. She was decidedly unpopular with her Celtic subjects, who now made a struggle against English influences.

In the year of her death died Fothadh, the last Celtic bishop of St Andrews, and the Celtic clergy were gradually superseded and replaced by monks of English name, English speech, and English ideas—or rather the ideas of western Europe. Scotland, under Margaret's influence, became more Catholic; the celibacy of the clergy was more strictly enforced (it had almost lapsed), but it will be observed throughout that, of all western Europe, Scotland was least overawed by Rome. Yet for centuries the Scottish Church was, in a peculiar degree, "the daughter of Rome," for not till about 1470 had she a Metropolitan, the Archbishop of St Andrews.

On the deaths, in one year, of Malcolm, Margaret, and Fothadh, the last Celtic bishop of St Andrews, the see for many years was vacant or merely filled by transient bishops. York and Canterbury were at feud for their superiority over the Scottish Church; and the other sees were not constituted and provided with bishops till the years 1115 (Glasgow), 1150,—Argyll not having a bishop till 1200. In the absence of a Metropolitan, episcopal elections had to be confirmed at Rome, which would grant no Metropolitan, but forbade the Archbishop of York to claim a superiority which would have implied, or prepared the way for, English superiority over Scotland. Meanwhile the expenses and delays of appeals from bishops direct to Rome did not stimulate the affection of the Scottish "daughter of Rome." The rights of the chapters of the Cathedrals to elect their bishops, and other appointments to ecclesiastical offices, in course of time were transferred to the Pope, who negotiated with the king, and thus all manner of jobbery increased, the nobles influencing the king in favour of their own needy younger sons, and the Pope being amenable to various secular persuasions, so that in every way the relations of Scotland with the Holy Father were anomalous and irksome.

Scotland was, indeed, a country predestined to much ill fortune, to tribulations against which human foresight could erect no defence. But the marriage of the Celtic Malcolm with the English Margaret, and the friendly arrival of great nobles from the south, enabled Scotland to receive the new ideas of feudal law in pacific fashion. They were not violently forced upon the English-speaking people of Lothian.

# Dynasty *of* Malcolm

On the death of Malcolm the contest for the Crown lay between his brother, Donald Ban, supported by the Celts; his son Duncan by his first wife, a Norse woman (Duncan being then a hostage at the English Court, who was backed by William Rufus); and thirdly, Malcolm's eldest son by Margaret, Eadmund, the favourite with the anglicised south of the country. Donald Ban, after a brief period of power, was driven out by Duncan (1094); Duncan was then slain by the Celts (1094). Donald was next restored, north of Forth, Eadmund ruling in the south, but was dispossessed and blinded by Malcolm's son Eadgar, who reigned for ten years (1097-1107), while Eadmund died in an English cloister. Eadgar had trouble enough on all sides, but the process of anglicising continued, under himself, and later, under his brother, Alexander I, who ruled north of Forth and Clyde; while the youngest brother, David, held Lothian and Cumberland, with the title of Earl. The sister of those sons of Malcolm, Eadgyth (Matilda), married Henry I of England in 1100. There seemed a chance that, north of Clyde and Forth, there would be a Celtic kingdom; while Lothian and Cumbria would be merged in England. Alexander was mainly engaged in fighting the Moray claimants of his crown in the north and in planting his religious houses, notably St Andrews, with English Augustinian canons from York. Canterbury and York contended for ecclesiastical superiority over Scotland; after various adventures, Robert, the prior of the Augustinians at Scone, was made Bishop of St Andrews, being consecrated by Canterbury, in 1124; while York consecrated David's bishop in Glasgow. Thanks to the quarrels of the sees of York and Canterbury, the Scottish clergy managed to secure their ecclesiastical independence from either English see; and became, finally, the most useful combatants in the long struggle for the independence of the nation. Rome, on the whole, backed that cause. The Scottish Catholic churchmen, in fact, pursued the old patriotic policy of resistance to England till the years just preceding the Reformation, when the people leaned to the reformed doctrines, and when Scottish national freedom was endangered more by France than by England.

# CHAPTER V

# David I & His Times

With the death of Alexander I (April 25, 1124) and the accession of his brother, David I, the deliberate Royal policy of introducing into Scotland English law and English institutions, as modified by the Norman rulers, was fulfilled. David, before Alexander's death, was Earl of the most English part of Lothian, the country held by Scottish kings, and Cumbria; and resided much at the court of his brother-in-law, Henry I. He associated, when Earl, with nobles of Anglo-Norman race and language, such as Moreville, Umfraville, Somerville, Gospatric, Bruce, Balliol, and others; men with a stake in both countries, England and Scotland. On coming to the throne, David endowed these men with charters of lands in Scotland. With him came a cadet of the great Anglo-Breton House of FitzAlan, who obtained the hereditary office of Seneschal or *Steward* of Scotland. His patronymic, FitzAlan, merged in Stewart (later Stuart), and the family cognizance, the *fesse chequy* in azure and argent, represents the Board of Exchequer. The earliest Stewart holdings of land were mainly in Renfrewshire; those of the Bruces were in Annandale. These two Anglo-Norman houses between them were to found the Stewart dynasty.

The wife of David, Matilda, widow of Simon de St Liz, was heiress of Waltheof, sometime the Conqueror's Earl in Northumberland; and to gain, through that connection, Northumberland for himself was the chief aim of David's foreign policy,—an aim fertile in contentions.

We have not space to disentangle the intricacies of David's first great domestic struggles; briefly, there was eternal dispeace caused by the Celts, headed by claimants to the throne, the MacHeths, representing the rights of Lulach, the ward of Macbeth.[4] In 1130 the Celts were defeated, and their leader, Angus, Earl of Moray, fell in fight near the North Esk in Forfarshire. His brother, Malcolm, by aid of David's Anglo-Norman friends, was taken and imprisoned in Roxburgh Castle. The result of this rising was that David declared the great and ancient Celtic Earldom of Moray—the home of his dynastic Celtic rivals—forfeit to the Crown. He planted the region with English, Anglo-Norman, and Lowland landholders, a great step in the anglicisation of his kingdom. Thereafter, for several centuries, the strength of the Celts lay in the west in Moidart, Knoydart, Morar, Mamore, Lochaber, and Kintyre, and in the western islands, which fell into the hands of "the sons of Somerled," the Macdonalds.

In 1135-1136, on the death of Henry I, David, backing his own niece, Matilda, as Queen of England in opposition to Stephen, crossed the Border in arms, but was bought off. His son Henry received the Honour of Huntingdom, with the Castle of Carlisle, and a vague promise of consideration of his claim to Northumberland. In 1138, after a disturbed interval, David led the whole force of his realm, from Orkney to Galloway, into Yorkshire. His Anglo-Norman friends, the Balliols and Bruces, with the Archbishop of York, now opposed him and his son Prince Henry. On August 22, 1138, at Cowton Moor, near Northallerton, was fought the great battle, named from the huge English sacred banner, "The Battle of the Standard."

In a military sense, the fact that here the men-at-arms and knights of England fought as dismounted infantry, their horses being held apart in reserve, is notable as preluding to the similar English tactics in their French wars of the fourteenth and fifteenth centuries.

Thus arrayed, the English received the impetuous charge of the wild Galloway men, not in armour, who claimed the right to form the van, and broke through the first line only to die beneath the spears of the second. But Prince David with his heavy cavalry scattered the force opposed to him, and stampeded the horses of the English that were held in reserve. This should have been fatal to the English, but Henry, like Rupert at Marston Moor, pursued too far, and the discipline of the Scots was broken by the cry that their King had fallen, and they fled. David fought his way to Carlisle in a series of rearguard actions, and at Carlisle was joined by Prince Henry with the remnant of his men-at-arms. It was no decisive victory for England.

---

[4] Lord Reay, according to the latest book on Scottish peerages, represents these MacHeths or Mackays.

In the following year (1139) David got what he wanted. His son Henry, by peaceful arrangement, received the Earldom of Northumberland, without the two strong places, Bamborough and Newcastle.

Through the anarchic weakness of Stephen's reign, Scotland advanced in strength and civilisation despite a Celtic rising headed by a strange pretender to the rights of the MacHeths, a "brother Wimund"; but all went with the death of David's son, Prince Henry, in 1152. Of the prince's three sons, the eldest, Malcolm, was but ten years old; next came his brothers William ("the Lion") and little David, Earl of Huntingdon. From this David's daughters descended the chief claimants to the Scottish throne in 1292—namely, Balliol, Bruce, and Comyn: the last also was descended, in the female line, from King Donald Ban, son of Malcolm Canmore.

David had done all that man might do to settle the crown on his grandson Malcolm; his success meant that standing curse of Scotland, "Woe to the kingdom whose king is a child,"—when, in a year, David died at Carlisle (May 24, 1153).

## Scotland Becomes Feudal

The result of the domestic policy of David was to bring all accessible territory under the social and political system of western Europe, "the Feudal System." Its principles had been perfectly familiar to Celtic Scotland, but had rested on a body of traditional customs (as in Homeric Greece), rather than on written laws and charters signed and sealed. Among the Celts the local tribe had been, theoretically, the sole source of property in land. In proportion as they were near of kin to the recognised tribal chief, families held lands by a tenure of three generations; but if they managed to acquire abundance of oxen, which they let out to poorer men for rents in kind and labour, they were apt to turn the lands which they held only temporarily, "in possession," into real permanent *property*. The poorer tribesmen paid rent in labour or "services," also in supplies of food and manure.

The Celtic tenants also paid military service to their superiors. The remotest kinsmen of each lord of land, poor as they might be, were valued for their swords, and were billeted on the unfree or servile tenants, who gave them free quarters.

In the feudal system of western Europe these old traditional customs had long been modified and stereotyped by written charters. The King gave gifts of land to his kinsmen or officers, who were bound to be "faithful" (*fideles*); in return the inferior did homage, while he received protection. From grade to grade of rank and wealth each inferior did homage to and received protection from his superior, who was also his judge. In this process, what had been the Celtic tribe became the new "thanage"; the Celtic king (*righ*) of the tribe became the thane; the province or group of tribes (say Moray) became the earldom; the Celtic Mormaer of the province became the earl; and the Crown appointed *vice-comites*, sub-earls, that is sheriffs, who administered the King's justice in the earldom.

But there were regions, notably the west Highlands and isles, where the new system penetrated slowly and with difficulty through a mountainous and almost townless land. The law, and written leases, "came slowly up that way."

Under David, where his rule extended, society was divided broadly into three classes—Nobles, Free, Unfree. All holders of "a Knight's fee," or part of one, holding by *free* service, hereditarily, and by charter, constituted the *communitas* of the realm (we are to hear of the *communitas* later), and were free, noble, or gentle,—men of coat armour. The "ignoble," "not noble," men with no charter from the Crown, or Earl, Thane, or Church, were, if lease-holders, though not "noble," still "free." Beneath them were the "unfree" *nativi*, sold or given with the soil.

The old Celtic landholders were not expropriated, as a rule, except where Celtic risings, in Galloway and Moray, were put down, and the lands were left in the King's hands. Often, when we find territorial surnames of families, "*de*" "of" this place or that,—the lords are really of Celtic blood with Celtic names; disguised under territorial titles; and finally disused. But in Galloway and Ayrshire the ruling Celtic name, Kennedy, remains Celtic, while the true Highlands of the west and northwest retained their native magnates. Thus the Anglicisation, except in very rebellious regions, was gradual. There was much less expropriation of the Celt than disguising of the Celt under new family names and regulation of the Celt under written charters and leases.

# Church Lands

David I was, according to James VI, nearly five centuries later, "a sair saint for the Crown." He gave Crown-lands in the southern lowlands to the religious orders with their priories and abbeys; for example, Holyrood, Melrose, Jedburgh, Kelso, and Dryburgh—centres of learning and art and of skilled agriculture. Probably the best service of the regular clergy to the State was its orderliness and attention to agriculture, for the monasteries did not, as in England, produce many careful chroniclers and historians.

Each abbey had its lands divided into baronies, captained by a lay "Church baron" to lead its levies in war. The civil centre of the barony was the great farm or grange, with its mill, for in the thirteenth century the Lowlands had water-mills which to the west Highlands were scarcely known in 1745, when the Highland husbandmen were still using the primitive hand-quern of two circular stones. Near the mill was a hamlet of some forty cottages; each head of a family had a holding of eight or nine acres and pasturage for two cows, and paid a small money rent and many arduous services to the Abbey.

The tenure of these cottars was, and under lay landlords long remained, extremely precarious; but the tenure of the "bonnet laird" (*hosbernus*) was hereditary. Below even the free cottars were the unfree serfs or *nativi*, who were handed over, with the lands they tilled, to the abbeys by benefactors: the Church was forward in emancipating these serfs; nor were lay landlords backward, for the freed man was useful as a spear-man in war.

We have only to look at the many now ruined abbeys of the Border to see the extent of civilisation under David I, and the relatively peaceful condition, then, of that region which later became the cockpit of the English wars, and the home of the raiding clans, Scotts, Elliots, and Armstrongs, Bells, Nixons, Robsons, and Croziers.

# The Burghs

David and his son and successor, William the Lion, introduced a stable middle and urban class by fostering, confirming, and regulating the rights, privileges, and duties of the already existing free towns. These became *burghs*, royal, seignorial, or ecclesiastical. In origin the towns may have been settlements that grew up under the shelter of a military castle. Their fairs, markets, rights of trading, internal organisation, and primitive police, were now, mainly under William the Lion, David's successor, regulated by charters; the burghers obtained the right to elect their own magistrates, and held their own burgh-courts; all was done after the English model. As the State had its "good men" (*probi homines*), who formed its recognised "community," so had the borough. Not by any means all dwellers in a burgh were free burghers; these free burghers had to do service in guarding the royal castle—later this was commuted for a payment in money. Though with power to elect their own chief magistrate, the burghers commonly took as Provost the head of some friendly local noble family, in which the office was apt to become practically hereditary. The noble was the leader and protector of the town. As to police, the burghers, each in his turn, provided men to keep watch and ward from curfew bell to cock-crow. Each ward in the town had its own elected Bailie. Each burgh had exclusive rights of trading in its area, and of taking toll on merchants coming within its *Octroi*. An association of four burghs, Berwick, Roxburgh, Edinburgh, and Stirling, was the root of the existing "Convention of Burghs."

# Justice

In early societies, justice is, in many respects, an affair to be settled between the kindreds of the plaintiff, so to speak, and the defendant. A man is wounded, killed, robbed, wronged in any way; his kin retaliate on the offender and *his* kindred. The blood-feud, the taking of blood for blood, endured for centuries in Scotland after the peace of the whole realm became, under David I, "the King's peace." Homicides, for example, were very frequently pardoned by Royal grace, but "the pardon was of no avail unless it had been issued with the full knowledge of the kin of the slaughtered man, who otherwise retained their *legal* right of vengeance on the homicide." They might accept pecuniary compensation, the blood-fine, or they might not, as in Homer's time.[5] At all events, under David, offences became offences against the King, not merely against this or that kindred. David introduced the "Judgment of the Country" or *Visnet del Pais* for

---

[5] 'Iliad,' xviii. 496-500.

the settlement of pleas. Every free man, in his degree, was "tried by his peers," but the old ordeal by fire and Trial by Combat or duel were not abolished. Nor did "compurgation" cease wholly till Queen Mary's reign. A powerful man, when accused, was then attended at his trial by hosts of armed backers. Men so unlike each other as Knox, Bothwell, and Lethington took advantage of this usage. All lords had their own Courts, but murder, rape, arson, and robbery could now only be tried in the royal Courts; these were "The Four Pleas of the Crown."

# The Courts

As there was no fixed capital, the King's Court, in David's time, followed the King in his annual circuits through his realm, between Dumfries and Inverness. Later, the regions of Scotia (north of Forth), Lothian, and the lawless realm of Galloway, had their Grand Justiciaries, who held the Four Pleas. The other pleas were heard in "Courts of Royalty" and by earls, bishops, abbots, down to the baron, with his "right of pit and gallows." At such courts, by a law of 1180, the Sheriff of the shire, or an agent of his, ought to be present; so that royal and central justice was extending itself over the minor local courts. But if the sheriff or his sergeant did not attend when summoned, local justice took its course.

The process initiated by David's son, William the Lion, was very slowly substituting the royal authority, the royal sheriffs of shires, juries, and witnesses, for the wild justice of revenge; and trial by ordeal, and trial by combat. But hereditary jurisdictions of nobles and gentry were not wholly abolished till after the battle of Culloden! Where Abbots held courts, their procedure, in civil cases, was based on laws sanctioned by popes and general councils. But, alas! the Abbot might give just judgment; to execute it, we know from a curious instance, was not within his power, if the offender laughed at a sentence of excommunication.

David and his successors, till the end of the thirteenth century, made Scotland a more civilised and kept it a much less disturbed country than it was to remain during the long war of Independence, while the beautiful abbeys with their churches and schools attested a high stage of art and education.

# CHAPTER VI

# Malcolm *the* Maiden

The prominent facts in the brief reign of David's son Malcolm the Maiden, crowned (1153) at the age of eleven, were, first, a Celtic rising by Donald, a son of Malcolm MacHeth (now a prisoner in Roxburgh Castle), and a nephew of the famous Somerled Macgillebride of Argyll. Somerled won from the Norse the Isle of Man and the Southern Hebrides; from his sons descend the great Macdonald Lords of the Isles, always the leaders of the long Celtic resistance to the central authority in Scotland. Again, Malcolm resigned to Henry II of England the northern counties held by David I; and died after subduing Galloway, and (on the death of Somerled, said to have been assassinated) the tribes of the isles in 1165.

## William *the* Lion

Ambition to recover the northern English counties revealed itself in the overtures of William the Lion,—Malcolm's brother and successor,—for an alliance between Scotland and France. "The auld Alliance" now dawned, with rich promise of good and evil. In hopes of French aid, William invaded Northumberland, later laid siege to Carlisle, and on July 13, 1174, was surprised in a morning mist and captured at Alnwick. Scotland was now kingless; Galloway rebelled, and William, taken a captive to Falaise in Normandy, surrendered absolutely the independence of his country, which, for fifteen years, really was a fief of England. When William was allowed to go home, it was to fight the Celts of Galloway, and subdue the pretensions, in

Moray, of the MacWilliams, descendants of William, son of Duncan, son of Malcolm Canmore.

During William's reign (1188) Pope Clement III decided that the Scottish Church was subject, not to York or Canterbury, but to Rome. Seven years earlier, defending his own candidate for the see of St Andrews against the chosen of the Pope, William had been excommunicated, and his country and he had unconcernedly taken the issue of an Interdict. The Pope was too far away, and William feared him no more than Robert Bruce was to do.

By 1188, William refused to pay to Henry II a "Saladin Tithe" for a crusade, and in 1189 he bought from Richard I, who needed money for a crusade, the abrogation of the Treaty of Falaise. He was still disturbed by Celts in Galloway and the north, he still hankered after Northumberland, but, after preparations for war, he paid a fine and drifted into friendship with King John, who entertained his little daughters royally, and knighted his son Alexander. William died on December 4, 1214. He was buried at the Abbey of Arbroath, founded by him in honour of St Thomas of Canterbury, who had worked a strange posthumous miracle in Scotland. William was succeeded by his son, Alexander II (1214-1249).

# Alexander II

Under this Prince, who successfully put down the usual northern risings, the old suit about the claims to Northumberland was finally abandoned for a trifling compensation (1237). Alexander had married Joanna, daughter of King John, and his brother-in-law, Henry III, did not press his demand for homage for Scotland. The usual Celtic pretenders to the throne were forever crushed. Argyll became a sheriffdom, Galloway was brought into order, and Alexander, who died in the Isle of Kerrera in the bay of Oban (1249), well deserved his title of "a King of Peace." He was buried in Melrose Abbey. In his reign the clergy were allowed to hold Provincial or Synodal Councils without the presence of a papal Legate (1225), and the Dominicans and Franciscans appeared in Scotland.

# Alexander III

The term King of Peace was also applied to Alexander III, son of the second wife of Alexander II, Marie de Coucy. Alexander came to the throne (1249) at the age of eight. As a child he was taken and held (like James II, James III, James V, and James VI) by contending factions of the nobles, Henry of England intervening. In 1251 he wedded another child, Margaret, daughter of Henry III of England, but Henry neither forced a claim to hold Scotland during the boy's minority (his right if Scotland were his fief), nor in other respects pressed his advantage. In February 1261-1262 a girl was born to Alexander at Windsor; she was Margaret, later wife of Eric of Norway. Her daughter, on the death of Alexander III (March 19, 1286), was the sole direct descendant in the male line.

After the birth of this heiress, Alexander won from Norway the isles of the western coast of Scotland in which Norse chieftains had long held sway. They complained to Hakon of Norway concerning raids made on them by the Earl of Ross, a Celtic potentate. Alexander's envoys to Hakon were detained, and in 1263, Hakon, with a great fleet, sailed through the islands. A storm blew most of his Armada to shore near Largs, where his men were defeated by the Scots. Hakon collected his ships, sailed north, and (December 15) died at Kirkwall. Alexander now brought the island princes, including the Lord of Man, into subjection; and by Treaty, in 1266, placed them under the Crown. In 1275 Benemund de Vicci (called Bagimont), at a council in Perth, compelled the clergy to pay a tithe for a crusade, the Pope insisting that the money should be assessed on the true value of benefices—that is, on "Bagimont's Roll,"—thenceforth recognised as the basis of clerical taxation. In 1278 Edward I laboured to extract from Alexander an acknowledgment that he was England's vassal. Edward signally failed; but a palpably false account of Alexander's homage was fabricated, and dated September 29, 1278. This was not the only forgery by which England was wont to back her claims.

A series of bereavements (1281-1283) deprived Alexander of all his children save his little grandchild, "the Maid of Norway." She was recognised by a great national assembly at Scone as heiress of the throne; and Alexander had no issue by his second wife, a daughter of the Comte de Dreux. On the night of March 19, 1285, while Alexander was riding from Edinburgh to visit his bride at Kinghorn, his horse slipped over a cliff and the rider was slain.

CHAPTER VII

# Encroachments *of* Edward I—Wallace

T he Estates of Scotland met at Scone (April 11, 1286) and swore loyalty to their child queen, "the Maid of Norway," granddaughter of Alexander III. Six guardians of the kingdom were appointed on April 11, 1286. They were the Bishops of St Andrews and Glasgow, two Comyns (Buchan and Badenoch), the Earl of Fife, and Lord James, the Steward of Scotland. No Bruce or Baliol was among the Custodians. Instantly a "band," or covenant, was made by the Bruces, Earls of Annandale and Carrick, to support their claims (failing the Maid) to the throne; and there were acts of war on their part against another probable candidate, John Balliol. Edward (like Henry VIII in the case of Mary Stuart) moved for the marriage of the infant queen to his son. A Treaty safeguarding all Scottish liberties as against England was made by clerical influences at Birgham (July 18, 1290), but by October 7 news of the death of the young queen reached Scotland: she had perished during her voyage from Norway. Private war now broke out between the Bruces and Balliols; and the party of Balliol appealed to Edward, through Fraser, Bishop of St Andrews, asking the English king to prevent civil war, and recommending Balliol as a person to be carefully treated. Next the Seven Earls, alleging some dim elective right, recommended Bruce, and appealed to Edward as their legal superior.

Edward came to Norham-on-Tweed in May 1291, proclaimed himself Lord Paramount, and was accepted as such by the twelve candidates for the Crown (June 3). The great nobles thus, to serve their ambitions, betrayed their country: *the communitas* (whatever that term may here mean) made a futile protest.

As lord among his vassals, Edward heard the pleadings and evidence in autumn 1292; and out of the descendants, in the female line, of David Earl of Huntingdon, youngest son of David I, he finally

30

(November 17, 1292) preferred John Balliol (*great-grandson* of the earl through his eldest daughter) to Bruce the Old, grandfather of the famous Robert Bruce, and *grandson* of Earl David's second daughter. The decision, according to our ideas, was just; no modern court could set it aside. But Balliol was an unpopular weakling—"an empty tabard," the people said—and Edward at once subjected him, king as he was, to all the humiliations of a petty vassal. He was summoned into his Lord's Court on the score of the bills of tradesmen. If Edward's deliberate policy was to goad Balliol into resistance and then conquer Scotland absolutely, in the first of these aims he succeeded.

In 1294 Balliol was summoned, with his Peers, to attend Edward in Gascony. Balliol, by advice of a council (1295), sought a French alliance and a French marriage for his son, named Edward; he gave the Annandale lands of his enemy Robert Bruce (father of the king to be) to Comyn, Earl of Buchan. He besieged Carlisle, while Edward took Berwick, massacred the people, and captured Sir William Douglas, father of the good Lord James.

In the war which followed, Edward broke down resistance by a sanguinary victory at Dunbar, captured John Comyn of Badenoch (the Red Comyn), received from Balliol (July 7, 1296) the surrender of his royal claims, and took the oaths of the Steward of Scotland and the Bruces, father and son. He carried to Westminster the Black Rood of St Margaret and the famous stone of Scone, a relic of the early Irish dynasty of the Scots; as far north as Elgin he rode, receiving the oaths of all persons of note and influence—except William Wallace. *His* name does not appear in the list of submissions called "The Ragman's Roll." Between April and October 1296 the country was subjugated; the castles were garrisoned by Englishmen. But by January 1297, Edward's governor, Warenne, Earl of Surrey, and Ormsby, his Chief Justice, found the country in an uproar, and at midsummer 1297 the levies of the northern counties of England were ordered to put down the disorders.

## The Year *of* Wallace

In May the *commune* of Scotland (whatever the term may here mean) had chosen Wallace as their leader; probably this younger son of Sir Malcolm Wallace of Elderslie, in Renfrewshire, had already been distinguished for his success in skirmishes against the English, as well as for strength and courage.[6] The popular account of his early adventures given in the poem by Blind Harry (1490?) is of no historical value. His men destroyed the English at Lanark (May 1297); he was abetted by Wishart, Bishop of Glasgow, and the Steward; but by July 7, Percy and Clifford, leading the English army, admitted the Steward, Robert Bruce (the future king), and Wishart to the English peace at Irvine in Ayrshire. But the North was up under Sir Andrew Murray, and "that thief Wallace" (to quote an English contemporary) left the siege of Dundee Castle which he was conducting to face Warenne on the north bank of the Forth. On September 11, the English, under Warenne, manœuvred vaguely at Stirling Bridge, and were caught on the flank by Wallace's army before they could deploy on the northern side of the river. They were cut to pieces, Cressingham was slain, and Warenne galloped to Berwick, while the Scots harried Northumberland with great ferocity, which Wallace seems to have been willing but not often able to control. By the end of March 1298 he appears with Andrew Murray as Guardian of the Kingdom for the exiled Balliol. This attitude must have aroused the jealousy of the nobles, and especially of Robert Bruce, who aimed at securing the crown, and who, after several changes of side, by June 1298 was busy in Edward's service in Galloway.

Edward then crossed the Border with a great army of perhaps 40,000 men, met the spearmen of Wallace in their serried phalanxes at Falkirk, broke the "schiltrom" or clump of spears by the arrows of his archers; slaughtered the archers of Ettrick Forest; scattered the mounted nobles, and avenged the rout of Stirling (July 22, 1298). The country remained unsubdued, but its leaders were at odds among themselves, and Wallace had retired to France, probably to ask for aid; he may also conceivably have visited Rome. The Bishop of St Andrews, Lamberton, with Bruce and the Red Comyn—deadly rivals—were Guardians of the Kingdom in 1299. But in June 1300, Edward, undeterred by remonstrances from the Pope, entered Scotland; an armistice, however, was accorded to the Holy Father, and the war, in which the Scots scored a victory at Roslin in February 1293, dragged on from summer to summer till July 1304. In these

---

[6] As Waleys was then an English as much as a Scottish name, I see no reason for identifying the William le Waleys, outlawed for bilking a poor woman who kept a beer house (Perth, June-August, 1296), with the great historical hero of Scotland.

years Bruce alternately served Edward and conspired against him; the intricacies of his perfidy are deplorable.

Bruce served Edward during the siege of Stirling, then the central key of the country. On its surrender Edward admitted all men to his peace, on condition of oaths of fealty, except "Messire Williame le Waleys." Men of the noblest Scottish names stooped to pursue the hero: he was taken near Glasgow, and handed over to Sir John Menteith, a Stewart, and son of the Earl of Menteith. As Sheriff of Dumbartonshire, Menteith had no choice but to send the hero in bonds to England. But, if Menteith desired to escape the disgrace with which tradition brands his name, he ought to have refused the English blood-price for the capture of Wallace. He made no such refusal. As an outlaw, Wallace was hanged at London; his limbs, like those of the great Montrose, were impaled on the gates of various towns.

What we really know about the chief popular hero of his country, from documents and chronicles, is fragmentary; and it is hard to find anything trustworthy in Blind Harry's rhyming "Wallace" (1490), plagiarised as it is from Barbour's earlier poem (1370) on Bruce.[7] But Wallace was truly brave, disinterested, and indomitable. Alone among the leaders he never turned his coat, never swore and broke oaths to Edward. He arises from obscurity, like Jeanne d'Arc; like her, he is greatly victorious; like her, he awakens a whole people; like her, he is deserted, and is unlawfully put to death; while his limbs, like her ashes, are scattered by the English. The ravens had not pyked his bones bare before the Scots were up again for freedom.

---

[7] See Dr Neilson on "Blind Harry's Wallace," in 'Essays and Studies by Members of the English Association,' p. 85 ff. (Oxford, 1910.)

# CHAPTER VIII

# Bruce *and the* War *of* Independence

The position towards France of Edward I made it really more desirable for him that Scotland should be independent and friendly, than half subdued and hostile to his rule. While she was hostile, England, in attacking France, always left an enemy in her rear. But Edward supposed that by clemency to all the Scottish leaders except Wallace, by giving them great appointments and trusting them fully, and by calling them to his Parliament in London, he could combine England and Scotland in affectionate union. He repaired the ruins of war in Scotland; he began to study her laws and customs; he hastily ran up for her a new constitution, and appointed his nephew, John of Brittany, as governor. But he had overlooked two facts: the Scottish clergy, from the highest to the lowest, were irreconcilably opposed to union with England; and the greatest and most warlike of the Scottish nobles, if not patriotic, were fickle and insatiably ambitious. It is hard to reckon how often Robert Bruce had turned his coat, and how often the Bishop of St Andrews had taken the oath to Edward. Both men were in Edward's favour in June 1304, but in that month they made against him a treasonable secret covenant. Through 1305 Bruce prospered in Edward's service, on February 10, 1306, Edward was conferring on him a new favour, little guessing that Bruce, after some negotiation with his old rival, the Red Comyn, had slain him (an uncle of his was also butchered) before the high altar of the Church of the Franciscans in Dumfries. Apparently Bruce had tried to enlist Comyn in his conspiracy, and had found him recalcitrant, or feared that he would be treacherous (February 10, 1306).

The sacrilegious homicide made it impossible for Bruce again to waver. He could not hope for pardon; he must be victorious or share the fate of Wallace. He summoned his adherents, including young James Douglas, received the support of the Bishops of St Andrews and Glasgow, hurried to Scone, and there was hastily crowned with a slight coronet, in the presence of but two earls and three bishops.

Edward made vast warlike preparations and forswore leniency, while Bruce, under papal excommunication, which he slighted, collected a few nobles, such as Lennox, Atholl, Errol, and a brother of the chief of the Frazers. Other chiefs, kinsmen of the slain Comyn, among them Macdowal of Argyll, banded to avenge the victim; Bruce's little force was defeated at Methven Wood, near Perth, by Aymer de Valence, and prisoners of all ranks were hanged as traitors, while two bishops were placed in irons. Bruce took to the heather, pursued by the Macdowals no less than by the English; his queen was captured, his brother Nigel was executed; he cut his way to the wild west coast, aided only by Sir Nial Campbell of Loch Awe, who thus founded the fortune of his house, and by the Macdonalds, under Angus Og of Islay. He wintered in the isle of Rathlin (some think he even went to Norway), and in spring, after surprising the English garrison in his own castle of Turnberry, he roamed, now lonely, now with a mobile little force, in Galloway, always evading and sometimes defeating his English pursuers. At Loch Trool and at London Hill (Drumclog) he dealt them heavy blows, while on June 7, 1307, his great enemy Edward died at Borough-on-Sands, leaving the crown and the war to the weakling Edward II.

Fortune had turned. We cannot follow Bruce through his campaign in the north, where he ruined the country of the Comyns (1308), and through the victories in Galloway of his hard-fighting brother Edward. With enemies on every side, Bruce took them in detail; early in March 1309 he routed the Macdowals at the west end of the Pass of Brander. Edward II was involved in disputes with his own barons, and Bruce was recognised by his country's Church in 1310 and aided by his great lieutenants, Sir James Douglas and Thomas Randolph, Earl of Murray. By August 1311 Bruce was carrying the war into England, sacking Durham and Chester, failing at Carlisle, but in January 1313, capturing Perth. In summer, Edward Bruce, in the spirit of chivalry, gave to Stirling Castle (Randolph had taken Edinburgh Castle) a set day, Midsummer Day 1314, to be relieved or to surrender; and Bruce kept tryst with Edward II and his English and Irish levies, and all his adventurous chivalry from France, Hainault, Bretagne, Gascony, and Aquitaine. All the world knows the story of the first battle, the Scottish Quatre Bras; the success of Randolph on the right; the slaying of Bohun when Bruce broke his battle-axe. Next day Bruce's position was strong; beneath the towers of Stirling the Bannockburn protected his front; morasses only to be crossed by narrow paths impeded the English advance. Edward Bruce commanded the right wing; Randolph the centre; Douglas and the Steward the left; Bruce the reserve, the Islesmen. His strength lay in his spearmen's "dark impenetrable wood"; his archers were ill-trained; of horse he had but a handful under Keith, the Marischal. But the heavy English cavalry could not break the squares of spears; Keith cut up the archers of England; the main body could not deploy, and the slow, relentless advance of the whole Scottish line covered the plain with the dying and the flying. A panic arose, caused by the sight of an approaching cloud of camp-followers on the Gillie's hill; Edward fled, and hundreds of noble prisoners, with all the waggons and supplies of England, fell into the hands of the Scots. In eight strenuous years the generalship of Bruce and his war-leaders, the resolution of the people, hardened by the cruelties of Edward, the sermons of the clergy, and the utter incompetence of Edward II, had redeemed a desperate chance. From a fief of England, Scotland had become an indomitable nation.

# Later Days *of* Bruce

Bruce continued to prosper, despite an ill-advised attempt to win Ireland, in which Edward Bruce fell (1318.) This left the succession, if Bruce had no male issue, to the children of his daughter, Marjory, and her husband, the Steward. In 1318 Scotland recovered Berwick, in 1319 routed the English at Mytton-on-Swale. In a Parliament at Aberbrothock (April 6, 1320) the Scots announced to the Pope, who had been interfering, that, while a hundred of them survive, they will never yield to England. In October 1322 Bruce utterly routed the English at Byland Abbey, in the heart of Yorkshire, and chased Edward II into York. In March 1324 a son was born to Bruce named David; on May 4, 1328, by the Treaty of Northampton, the independence of Scotland was recognised. In July the infant David married Joanna, daughter of Edward II.

On June 7, 1329, Bruce died and was buried at Dunfermline; his heart, by his order, was carried by Douglas towards the Holy Land, and when Douglas fell in a battle with the Moors in Spain, the heart was brought back by Sir Simon Lockhart of the Lee. The later career of Bruce, after he had been excommunicated, is that of the foremost knight and most sagacious man of action who ever wore the crown of

Scotland. The staunchness with which the clergy and estates disregarded papal fulminations (indeed under William the Lion they had treated an interdict as waste-paper) indicated a kind of protestant tendency to independence of the Holy See.

Bruce's inclusion of representatives of the Burghs in the first regular Scottish Parliament (at Cambuskenneth in 1326) was a great step forward in the constitutional existence of the country. The king, in Scotland, was expected to "live of his own," but in 1326 the expenses of the war with England compelled Bruce to seek permission for taxation.

# CHAPTER IX

# Decadence *and* Disasters
# Reign *of* David II

The heroic generation of Scotland was passing off the stage. The King was a child. The forfeiture by Bruce of the lands of hostile or treacherous lords, and his bestowal of the estates on his partisans, had made the disinherited nobles the enemies of Scotland, and had fed too full the House of Douglas. As the star of Scotland was thus clouded—she had no strong man for a King during the next ninety years—the sun of England rose red and glorious under a warrior like Edward III. The Scottish nobles in many cases ceased to be true to their proud boast that they would never submit to England. A very brief summary of the wretched reign of David II must here suffice.

First, the son of John Balliol, Edward, went to the English Court, and thither thronged the disinherited and forfeited lords, arranging a raid to recover their lands. Edward III, of course, connived at their preparations.

After Randolph's death (July 20, 1332), when Mar—a sister's son of Bruce—was Regent, the disinherited lords, under Balliol, invaded Scotland, and Mar, with young Randolph, Menteith, and a bastard of Bruce, "Robert of Carrick," leading a very great host, fell under the shafts of the English archers of Umfraville, Wake, the English Earl of Atholl, Talbot, Ferrers, and Zouche, at Dupplin, on the Earn (August 12, 1332). Rolled up by arrows loosed on the flanks of their charging columns, they fell, and their dead bodies lay in heaps as tall as a lance.

On September 24, Edward Balliol was crowned King at Scone. Later, Andrew Murray, perhaps a son of the Murray who had been Wallace's companion-in-arms, was taken, and Balliol acknowledged Edward III as his liege-lord at Roxburgh. In December the second son of Randolph, with Archibald, the new Regent, brother of the great

Black Douglas, drove Balliol, flying in his shirt, from Annan across the Border. He returned, and was opposed by this Archibald Douglas, called Tineman, the Unlucky, and on July 19, 1333, Tineman suffered, at Halidon Hill, near Berwick, a defeat as terrible as Flodden; Berwick, too, was lost, practically forever, Tineman fell, and Sir William Douglas, the Knight of Liddesdale, was a prisoner. These Scots defeats were always due to rash frontal attacks on strong positions, the assailants passing between lines of English bowmen who loosed into their flanks. The boy king, David, was carried to France (1334) for safety, while Balliol delivered to Edward Berwick and the chief southern counties, including that of Edinburgh, with their castles.

There followed internal wars between Balliol's partisans, while the patriots were led by young Randolph, by the young Steward, by Sir Andrew Murray, and the wavering and cruel Douglas, called the Knight of Liddesdale, now returned from captivity. In the desperate state of things, with Balliol and Edward ravaging Scotland at will, none showed more resolution than Bruce's sister, who held Kildrummie Castle; and Randolph's daughter, "Black Agnes," who commanded that of Dunbar. By vast gifts Balliol won over John, Lord of the Isles. The Celts turned to the English party; Edward III harried the province of Moray, but, in 1337, he began to undo his successes by formally claiming the crown of France: France and Scotland together could always throw off the English yoke.

Thus diverted from Scotland, Edward lost strength there while he warred with Scotland's ally: in 1341 the Douglas, Knight of Liddesdale, recovered Edinburgh Castle by a romantic surprise. But David returned home in 1341, a boy of eighteen, full of the foibles of chivalry, rash, sensual, extravagant, who at once gave deadly offence to the Knight of Liddesdale by preferring to him, as sheriff of Teviotdale, the brave Sir Alexander Ramsay, who had driven the English from the siege of Dunbar Castle. Douglas threw Ramsay into Hermitage Castle in Liddesdale and starved him to death.

In 1343 the Knight began to intrigue traitorously with Edward III; after a truce, David led his whole force into England, where his rash chivalry caused his utter defeat at Neville's Cross, near Durham (October 17, 1346). He was taken, as was the Bishop of St Andrews; his ransom became the central question between England and Scotland. In 1353 Douglas, Knight of Liddesdale, was slain at Williamshope on Yarrow by his godson, William, Lord Douglas: the fact is commemorated in a fragment of perhaps our oldest narrative Border ballad. French men-at-arms now helped the Scots to recover

Berwick, merely to lose it again in 1356; in 1357 David was set free: his ransom, 100,000 merks, was to be paid by instalment. The country was heavily taxed, but the full sum was never paid. Meanwhile the Steward had been Regent; between him, the heir of the Crown failing issue to David, and the King, jealousies arose. David was suspected of betraying the kingdom to England; in October 1363 he and the Earl of Douglas visited London and made a treaty adopting a son of Edward as king on David's demise, and on his ransom being remitted, but in March 1364 his Estates rejected the proposal, to which Douglas had assented. Till 1369 all was poverty and internal disunion; the feud, to be so often renewed, of the Douglas and the Steward raged. David was made contemptible by a second marriage with Margaret Logie, but the war with France drove Edward III to accept a fourteen years' truce with Scotland. On February 22, 1371, David died in Edinburgh Castle, being succeeded, without opposition, by the Steward, Robert II, son of Walter, and of Marjorie, daughter of Robert Bruce. This Robert II, somewhat outworn by many years of honourable war in his country's cause, and the father of a family, by Elizabeth Mure of Rowallan, which could hardly be rendered legitimate by any number of Papal dispensations, *was the first of the Royal Stewart line.* In him a cadet branch of the English FitzAlans, themselves of a very ancient Breton stock, blossomed into Royalty.

## Parliament *and the* Crown

With the coming of a dynasty which endured for three centuries, we must sketch the relations, in Scotland, of Crown and Parliament till the days of the Covenant and the Revolution of 1688. Scotland had but little of the constitutional evolution so conspicuous in the history of England. The reason is that while the English kings, with their fiefs and wars in France, had constantly to be asking their parliaments for money, and while Parliament first exacted the redress of grievances, in Scotland the king was expected "to live of his own" on the revenue of crown-lands, rents, feudal aids, fines exacted in Courts of Law, and duties on merchandise. No "tenths" or "fifteenths" were exacted from clergy and people. There could be no "constitutional resistance" when the Crown made no unconstitutional demands.

In Scotland the germ of Parliament is the King's court of vassals of the Crown. To the assemblies, held now in one place, now in another, would usually come the vassals of the district, with such officers of state as the Chancellor, the Chamberlain, the Steward, the Constable or Commander-in-Chief, the Justiciar, and the Marischal, and such Bishops, Abbots, Priors, Earls, Barons, and tenants-in-chief as chose to attend. At these meetings public business was done, charters were granted, and statutes were passed; assent was made to such feudal aids as money for the king's ransom in the case of William the Lion. In 1295 the seals of six Royal burghs are appended to the record of a negotiation; in 1326 burgesses, as we saw, were consulted by Bruce on questions of finance.

The misfortunes and extravagance of David II had to be paid for, and Parliament interfered with the Royal prerogative in coinage and currency, directed the administration of justice, dictated terms of peace with England, called to account even hereditary officers of the Crown (such as the Steward, Constable, and Marischal), controlled the King's expenditure (or tried to do so), and denounced the execution of Royal warrants against the Statutes and common form of law. They summarily rejected David's attempt to alter the succession of the Crown.

At the same time, as attendance of multitudes during protracted Parliaments was irksome and expensive, arose the habit of intrusting business to a mere "Committee of Articles," later "The Lords of the Articles," selected in varying ways from the Three Estates—Spiritual, Noble, and Commons. These Committees saved the members of Parliament from the trouble and expense of attendance, but obviously tended to become an abuse, being selected and packed to carry out the designs of the Crown or of the party of nobles in power. All members, of whatever Estate, sat together in the same chamber. There were no elected Knights of the Shires, no representative system.

The reign of David II saw two Scottish authors or three, whose works are extant. Barbour wrote the chivalrous rhymed epic-chronicle 'The Brus'; Wyntoun, an unpoetic rhymed "cronykil"; and "Hucheoun of the Awle Ryal" produced works of more genius, if all that he is credited with be his own.

CHAPTER X

# Early Stewart Kings:
# Robert II (1371-1390)

Robert II was crowned at Scone on March 26, 1371. He was elderly, jovial, pacific, and had little to fear from England when the deaths of Edward III and the Black Prince left the crown to the infant Richard II. There was fighting against isolated English castles within the Scottish border, to amuse the warlike Douglases and Percies, and there were truces, irregular and ill kept. In 1384 great English and Scottish raids were made, and gentlemen of France, who came over for sport, were scurvily entertained, and (1385) saw more plundering than honest fighting under James, Earl of Douglas, who merely showed them an army that, under Richard II, burned Melrose Abbey and fired Edinburgh, Perth, and Dundee. Edinburgh was a town of 400 houses. Richard insisted that not more than a third of his huge force should be English Borderers, who had no idea of hitting their Scottish neighbours, fathers-in-law and brothers-in-law, too hard. The one famous fight, that of Otterburn (August 15, 1388), was a great and joyous passage of arms by moonlight. The Douglas fell, the Percy was led captive away; the survivors gained advancement in renown and the hearty applause of the chivalrous chronicler, Froissart. The oldest ballads extant on this affair were current in 1550, and show traces of the reading of Froissart and the English chroniclers.

In 1390 died Robert II. Only his youth was glorious. The reign of his son, Robert III (crowned August 14, 1390), was that of a weakling who let power fall into the hands of his brother, the Duke of Albany, or his son David, Duke of Rothesay, who held the reins after the Parliament (a Parliament that bitterly blamed the Government) of January 1399. (With these two princes the title of Duke first appears in Scotland.) The follies of young David alienated all: he broke his betrothal to the daughter of the Earl of March; March retired to England, becoming the man of Henry IV; and though Rothesay wedded the daughter of the Earl of Douglas, he was arrested by Albany and Douglas and was starved to death (or died of dysentery) in Falkland Castle (1402). The Highlanders had been in anarchy throughout the reign; their blood was let in the great clan duel of thirty against thirty, on the Inch of Perth, in 1396. Probably clans Cameron and Chattan were the combatants.

On Rothesay's death Albany was Governor, while Douglas was taken prisoner in the great Border defeat of Homildon Hill, not far from Flodden. But then (1403) came the alliance of Douglas with Percy; Percy's quarrel with Henry IV and their defeat; and Hotspur's death, Douglas's capture at Shrewsbury. Between Shakespeare, in "Henry IV," and Scott, in 'The Fair Maid of Perth,' the most notable events in the reign of Robert III are immortalised. The King's last misfortune was the capture by the English at sea, on the way to France, of his son James in February-March 1406.[8] On April 4, 1406, Robert went to his rest, one of the most unhappy of the fated princes of his line.

# The Regency *of* Albany

The Regency of Albany, uncle of the captured James, lasted for fourteen years, ending with his death in 1420. He occasionally negotiated for his king's release, but more successfully for that of his son Murdoch. That James suspected Albany's ambition, and was irritated by his conduct, appears in his letters, written in Scots, to Albany and to Douglas, released in 1408, and now free in Scotland. The letters are of 1416.

The most important points to note during James's English captivity are the lawlessness and oppression which prevailed in Scotland, and the beginning of Lollard heresies, nascent Protestantism, nascent Socialism, even "free love." The Parliament of 1399, which had inveighed against the laxity of Government under Robert II, also demanded the extirpation of heresies, in accordance with the Coronation Oath. One Resby, a heretical English priest, was arraigned and burned at Perth in 1407, under Laurence of Lindores, the

---

[8] The precise date is disputed.

Dominican Inquisitor into heresies, who himself was active in promoting Scotland's oldest University, St Andrews. The foundation was by Henry Wardlaw, Bishop of St Andrews, by virtue of a bull from the anti-pope Benedict XIII, of February 1414. Lollard ideas were not suppressed; the chronicler, Bower, speaks of their existence in 1445; they sprang from envy of the wealth, and indignation against the corruptions of the clergy, and the embers of Lollardism in Kyle were not cold when, under James V, the flame of the Reformation was rekindled.

The Celtic North, never quiet, made its last united effort in 1411, when Donald, Lord of the Isles, who was in touch with the English Government, claimed the earldom of Ross, in right of his wife, as against the Earl of Buchan, a son of Albany; mustered all the wild clans of the west and the isles at Ardtornish Castle on the Sound of Mull; marched through Ross to Dingwall; defeated the great northern clan of Mackay, and was hurrying to sack Aberdeen when he was met by Alexander Stewart, Earl of Mar, the gentry of the northern Lowlands, mounted knights, and the burgesses of the towns, some eighteen miles from Aberdeen, at Harlaw. There was a pitched battle with great slaughter, but the Celts had no cavalry, and the end was that Donald withdrew to his fastnesses. The event is commemorated by an old literary ballad, and in Elspeth's ballad in Scott's novel, 'The Antiquary.'

In the year of Albany's death, at a great age (1420), in compliance with the prayer of Charles VII of France, the Earl of Buchan, Archibald, Douglas's eldest son, and Sir John Stewart of Derneley, led a force of some 7000 to 10,000 men to war for France. Henry V then compelled the captive James I to join him, and (1421) at Baugé Bridge the Scots, with the famed La Hire, routed the army of Henry's brother, the Duke of Clarence, who, with 2000 of the English, fell in the action. The victory was fruitless; at Crevant (1423) the Scots were defeated; at Verneuil (1424) they were almost exterminated. None the less the remnant, with fresh levies, continued to war for their old ally, and, under Sir Hugh Kennedy and others, suffered at Rouvray (February 1429), and were with the victorious French at Orleans (May 1429) under the leadership of Jeanne d'Arc. The combination of Scots and French, at the last push, always saved the independence of both kingdoms.

The character of Albany, who, under his father, Robert III, and during the captivity of James I, ruled Scotland so long, is enigmatic. He is well spoken of by the contemporary Wyntoun, author of a chronicle in rhyme; and in the Latin of Wyntoun's continuator, Bower. He kept on friendly terms with the Douglases, he was popular in so far as he was averse to imposing taxation; and perhaps the anarchy and oppression which preceded the return of James I to Scotland were due not to the weakness of Albany but to that of his son and successor, Murdoch, and to the iniquities of Murdoch's sons.

The death of Henry V (1422) and the ambition of Cardinal Beaufort, determined to wed his niece Jane Beaufort to a crowned king, may have been among the motives which led the English Government (their own king, Henry VI, being a child) to set free the royal captive (1424).

# CHAPTER XI

# James I

On March 28, 1424, James I was released, on a ransom of £40,000, and after his marriage with Jane Beaufort, grand-daughter of John of Gaunt, son of Edward III. The story of their wooing (of course in the allegorical manner of the age, and with poetical conventions in place of actual details) is told in James's poem, "The King's Quair," a beautiful composition in the school of Chaucer, of which literary scepticism has vainly tried to rob the royal author. James was the ablest and not the most scrupulous of the Stuarts. His captivity had given him an English education, a belief in order, and in English parliamentary methods, and a fiery determination to put down the oppression of the nobles. "If God gives me but a dog's life," he said, "I will make the key keep the castle and the bracken bush keep the cow." Before his first Parliament, in May 1424, James arrested Murdoch's eldest son, Sir Walter Fleming of Cumbernauld, and the younger Boyd of Kilmarnock. The Parliament left a Committee of the Estates ("The Lords of the Articles") to carry out the royal policy. Taxes for the payment of James's ransom were imposed; to impose them was easy, "passive resistance" was easier; the money was never paid, and James's noble hostages languished in England. He next arrested the old Earl of Lennox, and Sir Robert Graham of the Kincardine family, later his murderer.

These were causes of unpopularity. During a new Parliament (1425) James imprisoned the new Duke of Albany (Murdoch) and his son Alexander, and seized their castles.[9] The Albanys and Lennox were executed; their estates were forfeited; but resentment dogged a

---

[9] By a blunder which Sir James Ramsay corrected, history has accused James of arresting his "whole House of Lords"!

king who was too fierce and too hurried a reformer, perhaps too cruel an avenger of his own wrongs.

Our knowledge of the events of his reign is vague; but a king of Scotland could never, with safety, treat any of his nobles as criminals; the whole order was concerned to prevent or avenge severity of justice.

At a Parliament in Inverness (1427) he seized the greatest of the Highland magnates whom he had summoned; they were hanged or imprisoned, and, after resistance, Alastair, the new Lord of the Isles, did penance at Holyrood, before being immured in Tantallon Castle. His cousin, Donald Balloch, defeated Mar at Inverlochy (where Montrose later routed Argyll) (1431). Not long afterwards Donald fled to Ireland, whence a head, said to be his, was sent to James, but Donald lived to fight another day.

Without a standing army to garrison the inaccessible Highlands, the Crown could neither preserve peace in those regions nor promote justice. The system of violent and perfidious punishments merely threw the Celts into the arms of England.

Execution itself was less terrible to the nobles than the forfeiting of their lands and the disinheriting of their families. None the less, James (1425-1427) seized the lands of the late Earl of Lennox, made Malise Graham surrender the earldom of Strathearn in exchange for the barren title of Earl of Menteith, and sent the sufferer as a hostage into England. The Earl of March, son of the Earl who, under Robert III, had gone over to the English cause, was imprisoned and stripped of his ancient domains on the Eastern Border; and James, disinheriting Lord Erskine, annexed the earldom of Mar to the Crown.

In a Parliament at Perth (March 1428) James permitted the minor barons and freeholders to abstain from these costly assemblies on the condition of sending two "wise men" to represent each sheriffdom: a Speaker was to be elected, and the shires were to pay the expenses of the wise men. But the measure was unpopular, and in practice lapsed. Excellent laws were passed, but were not enforced.

In July-November 1428 a marriage was arranged between Margaret the infant daughter of James and the son (later Louis XI) of the still uncrowned Dauphin, Charles VIII of France. Charles announced to his subjects early in 1429 that an army of 6000 Scots was to land in France; that James himself, if necessary, would follow; but Jeanne d'Arc declared that there was no help from Scotland, none save from God and herself. She was right: no sooner had she won her victories at Orleans, Jargeau, Pathay, and elsewhere (May-June 1429) than James made a truce with England which enabled Cardinal Beaufort to throw his large force of anti-Hussite crusaders into France, where they secured Normandy. The Scots in France, nevertheless, fought under the Maid in her last successful action, at Lagny (April 1430).

An heir to the Crown, James, was born in October 1430, while the King was at strife with the Pope, and asserting for King and Parliament power over the Provincial Councils of the Church. An interdict was threatened, James menaced the rich and lax religious orders with secular reformation; settled the Carthusians at Perth, to show an example of holy living; and pursued his severities against many of his nobles.

His treatment of the Earl of Strathearn (despoiled and sent as a hostage to England) aroused the wrath of the Earl's uncle, Robert Graham, who bearded James in Parliament, was confiscated, fled across the Highland line, and, on February 20, 1437, aided, it is said by the old Earl of Atholl (a grandson of Robert II by his second marriage), led a force against the King in the monastery of the Black Friars at Perth, surprised him, and butchered him. The energy of his Queen brought the murderers, and Atholl himself, to die under unspeakable torments.

James's reforms were hurried, violent, and, as a rule, incapable of surviving the anarchy of his son's minority: his new Court of Session, sitting in judgment thrice a-year, was his most fortunate innovation.

# CHAPTER XII

# James II

Scone, with its sacred stone, being so near Perth and the Highlands, was perilous, and the coronation of James II was therefore held at Holyrood (March 25, 1437). The child, who was but seven years of age, was bandied to and fro like a shuttlecock between rival adventurers. The Earl of Douglas (Archibald, fifth Earl, died 1439) took no leading part in the strife of factions: one of them led by Sir William Crichton, who held the important post of Commander of Edinburgh Castle; the other by Sir Alexander Livingstone of Callendar.

The great old Houses had been shaken by the severities of James I, at least for the time. In a Government of factions influenced by private greed, there was no important difference in policy, and we need not follow the transference of the royal person from Crichton in Edinburgh to Livingstone in Stirling Castle; the coalitions between these worthies, the battles between the Boyds of Kilmarnock and the Stewarts, who had to avenge Stewart of Derneley, Constable of the Scottish contingent in France, who was slain by Sir Thomas Boyd. The queen-mother married Sir James Stewart, the Black Knight of Lorne, and (August 3, 1439) she was captured by Livingstone, while her husband, in the mysterious words of the chronicler, was "put in a pitt and bollit." In a month Jane Beaufort gave Livingstone an amnesty; he, not the Stewart family, not the queen-mother, now held James.

To all this the new young Earl of Douglas, a boy of eighteen, tacitly assented. He was the most powerful and wealthiest subject in Scotland; in France he was Duc de Touraine; he was descended in lawful wedlock from Robert II; "he micht ha'e been the king," as the ballad says of the bonny Earl of Moray. But he held proudly aloof from both Livingstone and Crichton, who were stealing the king alternately: they then combined, invited Douglas to Edinburgh Castle, with his brother David, and served up the ominous bull's head at that "black dinner" recorded in a ballad fragment.[10] They decapitated the two Douglas boys; the earldom fell to their granduncle, James the Fat, and presently, on *his* death (1443), to young William Douglas, after which "bands," or illegal covenants, between the various leaders of factions, led to private wars of shifting fortune. Kennedy, Bishop of St Andrews, opposed the Douglas party, now strong both in lands newly acquired, till (July 3, 1449) James married Mary of Gueldres, imprisoned the Livingstones, and relied on the Bishop of St Andrews and the clergy. While Douglas was visiting Rome in 1450, the Livingstones had been forfeited, and Crichton became Chancellor.

## Fall *of the* Black Douglases

The Douglases, through a royal marriage of an ancestor to a daughter of the more legitimate marriage of Robert II, had a kind of claim to the throne which they never put forward. The country was thus spared dynastic wars, like those of the White and Red Roses in England; but, none the less, the Douglases were too rich and powerful for subjects.

The Earl at the moment held Galloway and Annandale, two of his brothers were Earls of Moray and Ormond; in October 1448, Ormond had distinguished himself by defeating and taking Percy, urging a raid into Scotland, at a bloody battle on the Water of Sark, near Gretna.

During the Earl of Douglas's absence in Rome, James had put down some of his unruly retainers, and even after his return (1451) had persevered in this course. Later in the year Douglas resigned, and received back his lands, a not uncommon formula showing submission on the vassal's favour on the lord's part, as when Charles VII, at the request of Jeanne d'Arc, made this resignation to God!

Douglas, however, was suspected of intriguing with England and with the Lord of the Isles, while he had a secret covenant or "band" with the Earls of Crawford and Ross. If all this were true, he was planning a most dangerous enterprise.

---

[10] The ballad fragments on the Knight of Liddesdale's slaying, and on "the black dinner," are preserved in Hume of Godscroft's 'History of the House of Douglas,' written early in the seventeenth century.

He was invited to Stirling to meet the king under a safe-conduct, and there (February 22, 1452) was dirked by his king at the sacred table of hospitality.

Whether this crime was premeditated or merely passionate is unknown, as in the case of Bruce's murder of the Red Comyn before the high altar. Parliament absolved James on slender grounds. James, the brother of the slain earl, publicly defied his king, gave his allegiance to Henry VI of England, withdrew it, intrigued, and, after his brothers had been routed at Arkinholm, near Langholm (May 18, 1455), fled to England. His House was proclaimed traitorous; their wide lands in southern and south-western Scotland were forfeited and redistributed, the Scotts of Buccleuch profiting largely in the long-run. The leader of the Royal forces at Arkinholm, near Langholm, was another Douglas, one of "the Red Douglases," the Earl of Angus; and till the execution of the Earl of Morton, under James VI, the Red Douglases were as powerful, turbulent, and treacherous as the Black Douglases had been in their day. When attacked and defeated, these Douglases, red or black, always allied themselves with England and with the Lords of the Isles, the hereditary foes of the royal authority.

Meanwhile Edward IV wrote of the Scots as "his rebels of Scotland," and in the alternations of fortune between the Houses of York and Lancaster, James held with Henry VI. When Henry was defeated and taken at Northampton (July 10, 1460), James besieged Roxburgh Castle, an English hold on the Border, and (August 3, 1460) was slain by the explosion of a great bombard.

James was but thirty years of age at his death. By the dagger, by the law, and by the aid of the Red Douglases, he had ruined his most powerful nobles—and his own reputation. His early training, like that of James VI, was received while he was in the hands of the most treacherous, bloody, and unscrupulous of mankind; later, he met them with their own weapons. The foundation of the University of Glasgow (1451), and the building and endowment of St Salvator's College in St Andrews, by Bishop Kennedy, are the most permanent proofs of advancing culture in the reign of James.

Many laws of excellent tendency, including sumptuary laws, which suggest the existence of unexpected wealth and luxury, were passed; but such laws were never firmly and regularly enforced. By one rule, which does seem to have been carried out, no poisons were to be imported: Scottish chemical science was incapable of manufacturing them. Much later, under James VI, we find a parcel of arsenic, to be used for political purposes, successfully stopped at Leith.

# CHAPTER XIII

# James III

James II left three sons; the eldest, James III, aged nine, was crowned at Kelso (August 10, 1460); his brothers, bearing the titles of Albany and Mar, were not to be his supports. His mother, Mary of Gueldres, had the charge of the boys, and, as she was won over by her uncle, Philip of Burgundy, to the cause of the House of York, while Kennedy and the Earl of Angus stood for the House of Lancaster, there was strife between them and the queen-mother and nobles. Kennedy relied on France (Louis XL), and his opponents on England.

The battle of Towton (March 30, 1461) drove Henry VI and his queen across the Border, where Kennedy entertained the melancholy exile in the Castle of St Andrews. The grateful Henry restored Berwick to the Scots, who could not hold it long. In June 1461, while the Scots were failing to take Carlisle, Edward IV was crowned, and sent his adherent, the exiled Earl of Douglas, to treat for an alliance with the Celts, under John, Lord of the Isles, and that Donald Balloch who was falsely believed to have long before been slain in Ireland.

It is curious to think of the Lord of the Isles dealing as an independent prince, through a renegade Douglas, with the English king. A treaty was made at John's Castle of Ardtornish—now a shell of crumbling stone on the sea-shore of the Morvern side of the Sound of Mull—with the English monarch at Westminster. The Highland chiefs promise allegiance to Edward, and, if successful, the Celts are to recover the ancient kingdom from Caithness to the Forth, while Douglas is to be all-powerful from the Forth to the Border!

But other intrigues prevailed. The queen-mother and her son, in the most friendly manner, met the kingmaker Warwick at Dumfries, and again at Carlisle, and Douglas was disgraced by Edward, though restored to favour when Bishop Kennedy declined to treat with Edward's commissioners. The Treaty of England with Douglas and the Celts was then ratified; but Douglas, advancing in front of Edward's army to the Border, met old Bishop Kennedy in helmet and corslet, and was defeated. Louis XI, however, now deserted the Red for the White Rose. Kennedy followed his example; and peace was made between England and Scotland in October 1464. Kennedy died in the summer of 1465.

There followed the usual struggles between confederations of the nobles, and, in July 1466, James was seized, being then aged fourteen, by the party of the Boyds, Flemings, and Kennedys, aided by Hepburn of Hailes (ancestor of the turbulent Earl of Bothwell), and by the head of the Border House of Cessford, Andrew Ker.

It was a repetition of the struggles of Livingstone and Crichton, and now the great Border lairds begin to take their place in history. Boyd made himself Governor to the king, his son married the king's eldest sister, Mary, and became Earl of Arran. But brief was the triumph of the Boyds. In 1469 James married Margaret of Norway; Orkney and Shetland were her dower; but while Arran negotiated the affair abroad, at home the fall of his house was arranged. Boyd fled the country; the king's sister, divorced from young Arran, married the Lord Hamilton; and his family, who were Lords of Cadzow under Robert Bruce, and had been allies of the Black Douglases till their fall, became the nearest heirs of the royal Stewarts, if that family were extinct. The Hamiltons, the wealthiest house in Scotland, never produced a man of great ability, but their nearness to the throne and their ambition were storm-centres in the time of Mary Stuart and James VI, and even as late as the Union in 1707.

The fortunes of a nephew of Bishop Kennedy, Patrick Graham, Kennedy's successor as Bishop of St Andrews, now perplex the historian. Graham dealt for himself with the Pope, obtained the rank of Archbishop for the Bishop of St Andrews (1472), and thus offended the king and country, always jealous of interference from Rome. But he was reported on as more or less insane by a Papal Nuncio, and was deposed. Had he been defending (as used to be said) the right of election of Bishop for the Canons against the greed of the nobles, the Nuncio might not have taken an unfavourable view of his intellect. In any case, whether the clergy, backed by Rome, elected their bishops, or whether the king and nobles made their profit out of the Church appointments, jobbery was the universal rule. Ecclesiastical corruption and, as a rule, ignorance, were attaining their lowest level.[11] By 1476 the Lord of the Isles, the Celtic ally of Edward IV, was reduced by Argyll, Huntly, and Crawford, and lost the sheriffdom of Inverness, and the earldom of Ross, which was attached to the Crown (1476). His treaty of Ardtornish had come to light. But his bastard, Angus Og, filled the north and west with fire and tumult from Ross to Tobermory (1480-1490), while James's devotion to the arts—a thing intolerable—and to the society of low-born favourites, especially Thomas Cockburn, "a stone-cutter," prepared the sorrows and the end of his reign.

The intrigues which follow, and the truth about the character of James, are exceedingly obscure. We have no Scottish chronicle written at the time; the later histories, by Ferrerius, an Italian, and, much later, by Queen Mary's Bishop Lesley, and by George Buchanan, are full of rumours and contradictions, while the State Papers and Treaties of England merely prove the extreme treachery of James's brother Albany, and no evidence tells us how James contrived to get the better of the traitor. James's brothers Albany and Mar were popular; were good horsemen, men of their hands, and Cochrane is accused of persuading James to arrest Mar on a charge of treason and black magic. Many witches are said to have been burned: perhaps the only such case before the Reformation. However it fell out—all is obscure—Mar died in prison; while Albany, also a prisoner on charges of treasonable intrigues with the inveterate Earl of Douglas, in the English interest, escaped to France.

Douglas (1482) brought him to England, where he swore allegiance to Edward IV, under whom, like Edward Balliol, he would hold Scotland if crowned. He was advancing on the Border with Edward's support and with the Duke of Gloucester (Richard III), and James had gone to Lauder to encounter him, when the Earl of Angus headed a conspiracy of nobles, such as Huntly, Lennox, and Buchan, seized Cochrane and other favourites of James, and hanged them over Lauder Bridge. The most tangible grievance was the increasing debasement of the coinage. James was immured at Edinburgh, but, by a compromise, Albany was restored to rank and estates. Meanwhile Gloucester captured Berwick, never to be recovered by Scotland. In 1483 Albany renewed, with many of the nobles, his intrigues with Edward for the betrayal of Scotland. In some unknown way James

---

[11] The works of Messrs Herkless and Hannay on the Bishops of St Andrews may be consulted.

separated Albany from his confederates Atholl, Buchan, and Angus; Albany went to England, betrayed the Castle of Dunbar to England, and was only checked in his treasons by the death of Edward IV (April 9, 1483), after which a full Parliament (July 7, 1483) condemned him and forfeited him in his absence. On July 22, 1484, he invaded Scotland with his ally, Douglas; they were routed at Lochmaben, Douglas was taken, and, by singular clemency, was merely placed in seclusion in the Monastery of Lindores, while Albany, escaping to France, perished in a tournament, leaving a descendant, who later, in the minority of James V, makes a figure in history.

The death of Richard III (August 18, 1485) and the accession of the prudent Henry VII gave James a moment of safety. He turned his attention to the Church, and determined to prosecute for treason such Scottish clerics as purchased benefices through Rome. He negotiated for three English marriages, including that of his son James, Duke of Rothesay, to a daughter of Edward IV; he also negotiated for the recovery of Berwick, taken by Gloucester during Albany's invasion of 1482. After his death, and before it, James was accused, for these reasons, of disloyal dealings with England; and such nobles as Angus, up to the neck as they were in treason and rebellion, raised a party against him on the score that he was acting as they did. The almost aimless treachery of the Douglases, Red or Black, endured for centuries from the reign of David II to that of James VI. Many nobles had received no amnesty for the outrage of Lauder Bridge; their hopes turned to the heir of the Crown, James, Duke of Rothesay. We see them offering peace for an indemnity in a Parliament of October 1487; the Estates refused all such pardons for a space of seven years; the king's party was manifestly the stronger. He was not to be intimidated; he offended Home and the Humes by annexing the Priory of Coldingham (which they regarded as their own) to the Royal Chapel at Stirling. The inveterate Angus, with others, induced Prince James to join them under arms. James took the Chancellorship from Argyll and sent envoys to England.

The rebels, proclaiming the prince as king, intrigued with Henry VII; James was driven across the Forth, and was supported in the north by his uncle, Atholl, and by Huntly, Crawford, and Lord Lindsay of the Byres, Errol, Glamis, Forbes, and Tullibardine, and the chivalry of Angus and Strathtay. Attempts at pacification failed; Stirling Castle was betrayed to the rebels, and James's host, swollen by the loyal burgesses of the towns, met the Border spears of Home and Hepburn, the Galloway men, and the levies of Angus at Sauchie Burn, near Bannockburn.

In some way not understood, James, riding without a single knight or squire, fell from his horse, which had apparently run away with him, at Beaton's Mill, and was slain in bed, it was rumoured, by a priest, feigned or false, who heard his confession. The obscurity of his reign hangs darkest over his death, and the virulent Buchanan slandered him in his grave. Under his reign, Henryson, the greatest of the Chaucerian school in Scotland, produced his admirable poems. Many other poets whose works are lost were flourishing; and *The Wallace*, that elaborate plagiarism from Barbour's 'The Brus,' was composed, and attributed to Blind Harry, a paid minstrel about the Court.[12]

---

[12] As Waleys was then an English as much as a Scottish name, I see no reason for identifying the William le Waleys, outlawed for bilking a poor woman who kept a beer house (Perth, June-August, 1296), with the great historical hero of Scotland.

CHAPTER XIV

# James IV

The new king, with Angus for his Governor, Argyll for his Chancellor, and with the Kers and Hepburns in office, was crowned at Scone about June 25, 1488. He was nearly seventeen, no child, but energetic in business as in pleasure, though lifelong remorse for his rebellion gnawed at his heart. He promptly put down a rebellion of the late king's friends and of the late king's foe, Lennox, then strong in the possession of Dumbarton Castle, which, as it commands the sea-entrance by Clyde, is of great importance in the reign of Mary and James VI. James III must have paid attention to the navy, which, under Sir Andrew Wood, already faced English pirates triumphantly. James IV spent much money on his fleet, buying timber from France, for he was determined to make Scotland a power of weight in Europe. But at the pinch his navy vanished like a mist.

Spanish envoys and envoys from the Duchess of Burgundy visited James in 1488-1489; he was in close relations with France and Denmark, and caused anxieties to the first Tudor king, Henry VII, who kept up the Douglas alliance with Angus, and bought over Scottish politicians. While James, as his account-books show, was playing cards with Angus, that traitor was also negotiating the sale of Hermitage Castle, the main hold of the Middle Border, to England. He was detected, and the castle was intrusted to a Hepburn, Earl of Bothwell; it was still held by Queen Mary's Bothwell in 1567. The Hepburns rose to the earldom of Bothwell on the death of Ramsay, a favourite of James III, who (1491) had arranged to kidnap James IV with his brother, and hand them over to Henry VII, for £277, 13s. 4d.! Nothing came of this, and a truce with England was arranged in 1491. Through four reigns, till James VI came to the English throne, the Tudor policy was to buy Scottish traitors, and attempt to secure the person of the Scottish monarch.

Meanwhile, the Church was rent by jealousies between the holder of the newly-created Archbishop of Glasgow (1491) and the Archbishop of St Andrews, and disturbed by the Lollards, in the region which was later the centre of the fiercest Covenanters,—Kyle in Ayrshire. But James laughed away the charges against the heretics (1494), whose views were, on many points, those of John Knox. In 1493-1495 James dealt in the usual way with the Highlanders and "the wicked blood of the Isles": some were hanged, some imprisoned, some became sureties for the peacefulness of their clans. In 1495, by way of tit-for-tat against English schemes, James began to back the claims of Perkin Warbeck, pretending to be Richard, Duke of York, escaped from the assassins employed by Richard III. Perkin, whoever he was, had probably been intriguing between Ireland and Burgundy since 1488. He was welcomed by James at Stirling in November 1495, and was wedded to the king's cousin, Catherine Gordon, daughter of the Earl of Huntly, now supreme in the north. Rejecting a daughter of England, and Spanish efforts at pacification, James prepared to invade England in Perkin's cause; the scheme was sold by Ramsay, the would-be kidnapper, and came to no more than a useless raid of September 1496, followed by a futile attempt and a retreat in July 1497. The Spanish envoy, de Ayala, negotiated a seven-years' truce in September, after Perkin had failed and been taken at Taunton.

The Celts had again risen while James was busy in the Border; he put them down, and made Argyll Lieutenant of the Isles. Between the Campbells and the Huntly Gordons, as custodians of the peace, the fighting clans were expected to be more orderly. On the other hand, a son of Angus Og, himself usually reckoned a bastard of the Lord of the Isles, gave much trouble. Angus had married a daughter of the Argyll of his day; their son, Donald Dubh, was kidnapped (or, rather, his mother was kidnapped before his birth) for Argyll; he now escaped, and in 1503, found allies among the chiefs, did much scathe, was taken in 1506, but was as active as ever forty years later.

The central source of these endless Highland feuds was the family of the Macdonalds, Lords of the Isles, claiming the earldom of Ross, resisting the Lowland influences and those of the Gordons and Campbells (Huntly and Argyll), and seeking aid from England. With the capture of Donald Dubh (1506) the Highlanders became for the while comparatively quiescent; under Lennox and Argyll they suffered in the defeat of Flodden.

From 1497 to 1503 Henry VII was negotiating for the marriage of James to his daughter Margaret Tudor; the marriage was celebrated on

August 8, 1503, and a century later the great grandson of Margaret, James VI came to the English throne. But marriage does not make friendship. There had existed since 1491 a secret alliance by which Scotland was bound to defend France if attacked by England. Henry's negotiations for the kidnapping of James were of April of the same year. Margaret, the young queen, after her marriage, was soon involved in bitter quarrels over her dowry with her own family; the slaying of a Sir Robert Ker, Warden of the Marches, by a Heron in a Border fray (1508), left an unhealed sore, as England would not give up Heron and his accomplice. Henry VII had been pacific, but his death, in 1509, left James to face his hostile brother-in-law, the fiery young Henry VIII.

In 1511 the Holy League under the Pope, against France, imperilled James's French ally. He began to build great ships of war; his sea-captain, Barton, pirating about, was defeated and slain by ships under two of the Howards, sons of the Earl of Surrey (August 1511). James remonstrated, Henry was firm, and the Border feud of Ker and Heron was festering; moreover, Henry was a party to the League against France, and France was urging James to attack England. He saw, and wrote to the King of Denmark, that, if France were down, the turn of Scotland to fall would follow. In March 1513, an English diplomatist, West, found James in a wild mood, distraught "like a fey man."

Chivalry, and even national safety, called him to war; while his old remorse drove him into a religious retreat, and he was on hostile terms with the Pope. On May 24th, in a letter to Henry, he made a last attempt to obtain a truce, but on June 30th Henry invaded France. The French queen despatched to James, as to her true knight, a letter and a ring. He sent his fleet to sea; it vanished like a dream. He challenged Henry through a herald on July 26th, and, in face of strange and evil omens, summoned the whole force of his kingdom, crossed the Border on August 22nd, took Norham Castle on Tweed, with the holds of Eital, Chillingham, and Ford, which he made his headquarters, and awaited the approach of Surrey and the levies of the Stanleys. On September 5th he demolished Ford Castle, and took position on the crest of Flodden Edge, with the deep and sluggish water of Till at its feet. Surrey, commanding an army all but destitute of supplies, outmaneuvered James, led his men unseen behind a range of hills to a position where, if he could maintain himself, he was upon James's line of communications, and thence marched against him to Branxton Ridge, under Flodden Edge.

James was ignorant of Surrey's movement till he saw the approach of his standards. In place of retaining his position, he hurled his force down to Branxton, his gunners could not manage their new French ordnance, and though Home with the Border spears and Huntly had a success on the right, the Borderers made no more efforts, and, on the left, the Celts fled swiftly after the fall of Lennox and Argyll. In the centre Crawford and Rothes were slain, and James, with the steady spearmen of his command, drove straight at Surrey. James, as the Spaniard Ayala said, "was no general: he was a fighting man." He was outflanked by the Admiral (Howard) and Dacre; his force was surrounded by charging horse and foot, and rained on by arrows. But

"The stubborn spearmen still made good
Their dark impenetrable wood,"

when James rushed from the ranks, hewed his way to within a lance's length of Surrey (so Surrey writes), and died, riddled with arrows, his neck gashed by a bill-stroke, his left hand almost sundered from his body. Night fell on the unbroken Scottish phalanx, but when dawn arrived only a force of Border prickers was hovering on the fringes of the field. Thirteen dead earls lay in a ring about their master; there too lay his natural son, the young Archbishop of St Andrews, and the Bishops of Caithness and the Isles. Scarce a noble or gentle house of the Lowlands but reckons an ancestor slain at Flodden.

Surrey did not pursue his victory, which was won, despite sore lack of supplies, by his clever tactics, by the superior discipline of his men, by their marching powers, and by the glorious rashness of the Scottish king. It is easy, and it is customary, to blame James's adherence to the French alliance as if it were born of a foolish chivalry. But he had passed through long stress of mind concerning this matter. If he rejected the allurements of France, if France were overwhelmed, he knew well that the turn of Scotland would come soon. The ambitions and the claims of Henry VIII were those of the first Edwards. England was bent on the conquest of Scotland at the earliest opportunity, and through the entire Tudor period England was the home and her monarch the ally of every domestic foe and traitor to the Scottish Crown.

Scotland, under James, had much prospered in wealth and even in comfort. Ayala might flatter in some degree, but he attests the great increase in comfort and in wealth.

In 1495 Bishop Elphinstone founded the University of Aberdeen, while (1496) Parliament decreed a course of school and college for the sons of barons and freeholders of competent estate. Prior Hepburn founded the College of St Leonard's in the University of St Andrews; and in 1507 Chepman received a royal patent as a printer. Meanwhile Dunbar, reckoned by some the chief poet of Scotland before Burns, was already denouncing the luxury and vice of the clergy, though his own life set them a bad example. But with Dunbar, Henryson, and others, Scotland had a school of poets much superior to any that England had reared since the death of Chaucer. Scotland now enjoyed her brief glimpse of the Revival of Learning; and James, like Charles II, fostered the early movements of chemistry and physical science. But Flodden ruined all, and the country, under the long minority of James V, was robbed and distracted by English intrigues; by the follies and loves of Margaret Tudor; by actual warfare between rival candidates for ecclesiastical place; by the ambitions and treasons of the Douglases and other nobles; and by the arrival from France of the son of Albany, that rebel brother of James III.

The truth of the saying, "Woe to the kingdom whose king is a child," was never more bitterly proved than in Scotland between the day of Flodden and the day of the return of Mary Stuart from France (1513-1561). James V was not only a child and fatherless; he had a mother whose passions and passionate changes in love resembled those of her brother Henry VIII. Consequently, when the inevitable problem arose, was Scotland during the minority to side with England or with France? the queen-mother wavered ceaselessly between the party of her brother, the English king, and the party of France; while Henry VIII could not be trusted, and the policy of France in regard to England did not permit her to offer any stable support to the cause of Scottish independence. The great nobles changed sides constantly, each "fighting for his own hand," and for the spoils of a Church in which benefices were struggled for and sold like stocks in the Exchange.

The question, Was Scotland to ally herself with England or with France? later came to mean, Was Scotland to break with Rome or to cling to Rome? Owing mainly to the selfish and unscrupulous perfidy of Henry VIII, James V was condemned, as the least of two evils, to adopt the Catholic side in the great religious revolution; while the statesmanship of the Beatons, Archbishops of St Andrews, preserved Scotland from English domination, thereby preventing the country from adopting Henry's Church, the Anglican, and giving Calvinism and Presbyterianism the opportunity which was resolutely taken and held.

The real issue of the complex faction fight during James's minority was thus of the most essential importance; but the constant shiftings of parties and persons cannot be dealt with fully in our space. James's mother had a natural claim to the guardianship of her son, and was left Regent by the will of James IV, but she was the sister of Scotland's enemy, Henry VIII. Beaton, Archbishop of Glasgow (later of St Andrews), with the Earl of Arran (now the title of the Hamiltons), Huntly, and Angus were to advise the queen till the arrival of Albany (son of the brother of James III), who was summoned from France. Albany, of course, stood for the French alliance, but when the queen-mother (August 6, 1514) married the new young Earl of Angus, the grandson and successor of the aged traitor, "Bell the Cat," the earl began to carry on the usual unpatriotic policy of his house. The appointment to the see of St Andrews was competed for by the Poet Gawain Douglas, uncle of the new Earl of Angus; and himself of the English party; by Hepburn, Prior of St Andrews, who fortified the Abbey; and by Forman, Bishop of Moray, a partisan of France, and a man accused of having induced James IV to declare war against England.

After long and scandalous intrigues, Forman obtained the see. Albany was Regent for a while, and at intervals he repaired to France; he was in the favour of the queen-mother when later she quarrelled with her husband, Angus. At one moment, Margaret and Angus fled to England where was born her daughter Margaret, later Lady Lennox and mother of Henry Darnley.

Angus, with Home, now recrossed the Border (1516), and was reconciled to Albany; against all unity in Scotland Henry intrigued, bribing with a free hand, his main object being to get Albany sent out of the country. In early autumn, 1516, Home, the leader of the Borderers at Flodden, and his brother were executed for treason; in June, 1517, Albany went to seek aid and counsel in France; when the queen-mother returned from England to Scotland, where, if she retained any influence, she might be useful to her brother's schemes. But, contrary to Henry's interests, in this year Albany renewed the old alliance with France; while, in 1518, the queen-mother desired to divorce Angus. But Angus was a serviceable tool of Henry, who prevented his sister from having her way; and now the heads of the parties in the distracted country were Arran, chief of the Hamiltons, and Beaton, Archbishop of Glasgow, standing for France; and Angus representing the English party.

Their forces met at Edinburgh in the street battle of "Cleanse the Causeway," wherein the Archbishop of Glasgow wore armour, and the Douglases beat the Hamiltons out of the town (April 30, 1520). Albany returned (1521), but the nobles would not join with him in an English war (1522). Again he went to France, while Surrey devastated the Scottish Border (1523). Albany returned while Surrey was burning Jedburgh, was once more deserted by the Scottish forces on the Tweed, and left the country for ever in 1524. Angus now returned from England; but the queen-mother cast her affections on young Henry Stewart (Lord Methven), while Angus got possession of the boy king (June 1526) and held him, a reluctant ward, in the English interest.

Lennox was now the chief foe of Arran, and Angus, with whom Arran had coalesced; and Lennox desired to deliver James out of Angus's hands. On July 26, 1526, not far from Melrose, Walter Scott of Buccleuch attacked the forces guarding the prince; among them was Ker of Cessford, who was slain by an Elliot when Buccleuch's men rallied at the rock called "Turn Again." Hence sprang a long-enduring blood-feud of Scotts and Kers; but Angus retained the prince, and in a later fight in the cause of James's delivery, Lennox was slain by the Hamiltons, near Linlithgow. The spring of 1528 was marked by the burning of a Hamilton, Patrick, Abbot of Ferne, at St Andrews, for his Lutheran opinions. Angus had been making futile attacks on the Border thieves, mainly the Armstrongs, who now became very prominent and picturesque robbers. He meant to carry James with him on one of these expeditions; but in June 1528 the young king escaped from Edinburgh Castle, and rode to Stirling, where he was welcomed by his mother and her partisans. Among them were Arran, Argyll, Moray, Bothwell, and other nobles, with Maxwell and the Laird of Buccleuch, Sir Walter Scott. Angus and his kin were forfeited; he was driven across the Border in November, to work what mischief he might against his country; he did not return till the death of James V. Meanwhile James was at peace with his uncle, Henry VIII. He (1529-1530) attempted to bring the Border into his peace, and hanged Johnnie Armstrong of Gilnockie, with circumstances of treachery, says the ballad,—as a ballad-maker was certain to say.

Campbells, Macleans, and Macdonalds had all this while been burning each other's lands, and cutting each other's throats. James visited them, and partly quieted them, incarcerating the Earl of Argyll.

Bothwell and Angus now conspired together to crown Henry VIII in Edinburgh; but, in May 1534, a treaty of peace was made, to last till the death of either monarch and a year longer.

CHAPTER XV

# James V *and the* Reformation

The new times were at the door. In 1425 the Scottish Parliament had forbidden Lutheran books to be imported. But they were, of course, smuggled in; and the seed of religious revolution fell on minds disgusted by the greed and anarchy of the clerical fighters and jobbers of benefices.

James V, after he had shaken off the Douglases and become "a free king," had to deal with a political and religious situation, out of which we may say in the Scots phrase, "there was no outgait." His was the dilemma of his father before Flodden. How, against the perfidious ambition, the force in war, and the purchasing powers of Henry VIII, was James to preserve the national independence of Scotland? His problem was even harder than that of his father, because when Henry broke with Rome and robbed the religious houses a large minority, at least, of the Scottish nobles, gentry, and middle classes were, so far, heartily on the anti-Roman side. They were tired of Rome, tired of the profligacy, ignorance, and insatiable greed of the ecclesiastical dignitaries who, too often, were reckless cadets of the noble families. Many Scots had read the Lutheran books and disbelieved in transubstantiation; thought that money paid for prayers to the dead was money wasted; preferred a married and preaching to a celibate and licentious clergy who celebrated Mass; were convinced that saintly images were idols, that saintly miracles were impostures. Above all, the nobles coveted the lands of the Church, the spoils of the religious houses.

In Scotland, as elsewhere, the causes of the religious revolution were many. The wealth and luxury of the higher clergy, and of the dwellers in the abbeys, had long been the butt of satire and of the fiercer indignation of the people. Benefices, great and small, were jobbed on every side between the popes, the kings, and the great

65

nobles. Ignorant and profligate cadets of the great houses were appointed to high ecclesiastical offices, while the minor clergy were inconceivably ignorant just at the moment when the new critical learning, with knowledge of Hebrew and Greek, was revolutionising the study of the sacred books. The celibacy of the clergy had become a mere farce; and they got dispensations enabling them to obtain ecclesiastical livings for their bastards. The kings set the worst example: both James IV and James V secured the richest abbeys, and, in the case of James IV, the Primacy, for their bastard sons. All these abuses were of old standing. "Early in the thirteenth century certain of the abbots of Jedburgh, supported by their chapters, had granted certain of their appropriate churches to priests with a right of succession to their sons" (see 'The Mediæval Church in Scotland,' by the late Bishop Dowden, chap. xix. Mac-Lehose, 1910.) Oppressive customs by which "the upmost claith," or a pecuniary equivalent, was extorted as a kind of death-duty by the clergy, were sanctioned by excommunication: no grievance was more bitterly felt by the poor. The once-dreaded curses on evil-doers became a popular jest: purgatory was a mere excuse for getting money for masses.

In short, the whole mediæval system was morally rotten; the statements drawn up by councils which made vain attempts to check the stereotyped abuses are as candid and copious concerning all these things as the satires of Sir David Lyndsay.

Then came disbelief in mediæval dogmas: the Lutheran and other heretical books were secretly purchased and their contents assimilated. Intercession of saints, images, pilgrimages, the doctrine of the Eucharist, all fell into contempt.

As early as February 1428, as we have seen, the first Scottish martyr for evangelical religion, Patrick Hamilton, was burned at St Andrews. This sufferer was the son of a bastard of that Lord Hamilton who married the sister of James III. As was usual, he obtained, when a little boy, an abbey, that of Ferne in Ross-shire. He drew the revenues, but did not wear the costume of his place; in fact, he was an example of the ordinary abuses. Educated at Paris and Louvain, he came in contact with the criticism of Erasmus and the Lutheran controversy. He next read at St Andrews, and he married. Suspected of heresy in 1427, he retired to Germany; he wrote theses called 'Patrick's Places,' which were reckoned heretical; he was arrested, was offered by Archbishop Beaton a chance to escape, disdained it, and was burned with unusual cruelty,—as a rule, heretics in Scotland were strangled before burning. There were other similar cases, nor could James interfere—he was bound by his Coronation Oath; again, he found in the bishops his best diplomatists, and they, of course, were all for the French alliance, in the cause of the independence of their country and Church as against Henry VIII.

Thus James, in justifiable dread of the unscrupulous ambition of Henry VIII, could not run the English course, could not accept the varying creeds which Henry, who was his own Pope, put forward as his spirit moved him. James was thus inevitably committed to the losing cause—the cause of Catholicism and of France—while the intelligence no less than the avarice of his nobles and gentry ran the English course.

James had practically no choice. In 1536 Henry proposed a meeting with James "as far within England as possible." Knowing, as we do, that Henry was making repeated attempts to have James kidnapped and Archbishop Beaton also, we are surprised that James was apparently delighted at the hope of an interview with his uncle—in England. Henry declined to explain why he desired a meeting when James put the question to his envoy. James said, in effect, that he must act by advice of his Council, which, so far as it was clerical, opposed the scheme. Henry justified the views of the Council, later, when James, returning from a visit to France, asked permission to pass through England. "It is the king's honour not to receive the King of Scots in his realm except as a vassal, for there never came King of Scots into England in peaceful manner otherwise." Certain it is that, however James might enter England, he would leave it only as a vassal. Nevertheless his Council, especially his clergy, are blamed for embroiling James with Henry by dissuading him from meeting his uncle in England. Manifestly they had no choice. Henry had shown his hand too often.

At this time James, by Margaret Erskine, became the father of James, later the Regent Moray. Strange tragedies would never have occurred had the king first married Margaret Erskine, who, by 1536, was the wife of Douglas of Loch Leven. He is said to have wished for her a divorce that he might marry her; this could not be: he visited France, and on New Year's Day, 1537, wedded Madeline, daughter of Francis I. Six months later she died in Scotland.

Marriage for the king was necessary, and David Beaton, later Cardinal Beaton and Archbishop of St Andrews, obtained for his lord a lady coveted by Henry VIII, Mary, of the great Catholic house of Lorraine, widow of the Duc de Longueville, and sister of the popular and ambitious Guises. The pair were wedded on June 10, 1538; there was fresh offence to Henry and a closer tie to the Catholic cause. The appointment of Cardinal Beaton (1539) to the see of St Andrews, in succession to his uncle, gave James a servant of high ecclesiastical rank, great subtlety, and indomitable resolution, but remote from chastity of life and from clemency to heretics. Martyrdoms became more frequent, and George Buchanan, who had been tutor of James's son by Margaret Erskine, thought well to open a window in a house where he was confined, walk out, and depart to the Continent. Meanwhile Henry, no less than Beaton, was busily burning his own martyrs. In 1539 Henry renewed his intercourse with James, attempting to shake his faith in David Beaton, and to make him rob his Church. James replied that he preferred to try to reform it; and he enjoyed, in 1540, Sir David Lyndsay's satirical play on the vices of the clergy, and, indeed, of all orders of men. In 1540 James ratified the College of Justice, the fifteen Lords of Session, sitting as judges in Edinburgh.

In 1541 the idea of a meeting between James and Henry was again mooted, and Henry actually went to York, where James did not appear. Henry, who had expected him, was furious. In August 1542, on a futile pretext, he sent Norfolk with a great force to harry the Border. The English had the worse at the battle of Hadden Rig; negotiations followed; Henry proclaimed that Scottish kings had always been vassals of England, and horrified his Council by openly proposing to kidnap James. Henry's forces were now wrecking an abbey and killing women on the Border. James tried to retaliate, but his levies (October 31) at Fala Moor declined to follow him across the Border: they remembered Flodden, moreover they could not risk the person of a childless king. James prepared, however, for a raid on a great scale on the western Border, but the fact had been divulged by Sir George Douglas, Angus's brother, and had also been sold to Dacre, cheap, by another Scot. The English despatches prove that Wharton had full time for preparation, and led a competent force of horse, which, near Arthuret, charged on the right flank of the Scots, who slowly retreated, till they were entangled between the Esk and a morass, and lost their formation and their artillery, with 1200 men: a few were slain, most were drowned or were taken prisoners. The raid was no secret of the king and the priests, as Knox absurdly states; nobles of the Reforming no less than of the Catholic party were engaged; the English had full warning and a force of 3000 men, not of 400 farmers; the Scots were beaten through their own ignorance of the ground in which they had been burning and plundering. As to confusion caused by the claim of Oliver Sinclair to be commander, it is not corroborated by contemporary despatches, though Sir George Douglas reports James's lament for the conduct of his favourite, "Fled Oliver! fled Oliver!" The misfortune broke the heart of James. He went to Edinburgh, did some business, retired for a week to Linlithgow,[13] where his queen was awaiting her delivery, and thence went to Falkland, and died of nothing more specific than shame, grief, and despair. He lived to hear of the birth of his daughter, Mary (December 8, 1542). "It came with a lass and it will go with a lass," he is said to have muttered.

On December 14th James passed away, broken by his impossible task, lost in the bewildering paths from which there was no outgait.

James was personally popular for his gaiety and his adventures while he wandered in disguise. Humorous poems are attributed to him. A man of greater genius than his might have failed when confronted by a tyrant so wealthy, ambitious, cruel, and destitute of honour as Henry VIII; constantly engaged with James's traitors in efforts to seize or slay him and his advisers. It is an easy thing to attack James because he would not trust Henry, a man who ruined all that did trust to his seeming favour.

---

[13] Knox gives another account. Our evidence is from a household book of expenses, *Liber Emptorum*, in MS.

# CHAPTER XVI

# The Minority *of* Mary Stuart

When James died, Henry VIII seemed to hold in his hand all the winning cards in the game of which Scotland was the stake. He held Angus and his brother George Douglas; when he slipped them they would again wield the whole force of their House in the interests of England and of Henry's religion. Moreover, he held many noble prisoners taken at Solway—Glencairn, Maxwell, Cassilis, Fleming, Grey, and others,—and all of these, save Sir George Douglas, "have not sticked," says Henry himself, "to take upon them to set the crown of Scotland on our head." Henry's object was to get "the child, the person of the Cardinal, and of such as be chief hindrances to our purpose, and also the chief holds and fortresses into our hands." By sheer brigandage the Reformer king hoped to succeed where the Edwards had failed. He took the oaths of his prisoners, making them swear to secure for him the child, Beaton, and the castles, and later released them to do his bidding.

Henry's failure was due to the genius and resolution of Cardinal Beaton, heading the Catholic party.

What occurred in Scotland on James's death is obscure. Later, Beaton was said to have made the dying king's hand subscribe a blank paper filled up by appointment of Beaton himself as one of a Regency Council of four or five. There is no evidence for the tale. What actually occurred was the proclamation of the Earls of Arran, Argyll, Huntly, Moray, and of Beaton as Regents (December 19, 1542). Arran, the chief of the Hamiltons, was, we know, unless ousted by Henry VIII, the next heir to the throne after the new-born Mary. He was a good-hearted man, but the weakest of mortals, and his constant veerings from the Catholic and national to the English and reforming side were probably caused by his knowledge of his very doubtful legitimacy.

Either party could bring up the doubt; Beaton, having the ear of the Pope, could be specially dangerous, but so could the opposite party if once firmly seated in office. Arran, in any case, presently ousted the Archbishop of Glasgow from the Chancellorship and gave the seals to Beaton—the man whom he presently accused of a shameless forgery of James's will.[14]

The Regency soon came into Arran's own hands: the Solway Moss prisoners, learning this as they journeyed north, began to repent of their oaths of treachery, especially as their oaths were known or suspected in Scotland. George Douglas prevailed on Arran to seize and imprison Beaton till he answered certain charges; but no charges were ever made public, none were produced. The clergy refused to christen or bury during his captivity. Parliament met (March 12, 1543), and still there was silence as to the nature of the accusations against Beaton; and by March 22 George Douglas himself released the Cardinal (of course for a consideration) and carried him to his own strong castle of St Andrews.

Parliament permitted the reading but forbade the discussion of the Bible in English. Arran was posing as a kind of Protestant. Ambassadors were sent to Henry to negotiate a marriage between his son Edward and the baby Queen; but Scotland would not give up a fortress, would never resign her independence, would not place Mary in Henry's hands, would never submit to any but a native ruler.

The airy castle of Henry's hopes fell into dust, built as it was on the oaths of traitors. Love of such a religion as Henry professed, retaining the Mass and making free use of the stake and the gibbet, was not, even to Protestants, so attractive as to make them run the English course and submit to the English Lord Paramount. Some time was needed to make Scots, whatever their religious opinions, lick the English rod. But the scale was soon to turn; for every reforming sermon was apt to produce the harrying of religious houses, and every punishment of the robbers was persecution intolerable against which men sought English protection.

Henry VIII now turned to Arran for support. To Arran he offered the hand of his daughter, the Princess Elizabeth, who should later marry the heir of the Hamiltons. But by mid-April Arran was under the influence of his bastard brother, the Abbot of Paisley (later Archbishop Hamilton). The Earl of Lennox, a Stuart, and Keeper of

---

[14] As to the story of forgery, see a full discussion in the author's 'History of Scotland,' i. 460-467. 1900.

Dumbarton Castle, arrived from France. He was hostile to Arran; for, if Arran were illegitimate, Lennox was next heir to the crown after Mary: he was thus, for the moment, the ally of Beaton against Arran. George Douglas visited Henry, and returned with his terms—Mary to be handed over to England at the age of ten, and to marry Prince Edward at twelve; Arran (by a prior arrangement) was to receive Scotland north of Forth, an auxiliary English army, and the hand of Elizabeth for his son. To the English contingent Arran preferred £5000 in ready money—that was his price.

Sadleyr, Henry's envoy, saw Mary of Guise, and saw her little daughter unclothed; he admired the child, but could not disentangle the cross-webs of intrigue. The national party—the Catholic party—was strongest, because least disunited. When the Scottish ambassadors who went to Henry in spring returned (July 21), the national party seized Mary and carried her to Stirling, where they offered Arran a meeting, and (he said) the child queen's hand for his son. But Arran's own partisans, Glencairn and Cassilis, told Sadleyr that he fabled freely. Representatives of both parties accepted Henry's terms, but delayed the ratification. Henry insisted that it should be ratified by August 24, but on August 16 he seized six Scottish merchant ships. Though the Treaty was ratified on August 25, Arran was compelled to insist on compensation for the ships, but on August 28 he proclaimed Beaton a traitor. In the beginning of September Arran favoured the wrecking of the Franciscan monastery in Edinburgh; and at Dundee the mob, moved by sermons from the celebrated martyr George Wishart, did sack the houses of the Franciscans and the Dominicans; Beaton's Abbey of Arbroath and the Abbey of Lindores were also plundered. Clearly it was believed that Beaton was down, and that church-pillage was authorised by Arran. Yet on September 3 Arran joined hands with Beaton! The Cardinal, by threatening to disprove Arran's legitimacy and ruin his hopes of the crown, or in some other way, had dominated the waverer, while Henry (August 29) was mobilising an army of 20,000 men for the invasion of Scotland. On September 9 Mary was crowned at Stirling. But Beaton could not hold both Arran and his rival Lennox, who committed an act of disgraceful treachery. With Glencairn he seized large supplies of money and stores sent by France to Dumbarton Castle. In 1544 he fled to England and to the protection of Henry, and married Margaret, daughter of Angus and Margaret Tudor, widow of James IV. He became the father of Darnley, Mary's husband in later years, and the fortunes of Scotland were fatally involved in the feud between the Lennox Stewarts and the House of Hamilton.

Meanwhile (November 1543) Arran and Beaton together broke and persecuted the abbey robbers of Perthshire and Angus, making "martyrs" and incurring, on Beaton's part, fatal feuds with Leslies, Greys, Learmonths, and Kirkcaldys. Parliament (December 11) declared the treaty with England void; the party of the Douglases, equally suspected by Henry and by Beaton, was crushed, and George Douglas was held a hostage, still betraying his country in letters to England. Martyrs were burned in Perth and Dundee, which merely infuriated the populace. In April 1544, while Henry was giving the most cruel orders to his army of invasion, one Wishart visited him with offers, which were accepted, for the murder of the Cardinal.[15] Early in May the English army under Hertford took Leith, "raised a jolly fire," says Hertford, in Edinburgh; he burned the towns on his line of march, and retired.

On May 17 Lennox and Glencairn sold themselves to Henry; for ample rewards they were to secure the teaching of God's word "as the mere and only foundation whence proceeds all truth and honour"! Arran defeated Glencairn when he attempted his godly task, and Lennox was driven back into England.

In June Mary of Guise fell into the hands of nobles led by Angus, while the Fife, Perthshire, and Angus lairds, lately Beaton's deadly foes, came into the Cardinal's party. With him and Arran, in November, were banded the Protestants who were to be his murderers, while the Douglases, in December, were cleared by Parliament of all their offences, and Henry offered 3000 crowns for their "trapping." Angus, in February 1545, protested that he loved Henry "best of all men," and would make Lennox Governor of Scotland, while Wharton, for Henry, was trying to kidnap Angus. Enraged by the English desecration of his ancestors' graves at Melrose Abbey, Angus united with Arran, Norman Leslie, and Buccleuch to annihilate an English force at Ancrum Moor, where Henry's men lost 800 slain and 2000 prisoners. The loyalty of Angus to his country was now, by innocents like Arran, thought assured. The plot for Beaton's murder was in 1545 negotiated between Henry and Cassilis, backed by George Douglas; and Crichton of Brunston, as before, was engaged, a godly laird in Lothian. In August the Douglases boast that, as Henry's

---

[15] There is no proof that this man was the preacher George Wishart, later burned.

friends, they have frustrated an invasion of England with a large French contingent, which they pretended to lead, while they secured its failure. Meanwhile, after forty years, Donald Dubh, and all the great western chiefs, none of whom could write, renewed the alliance of 1463 with England, calling themselves "auld enemies of Scotland." Their religious predilections, however, were not Protestant. They promised to destroy or reduce half of Scotland, and hailed Lennox as Governor, as in Angus's offer to Henry in spring 1545. Lennox did make an attempt against Dumbarton in November with Donald Dubh. They failed, and Donald died, without legitimate issue, at Drogheda. The Macleans, Macleods, and Macneils then came into the national party.

In September 1545 Hertford, with an English force, destroyed the religious houses at Melrose, Kelso, Dryburgh, and Jedburgh.[16] Meanwhile the two Douglases skulked with the murderous traitor Cassilis in Ayrshire, and Henry tried to induce French deserters from the Scottish flag to murder Beaton and Arran.

Beaton could scarcely escape for ever from so many plots. His capture, in January 1546, of George Wishart, an eminently learned and virtuous Protestant preacher, and an intimate associate of the murderous, double-dyed traitor Brunston and of other Lothian pietists of the English party; and his burning of Wishart at St Andrews, on March 1, 1546, sealed the Cardinal's doom. On May 29th he was surprised in his castle of St Andrews and slain by his former ally, Norman Leslie, Master of Rothes, with Kirkcaldy of Grange, and James Melville who seems to have dealt the final stab after preaching at his powerless victim. They insulted the corpse, and held St Andrews Castle against all comers.

How gallant a fight Beaton had waged against adversaries how many and multifarious, how murderous, self-seeking, treacherous, and hypocritical, we have seen. He maintained the independence of Scotland against the most recklessly unscrupulous of assailants, though probably he was rather bent on defending the lost cause of a Church entirely and intolerably corrupt.

---

[16] A curious controversy is constantly revived in this matter. It is urged that Knox's mobs did not destroy the abbey churches of Kelso, Melrose, Dryburgh, Roxburgh, and Coldingham: that was done by Hertford's army. If so, they merely deprived the Knoxian brethren of the pleasures of destruction which they enjoyed almost everywhere else. The English, if guilty, left at Melrose, Jedburgh, Coldingham, and Kelso more beautiful remains of mediæval architecture than the Reformers were wont to spare.

The two causes were at the moment inseparable, and, whatever we may think of the Church of Rome, it was not more bloodily inclined than the Church of which Henry was Pope, while it was less illogical, not being the creature of a secular tyrant. If Henry and his party had won their game, the Church of Scotland would have been Henry's Church—would have been Anglican. Thus it was Beaton who, by defeating Henry, made Presbyterian Calvinism possible in Scotland.

# CHAPTER XVII

# Regency *of* Arran

The death of Cardinal Beaton left Scotland and the Church without a skilled and resolute defender. His successor in the see, Archbishop Hamilton, a half-brother of the Regent, was more licentious than the Cardinal (who seems to have been constant to Mariotte Ogilvy), and had little of his political genius. The murderers, with others of their party, held St Andrews Castle, strong in its new fortifications, which the queen-mother and Arran, the Regent, were unable to reduce. Receiving supplies from England by sea, and abetted by Henry VIII, the murderers were in treaty with him to work all his will, while some nobles, like Argyll and Huntly, wavered; though the Douglases now renounced their compact with England, and their promise to give the child queen in marriage to Henry's son. At the end of November, despairing of success in the siege, Arran asked France to send men and ships to take St Andrews Castle from the assassins, who, in December, obtained an armistice. They would surrender, they said, when they got a pardon for their guilt from the Pope; but they begged Henry VIII to move the Emperor to move the Pope to give no pardon! The remission, none the less, arrived early in April 1547, but was mocked at by the garrison of the castle.[17]

The garrison and inmates of the castle presently welcomed the arrival of John Knox and some of his pupils. Knox (born in Haddington, 1513-1515?), a priest and notary, had borne a two-handed sword and been of the body-guard of Wishart. He was now invited by

---

[17] This part of our history is usually and erroneously told as given by Knox, writing fifteen years later. He needs to be corrected by the letters and despatches of the day, which prove that the Reformer's memory, though picturesque, had, in the course of fifteen years, become untrustworthy. He is the chief source of the usual version of Solway Moss.

John Rough, the chaplain, to take on him the office of preacher, which he did, weeping, so strong was his sense of the solemnity of his duties. He also preached and disputed with feeble clerical opponents in the town. The congregation in the castle, though devout, were ruffianly in their lives, nor did he spare rebukes to his flock.

Before Knox arrived, Henry VIII and Francis II had died; the successor of Francis, Henri II, sent to Scotland Monsieur d'Oysel, who became the right-hand man of Mary of Guise in the Government. Meanwhile the advance of an English force against the Border, where they occupied Langholm, caused Arran to lead thither the national levies. But this gave no great relief to the besieged in the castle of St Andrews. In mid-July a well-equipped French fleet swept up the east coast; men were landed with guns; French artillery was planted on the cathedral roof and the steeple of St Salvator's College, and poured a plunging fire into the castle. In a day or two, on the last of July, the garrison surrendered. Knox, with many of his associates, was placed in the galleys and carried captive to France. On one occasion the galleys were within sight of St Andrews, and the Reformer predicted (so he says) that he would again preach there—as he did, to some purpose.

But the castle had not fallen before the English party among the nobles had arranged to betray Scottish fortresses to England; and to lead 2000 Scottish "favourers of the Word of God" to fight under the flag of St George against their country. An English host of 15,000 was assembled, and marched north accompanied by a fleet. On the 9th of September 1547 the leader, Somerset, found the Scottish army occupying a well-chosen position near Musselburgh: on their left lay the Firth, on their front a marsh and the river Esk. But next day the Scots, as when Cromwell defeated them at Dunbar, left an impregnable position in their eagerness to cut Somerset off from his ships, and were routed with great slaughter in the battle of Pinkie. Somerset made no great use of his victory: he took and held Broughty Castle on Tay, fortified Inchcolme in the Firth of Forth, and devastated Holyrood. Mischief he did, to little purpose.

The child queen was conveyed to an isle in the loch of Menteith, where she was safe, and her marriage with the Dauphin was negotiated. In June 1548 a large French force under the Sieur d'Essé arrived, and later captured Haddington, held by the English, while, despite some Franco-Scottish successes in the field, Mary was sent with her Four Maries to France, where she landed in August, the only passenger who had not been sea-sick! By April 1550 the English made peace, abandoning all their holds in Scotland. The great essential prize, the child queen, had escaped them.

The clergy burned a martyr in 1550; in 1549 they had passed measures for their own reformation: too late and futile was the scheme. Early in 1549 Knox returned from France to England, where he was minister at Berwick and at Newcastle, a chaplain of the child Edward VI, and a successful opponent of Cranmer as regards kneeling at the celebration of the Holy Communion. He refused a bishopric, foreseeing trouble under Mary Tudor, from whom he fled to the Continent. In 1550-51 Mary of Guise, visiting France, procured for Arran the Duchy of Châtelherault, and for his eldest son the command of the Scottish Archer Guard, and, by way of exchange, in 1554 took from him the Regency, surrounding herself with French advisers, notably De Roubay and d'Oysel.

CHAPTER XVIII

# Regency *of* Mary *of* Guise

In England, on the death of Edward VI, Catholicism rejoiced in the accession of Mary Tudor, which, by driving Scottish Protestant refugees back into their own country, strengthened there the party of revolt against the Church, while the queen-mother's preference of French over Scottish advisers, and her small force of trained French soldiers in garrisons, caused even the Scottish Catholics to hold France in fear and suspicion. The French counsellors (1556) urged increased taxation for purposes of national defence against England; but the nobles would rather be invaded every year than tolerate a standing army in place of their old irregular feudal levies. Their own independence of the Crown was dearer to the nobles and gentry than safety from their old enemy. They might have reflected that a standing army of Scots, officered by themselves, would be a check on the French soldiers in garrison.

Perplexed and opposed by the great clan of Hamilton, whose chief, Arran, was nearest heir to the crown, Mary of Guise was now anxious to conciliate the Protestants, and there was a "blink," as the Covenanters later said,—a lull in persecution.

After Knox's release from the French galleys in 1549, he had played, as we saw, a considerable part in the affairs of the English Church, and in the making of the second Prayer-Book of Edward VI, but had fled abroad on the accession of Mary Tudor. From Dieppe he had sent a tract to England, praying God to stir up some Phineas or Jehu to shed the blood of "abominable idolaters,"—obviously of Mary of England and Philip of Spain. On earlier occasions he had followed Calvin in deprecating such sanguinary measures. The Scot, after a stormy period of quarrels with Anglican refugees in Frankfort, moved to Geneva, where the city was under a despotism of preachers and of

Calvin. Here Knox found the model of Church government which, in a form if possible more extreme, he later planted in Scotland.

There, in 1549-52, the Church, under Archbishop Hamilton, Beaton's successor, had been confessing her iniquities in Provincial Councils, and attempting to purify herself on the lines of the tolerant and charitable Catechism issued by the Archbishop in 1552. Apparently a *modus vivendi* was being sought, and Protestants were inclined to think that they might be "occasional conformists" and attend Mass without being false to their convictions. But in this brief lull Knox came over to Scotland at the end of harvest, in 1555. On this point of occasional conformity he was fixed. The Mass was idolatry, and idolatry, by the law of God, was a capital offence. Idolaters must be converted or exterminated; they were no better than Amalekites.

This was the central rock of Knox's position: tolerance was impossible. He remained in Scotland, preaching and administering the Sacrament in the Genevan way, till June 1556. He associated with the future leaders of the religious revolution: Erskine of Dun, Lord Lorne (in 1558, fifth Earl of Argyll), James Stewart, bastard of James V, and lay Prior of St Andrews, and of Macon in France; and the Earl of Glencairn. William Maitland of Lethington, "the flower of the wits of Scotland," was to Knox a less congenial acquaintance. Not till May 1556 was Knox summoned to trial in Edinburgh, but he had a strong backing of the laity, as was the custom in Scotland, where justice was overawed by armed gatherings, and no trial was held. By July 1556 he was in France, on his way to Geneva.

The fruits of Knox's labours followed him, in March 1557, in the shape of a letter, signed by Glencairn, Lorne, Lord Erskine, and James Stewart, Mary's bastard brother. They prayed Knox to return. They were ready "to jeopardy lives and goods in the forward setting of the glory of God." This has all the air of risking civil war. Knox was not eager. It was October before he reached Dieppe on his homeward way. Meanwhile there had been hostilities between England and Scotland (as ally of France, then at odds with Philip of Spain, consort King of England), and there were Protestant tumults in Edinburgh. Knox had scruples as to raising civil war by preaching at home. The Scottish nobles had no zeal for the English war; but Knox, who received at Dieppe discouraging letters from unknown correspondents, did not cross the sea. He remained at Dieppe, preaching, till the spring of 1558.

In Knox's absence even James Stewart and Erskine of Dun agreed to hurry on the marriage between Mary, Queen of Scots, and Francis,

Dauphin of France, a feeble boy, younger than herself. Their faces are pitiably young as represented in their coronation medal.

While negotiations for the marriage were begun in October, on December 3, 1557, a godly "band" or covenant for mutual aid was signed by Argyll (then near his death, in 1558); his son, Lorne; the Earl of Morton (son of the traitor, Sir George Douglas); Glencairn; and Erskine of Dun, one of the commissioners who were to visit France for the Royal marriage. They vow to risk their lives against "the Congregation of Satan" (the Church), and in defence of faithful Protestant preachers. They will establish "the blessed Word of God and His Congregation," and henceforth the Protestant party was commonly styled "The Congregation."

Parliament (November 29, 1557) had accepted the French marriage, all the ancient liberties of Scotland being secured, and the right to the throne, if Mary died without issue, being confirmed to the House of Hamilton, not to the Dauphin. The marriage-contract (April 19, 1558) did ratify these just demands; but, on April 4, Mary had been induced to sign them all away to France, leaving Scotland and her own claims to the English crown to the French king.

The marriage was celebrated on April 24, 1558. In that week the last Protestant martyr, Walter Milne, an aged priest and a married man, was burned for heresy at St Andrews. This only increased the zeal of the Congregation.

Among the Protestant preachers then in Scotland, of whom Willock, an Englishman, seems to have been the most reasonable, a certain Paul Methuen, a baker, was prominent. He had been summoned (July 28) to stand his trial for heresy, but his backing of friends was considerable, and they came before Mary of Guise in armour and with a bullying demeanour. She tried to temporise, and on September 3 a great riot broke out in Edinburgh, the image of St Giles was broken, and the mob violently assaulted a procession of priests. The country was seething with discontent, and the death of Mary Tudor (November 17, 1558), with the accession of the Protestant Elizabeth, encouraged the Congregation. Mary of Guise made large concessions: only she desired that there should be no public meetings in the capital. On January 1, 1559, church doors were placarded with "The Beggars' Warning." The Beggars (really the Brethren in their name) claimed the wealth of the religious orders. Threats were pronounced, revolution was menaced at a given date, Whitsunday, and the threats were fulfilled.

All this was the result of a plan, not of accident. Mary of Guise was intending to visit France, not longing to burn heretics. But she fell into the worst of health, and her recovery was doubted, in April 1559. Willock and Methuen had been summoned to trial (February 2, 1559), for their preachings were always apt to lead to violence on the part of their hearers. The summons was again postponed in deference to renewed menaces: a Convention had met at Edinburgh to seek for some remedy, and the last Provincial Council of the Scottish Church (March 1559) had considered vainly some proposals by moderate Catholics for internal reform.[18]

Again the preachers were summoned to Stirling for May 10, but just a week earlier Knox arrived in Scotland. The leader of the French Protestant preachers, Morel, expressed to Calvin his fear that Knox "may fill Scotland with his madness." Now was his opportunity: the Regent was weak and ill; the Congregation was in great force; England was at least not unfavourable to its cause. From Dundee Knox marched with many gentlemen—unarmed, he says—accompanying the preachers to Perth: Erskine of Dun went as an envoy to the Regent at Stirling; she is accused by Knox of treacherous dealing (other contemporary Protestant evidence says nothing of treachery); at all events, on May 10 the preachers were outlawed for non-appearance to stand their trial. The Brethren, "the whole multitude with their preachers," says Knox, who were in Perth were infuriated, and, after a sermon from the Reformer, wrecked the church, sacked the monasteries, and, says Knox, denounced death against any priest who celebrated Mass (a circumstance usually ignored by our historians), at the same time protesting, "We require nothing but liberty of conscience"!

On May 31 a composition was made between the Regent and the insurgents, whom Argyll and James Stewart promised to join if the Regent broke the conditions. Henceforth the pretext that she had broken faith was made whenever it seemed convenient, while the Congregation permitted itself a godly liberty in construing the terms of treaties. A "band" was signed for "the destruction of idolatry" by Argyll, James Stewart, Glencairn, and others; and the Brethren scattered from Perth, breaking down altars and "idols" on their way home. Mary of Guise had promised not to leave a French garrison in Perth. She did leave some Scots in French pay, and on this slim pretext

---

[18] The dates and sequence of events are perplexing. In 'John Knox and the Reformation' (pp. 86-95) I have shown the difficulties.

of her treachery, Argyll and James Stewart proclaimed the Regent perfidious, deserted her cause, and joined the crusade against "idolatry."

# Note

It is far from my purpose to represent Mary of Guise as a kind of stainless Una with a milk-white lamb. I am apt to believe that she caused to be forged a letter, which she attributed to Arran. See my 'John Knox and the Reformation,' pp. 280, 281, where the evidence is discussed. But the critical student of Knox's chapters on these events, generally accepted as historical evidence, cannot but perceive his personal hatred of Mary of Guise, whether shown in thinly veiled hints that Cardinal Beaton was her paramour; or in charges of treacherous breach of promise, which rest primarily on his word. Again, that "the Brethren" wrecked the religious houses of Perth is what he reports to a lady, Mrs Locke; that "the rascal multitude" was guilty is the tale he tells "to all Europe" in his History. I have done my best to compare Knox's stories with contemporary documents, including his own letters. These documents throw a lurid light on his versions of events, as given in this part of his History, which is merely a partisan pamphlet of autumn 1559. The evidence is criticised in my 'John Knox and the Reformation,' pp. 107-157 (1905). Unhappily the letter of Mary of Guise to Henri II, after the outbreak at Perth, is missing from the archives of France.

# CHAPTER XIX

# The Great Pillage

The revolution was now under way, and as it had begun so it continued. There was practically no resistance by the Catholic nobility and gentry: in the Lowlands, apparently, almost all were of the new persuasion. The Duc de Châtelherault might hesitate while his son, the Protestant Earl of Arran, who had been in France as Captain of the Scots Guard, was escaping into Switzerland, and thence to England; but, on Arran's arrival there, the Hamiltons saw their chance of succeeding to the crown in place of the Catholic Mary. The Regent had but a small body of professional French soldiers. But the other side could not keep their feudal levies in the field, and they could not coin the supplies of church plate which must have fallen into their hands, until they had seized the Mint at Edinburgh, so money was scarce with them. It was plain to Knox and Kirkcaldy of Grange, and it soon became obvious to Maitland of Lethington, who, of course, forsook the Regent, that aid from England must be sought,—aid in money, and if possible in men and ships.

Meanwhile the reformers dealt with the ecclesiastical buildings of St Andrews as they had done at Perth, Knox urging them on by his sermons. We may presume that the boys broke the windows and images with a sanctified joy. A mutilated head of the Redeemer has been found in a *latrine* of the monastic buildings. As Commendator, or lay Prior, James Stewart may have secured the golden sheath of the arm-bone of the Apostle, presented by Edward I, and the other precious things, the sacred plate of the Church in a fane which had been the Delphi of Scotland. Lethington appears to have obtained most of the portable property of St Salvator's College except that beautiful monument of idolatry, the great silver mace presented by Kennedy, the Founder, work of a Parisian silversmith, in 1461: this, with maces of rude native work, escaped the spoilers. The monastery of the Franciscans is now levelled with the earth; of the Dominicans' chapel a small fragment remains. Of the residential part of the abbey a house was left: when the lead had been stripped from the roof of the church it became a quarry.

"All churchmen's goods were spoiled and reft from them... for every man for the most part that could get anything pertaining to any churchmen thought the same well-won gear," says a contemporary Diary. Arran himself, when he arrived in Scotland, robbed a priest of all that he had, for which Châtelherault made compensation.

By the middle of June the Regent was compelled to remove almost all her French soldiers out of Fife. Perth was evacuated. The abbey of Scone and the palace were sacked. The Congregation entered Edinburgh: they seem to have found the monasteries already swept bare, but they seized Holyrood, and the stamps at the Mint. The Regent proclaimed that this was flat rebellion, and that the rebels were intriguing with England.

Knox denied it, in the first part of his History (in origin a contemporary tract written in the autumn), but the charge was true, and Knox and Kirkcaldy were, since June, the negotiators. Already his party were offering Arran (the heir of the crown after Mary) as a husband for Elizabeth, who saw him but rejected his suit. Arran's father, Châtelherault, later openly deserted the Regent (July 1). The death of Henri II, wounded in a tournament, did not accelerate the arrival of French reinforcements for the Regent. The weaker Brethren, however, waxed weary; money was scarce, and on July 24, the Congregation evacuated Edinburgh and Leith, after a treaty which they misrepresented, broke, and accused the Regent of breaking.[19]

Knox visited England, about August 1, but felt dissatisfied with his qualification for diplomacy. Nothing, so far, was gained from Elizabeth, save a secret supply of £3000. On the other hand, fresh French forces arrived at Leith: the place was fortified; the Regent was again accused of perfidy by the perfidious; and on October 21 the Congregation proclaimed her deposition on the alleged authority of her daughter, now Queen of France, whose seal they forged and used in their documents. One Cokky was the forger; he saw Arran use the seal on public papers.[20] Cokky had made a die for the coins of the Congregation—a crown of thorns, with the words *Verbum Dei*. Leith,

---

[19] The details of these proceedings and the evidence for them may be found in the author's book, 'John Knox and the Reformation,' pp. 135-141. Cf. also my 'History of Scotland,' ii. 58-60.

[20] See 'Affaires Etrangères: Angleterre,' xv. 131-153. MS.

manned by French soldiers, was, till in the summer of 1560 it surrendered to the Congregation and their English allies, the centre of Catholic resistance.

In November the Congregation, after a severe defeat, fled in grief from Edinburgh to Stirling, where Knox reanimated them, and they sent Lethington to England to crave assistance. Lethington, who had been in the service of the Regent, is henceforth the central figure of every intrigue. Witty, eloquent, subtle, he was indispensable, and he had one great ruling motive, to unite the crowns and peoples of England and Scotland. Unfortunately he loved the crafty exercise of his dominion over men's minds for its own sake, and when, in some inscrutable way, he entered the clumsy plot to murder Darnley, and knew that Mary could prove his guilt, his shiftings and changes puzzle historians. In Scotland he was called Michael Wily, that is, Macchiavelli, and "the necessary evil."

In his mission to England Lethington was successful. By December 21 the English diplomatist, Sadleyr, informed Arran that a fleet was on its way to aid the Congregation, who were sacking Paisley Abbey, and issuing proclamations in the names of Francis and Mary. The fleet arrived while the French were about to seize St Andrews (January 23, 1560), and the French plans were ruined. The Regent, who was dying, found shelter in Edinburgh Castle, which stood neutral. On February 27, 1560, at Berwick, the Congregation entered into a regular league with England, Elizabeth appearing as Protectress of Scotland, while the marriage of Mary and Francis endured.

Meanwhile, owing to the Huguenot disturbances in France (such as the Tumult of Amboise, directed against the lives of Mary's uncles the Cardinal and Duc de Guise), Mary and Francis could not help the Regent, and Huntly, a Catholic, presently, as if in fear of the western clans, joined the Congregation. Mary of Guise had found the great northern chief treacherous, and had disgraced him, and untrustworthy he continued to be. On May 7 the garrison of Leith defeated with heavy loss an Anglo-Scottish attack on the walls; but on June 16 the Regent made a good end, in peace with all men. She saw Châtelherault, James Stewart, and the Earl Marischal; she listened patiently to the preacher Willock; she bade farewell to all, and died, a notable woman, crushed by an impossible task. The garrison of Leith, meanwhile, was starving on rats and horseflesh: negotiations began, and ended in the Treaty of Edinburgh (July 6, 1560).

This Treaty, as between Mary, Queen of France and Scotland, on one hand, and England on the other, was never ratified by Mary

Stuart: she appears to have thought that one clause implied her abandonment of all her claims to the English succession, typified by her quartering of the Royal English arms on her own shield. Thus there never was nor could be amity between her and her sister and her foe, Elizabeth, who was justly aggrieved by her assumption of the English arms, while Elizabeth quartered the arms of France. Again, the ratification of the Treaty as regarded Mary's rebels depended on their fulfilling certain clauses which, in fact, they instantly violated.

Preachers were planted in the larger town, some of which had already secured their services; Knox took Edinburgh. "Superintendents,"—by no means bishops—were appointed, an order which soon ceased to exist in the Kirk: their duties were to wander about in their provinces, superintending and preaching. By request of the Convention (which was crowded by persons not used to attend), some preachers drew up, in four days, a Confession of Faith, on the lines of Calvin's rule at Geneva: this was approved and passed on August 17. The makers of the document profess their readiness to satisfy any critic of any point "from the mouth of God" (out of the Bible), but the pace was so good that either no criticism was offered or it was very rapidly "satisfied." On August 24 four acts were passed in which the authority of "The Bishop of Rome" was repudiated. All previous legislation, not consistent with the new Confession, was rescinded. Against celebrants and attendants of the Mass were threatened (1) confiscation and corporal punishment; (2) exile; and (3) for the third offence, Death. The death sentence is not known to have been carried out in more than one or two cases. (Prof. Hume-Brown writes that "the penalties attached to the breach of these enactments" (namely, the abjuration of Papal jurisdiction, the condemnation of all practices and doctrines contrary to the new creed, and of the celebration of Mass in Scotland) "were those approved and sanctioned by the example of every country in Christendom." But not, surely, for the same offences, such as "the saying or hearing of Mass"?—' History of Scotland,' ii. 71, 72: 1902.) Suits in ecclesiastical were removed into secular courts (August 29).

In the Confession the theology was that of Calvin. Civil rulers were admitted to be of divine institution, their duty is to "suppress idolatry," and they are not to be resisted "when doing that which pertains to their charge." But a Catholic ruler, like Mary, or a tolerant ruler, as James VI would fain have been, apparently may be resisted for his tolerance. Resisted James was, as we shall see, whenever he attempted to be lenient to Catholics.

The Book of Discipline, by Knox and other preachers, never was ratified by the Estates, as the Confession of Faith had been. It made admirable provisions for the payment of preachers and teachers, for the Universities, and for the poor; but somebody, probably Lethington, spoke of the proposals as "devout imaginations." The Book of Discipline approved of what was later accepted by the General Assembly, The Book of Common Order in Public Worship. This book was not a stereotyped Liturgy, but it was a kind of guide to the ministers in public prayers: the minister may repeat the prayers, or "say something like in effect." On the whole, he prayed "as the Spirit moved him," and he really seems to have been regarded as inspired; his prayers were frequently political addresses. To silence these the infatuated policy of Charles I thrust the Laudian Liturgy on the nation.

The preachers were to be chosen by popular election, after examination in knowledge and as to morals. There was to be no ordination "by laying on of hands." "Seeing the miracle is ceased, the using of the ceremony we deem not necessary"; but, if the preachers were inspired, the miracle had not ceased, and the ceremony was soon reinstated. Contrary to Genevan practice, such festivals as Christmas and Easter were abolished. The Scottish Sabbath was established in great majesty. One "rag of Rome" was retained, clerical excommunication—the Sword of Church Discipline. It was the cutting off from Christ of the excommunicated, who were handed over to the devil, and it was attended by civil penalties equivalent to universal boycotting, practical outlawry, and followed by hell fire: "which sentence, lawfully pronounced on earth, is ratified in heaven." The strength of the preachers lay in this terrible weapon, borrowed from the armoury of Rome.

Private morals were watched by the elders, and offenders were judged in kirk-sessions. Witchcraft, Sabbath desecration, and sexual laxities were the most prominent and popular sins. The mainstay of the system is the idea that the Bible is literally inspired; that the preachers are the perhaps inspired interpreters of the Bible, and that the country must imitate the old Hebrew persecution of "idolaters," that is, mainly Catholics. All this meant a theocracy of preachers elected by the populace, and governing the nation by their General Assembly in which nobles and other laymen sat as elders. These peculiar institutions came hot from Geneva, and the country could never have been blessed with them, as we have observed, but for that instrument of Providence, Cardinal Beaton. Had he disposed of himself and Scotland to Henry VIII (who would not have tolerated Presbyterian claims for an hour), Scotland would not have received the Genevan discipline, and the Kirk would have groaned under bishops.

The Reformation supplied Scotland with a class of preachers who were pure in their lives, who were not accessible to bribes (a virtue in which they stood almost alone), who were firm in their faith, and soon had learning enough to defend it; who were constant in their parish work, and of whom many were credited with prophetic and healing powers. They could exorcise ghosts from houses, devils from men possessed.

The baldness of the services, the stern nature of the creed, were congenial to the people. The drawbacks were the intolerance, the spiritual pretensions of the preachers to interference in secular affairs, and the superstition which credited men like Knox, and later, Bruce, with the gifts of prophecy and other miraculous workings, and insisted on the burning of witches and warlocks, whereof the writer knows scarcely an instance in Scotland before the Reformation.

The pulpit may be said to have discharged the functions of the press (a press which was all on one side). When, in 1562, Ninian Winzet, a Catholic priest and ex-schoolmaster, was printing a controversial tractate addressed to Knox, the magistrates seized the manuscript at the printer's house, and the author was fortunate in making his escape. The nature of the Confession of Faith, and of the claims of the ministers to interfere in secular affairs, with divine authority, was certain to cause war between the Crown and the Kirk. That war, whether open and armed, or a conflict in words, endured till, in 1690, the weapon of excommunication with civil penalties was quietly removed from the ecclesiastical armoury. Such were the results of a religious revolution hurriedly effected.

The Lords now sent an embassy to Elizabeth about the time of the death of Amy Robsart, and while Amy's husband, Robert Dudley, was very dear to the English queen, to urge, vainly, her marriage with Arran. On December 5, 1560, Francis II died, leaving Mary Stuart a mere dowager; while her kinsmen, the Guises, lost power, which fell into the unfriendly hands of Catherine de Medici. At once Arran, who made Knox his confidant, began to woo Mary with a letter and a ring. Her reply perhaps increased his tendency to madness, which soon became open and incurable by the science of the day.

Here we must try to sketch Mary, *la, Reine blanche*, in her white royal mourning. Her education had been that of the learned ladies of her age; she had some knowledge of Latin, and knew French and Italian. French was to her almost a mother-tongue, but not quite; she had retained her Scots, and her attempts to write English are, at first, curiously imperfect. She had lived in a profligate Court, but she was not the wanton of hostile slanders. She had all the guile of statesmanship, said the English envoy, Randolph; and she long exercised great patience under daily insults to her religion and provocations from Elizabeth. She was generous, pitiful, naturally honourable, and most loyal to all who served her. But her passions, whether of love or hate, once roused, were tyrannical. In person she was tall, like her mother, and graceful, with beautiful hands. Her face was somewhat long, the nose long and straight, the lips and chin beautifully moulded, the eyebrows very slender, the eyes of a reddish brown, long and narrow. Her hair was russet, drawn back from a lofty brow; her smile was captivating; she was rather fascinating than beautiful; her courage and her love of courage in others were universally confessed.[21]

In January, 1561, the Estates of Scotland ordered James Stuart, Mary's natural brother, to visit her in France. In spring she met him, and an envoy from Huntly (Lesley, later Bishop of Ross), who represented the Catholic party, and asked Mary to land in Aberdeen, and march south at the head of the Gordons and certain northern clans. The proposal came from noblemen of Perthshire, Angus, and the north, whose forces could not have faced a Lowland army. Mary, who had learned from her mother that Huntly was treacherous, preferred to take her chance with her brother, who, returning by way of England, moved Elizabeth to recognise the Scottish queen as her heir. But Elizabeth would never settle the succession, and, as Mary refused to ratify the Treaty of Edinburgh, forbade her to travel home through England.

---

[21] Mary's one good portrait is that owned by Lord Leven and Melville.

# CHAPTER XX

# Mary *in* Scotland

On August 19, 1561, in a dense fog, and almost unexpected and unwelcomed, Mary landed in Leith. She had told the English ambassador to France that she would constrain none of her subjects in religion, and hoped to be unconstrained. Her first act was to pardon some artisans, under censure for a Robin Hood frolic: her motive, says Knox, was her knowledge that they had acted "in despite of religion."

The Lord James had stipulated that she might have her Mass in her private chapel. Her priest was mobbed by the godly; on the following Sunday Knox denounced her Mass, and had his first interview with her later. In vain she spoke of her conscience; Knox said that it was unenlightened. Lethington wished that he would "deal more gently with a young princess unpersuaded." There were three or four later interviews, but Knox, strengthened by a marriage with a girl of sixteen, daughter of Lord Ochiltree, a Stewart, was proof against the queen's fascination. In spite of insults to her faith offered even at pageants of welcome, Mary kept her temper, and, for long, cast in her lot with Lethington and her brother, whose hope was to reconcile her with Elizabeth.

The Court was gay with riotous young French nobles, well mated with Bothwell, who, though a Protestant, had sided with Mary of Guise during the brawls of 1559. He was now a man of twenty-seven, profligate, reckless, a conqueror of hearts, a speaker of French, a ruffian, and well educated.

In December it was arranged that the old bishops and other high clerics should keep two-thirds of their revenues, the other third to be divided between the preachers and the queen, "between God and the devil," says Knox. Thenceforth there was a rift between the preachers and the politicians, Lethington and Lord James (now Earl of Mar), on whom Mary leaned. The new Earl of Mar was furtively created Earl of Murray and enjoyed the gift after the overthrow of Huntly.

In January 1562 Mary asked for an interview with Elizabeth. Certainly Lethington hoped that Elizabeth "would be able to do much with Mary in religion," meaning that, if Mary's claims to succeed Elizabeth were granted, she might turn Anglican. The request for a meeting, dallied with but never granted, occupied diplomatists, while, at home, Arran (March 31) accused Bothwell of training him into a plot to seize Mary's person. Arran probably told truth, but he now went mad; Bothwell was imprisoned in the castle till his escape to England in August 1562. Lethington, in June, was negotiating for Mary's interview with Elizabeth; Knox bitterly opposed it; the preachers feared that the queen would turn Anglican, and bishops might be let loose in Scotland. The masques for Mary's reception were actually being organised, when, in July, Elizabeth, on the pretext of persecutions by the Guises in France, broke off the negotiations.

The rest of the year was occupied by an affair of which the origins are obscure. Mary, with her brother and Lethington, made a progress into the north, were affronted by and attacked Huntly, who died suddenly (October 28) at the fight of Corrichie; seized a son of his, who was executed (November 2), and spoiled his castle which contained much of the property of the Church of Aberdeen. Mary's motives for destroying her chief Catholic subject are not certainly known. Her brother, Lord James, in February made Earl of Mar, now received the lands and title of Earl of Murray. At some date in this year Knox preached against Mary because she gave a dance. He chose to connect her dance with some attack on the Huguenots in France. According to 'The Book of Discipline' he should have remonstrated privately, as Mary told him. The dates are inextricable. (See my 'John Knox and the Reformation,' pp. 215-218.) Till the spring of 1565 the main business was the question of the queen's marriage. This continued to divide the ruling Protestant nobles from the preachers. Knox dreaded an alliance with Spain, a marriage with Don Carlos. But Elizabeth, to waste time, offered Mary the hand of Lord Robert Dudley (Leicester), and, strange as it appears, Mary would probably have accepted him, as late as 1565, for Elizabeth let it be understood that to marry a Catholic prince would be the signal for war, while Mary hoped that, if she accepted Elizabeth's favourite, Dudley, she would be acknowledged as Elizabeth's heiress. Mary was young, and showed little knowledge of the nature of woman.

In 1563 came the affair of Châtelard, a French minor poet, a Huguenot apparently, who, whether in mere fatuity or to discredit Mary, hid himself under her bed at Holyrood, and again at Burntisland. Mary had listened to his rhymes, had danced with him, and smiled on him, but Châtelard went too far. He was decapitated in the market street of St Andrews (Feb. 22, 1563). It is clear, if we may trust Knox's account, singularly unlike Brantôme's, that Châtelard was a Huguenot.

About Easter priests were locked up in Ayrshire, the centre of Presbyterian fanaticism, for celebrating Mass. This was in accordance with law, and to soften Knox the girl queen tried her personal influence. He resisted "the devil"; Mary yielded, and allowed Archbishop Hamilton and some fifty other clerics to be placed "in prison courteous." The Estates, which met on May 27 for the first time since the queen landed, were mollified, but were as far as ever from passing the Book of Discipline. They did pass a law condemning witches to death, a source of unspeakable cruelties. Knox and Murray now ceased to be on terms till their common interests brought them together in 1565.

In June 1563 Elizabeth requested Mary to permit the return to Scotland of Lennox (the traitor to the national cause and to Cardinal Beaton, and the rival of the Hamiltons for the succession to the thrones), apparently for the very purpose of entangling Mary in a marriage with Lennox's son Darnley, and then thwarting it. (It was not Mary who asked Elizabeth to send Lennox.) Knox's favourite candidate was Lord Robert Dudley: despite his notorious character he sometimes favoured the English Puritans. When Holyrood had been invaded by a mob who, in Mary's absence in autumn 1563, broke up the Catholic attendants on Mass (such attendance, in Mary's absence, was illegal), and when both parties were summoned to trial, Knox called together the godly. The Council cleared him of the charge of making an unlawful convocation (they might want to make one, any day, themselves), and he was supported by the General Assembly. Similar conduct of the preachers thirty years later gave James VI the opportunity to triumph over the Kirk.

In June 1564 there was still discord between the Kirk and the Lords, and, in a long argument with Lethington, Knox maintained the right of the godly to imitate the slayings of idolaters by Phineas and Jehu: the doctrine bore blood-red fruits among the later Covenanters. Elizabeth, in May 1564, in vain asked Mary to withdraw the permission (previously asked for by her) to allow Lennox to visit Scotland and plead for the restitution of his lands. The objection to

Lennox's appearance had come, through Randolph, from Knox. "You may cause us to take the Lord Darnley," wrote Kirkcaldy to Cecil, to stop Elizabeth's systems of delays; and Sir James Melville, after going on a mission to Elizabeth, warned Mary that she would never part with her minion, now Earl of Leicester.

Lennox, in autumn 1564, arrived and was restored to his estates, while Leicester and Cecil worked for the sending of his son Darnley to Scotland. Leicester had no desire to desert Elizabeth's Court and his chance of touching her maiden heart.

The intrigues of Cecil, Leicester, and Elizabeth resemble rather a chapter in a novel than a page in history. Elizabeth notoriously hated and, when she could, thwarted all marriages. She desired that Mary should never marry: a union with a Catholic prince she vetoed, threatening war; and Leicester she offered merely "to drive time." But Mary, evasively tempted by hints, later withdrawn, of her recognition as Elizabeth's successor, was, till the end of March 1565, encouraged by Randolph, the English ambassador at her Court, to remain in hope of wedding Leicester.

Randolph himself was not in the secret of the English intrigue, which was to slip Darnley at Mary. He came (February 1565): Cecil and Leicester had "used earnest means" to ensure his coming. On March 17 Mary was informed that she would never be recognised as Elizabeth's successor till events should occur which never could occur. On receiving this news Mary wept; she also was indignant at the long and humiliating series of Elizabeth's treacheries. Her patience broke down; she turned to Darnley, thereby, as the English intriguers designed, breaking up the concord of her nobles. To marry Darnley involved the feud of the Hamiltons, and the return of Murray (whom Darnley had offended), of Châtelherault, Argyll, and many other nobles to the party of Knox and the preachers. Leicester would have been welcome to Knox; Darnley was a Catholic, if anything, and a weak passionate young fool. Mary, in the clash of interests, was a lost woman, as Randolph truly said, with sincere pity. Her long endurance, her attempts to "run the English course," were wasted.

David Riccio, who came to Scotland as a musician in 1561, was now high in her and in Darnley's favour. Murray was accused of a conspiracy to seize Darnley and Lennox; the godly began to organise an armed force (June 1565); Mary summoned from exile Bothwell, a man of the sword. On July 29th she married Darnley, and on August 6th Murray, who had refused to appear to answer the charges of treason brought against him, though a safe-conduct was offered, was outlawed and proclaimed a rebel, while Huntly's son, Lord George, was to be restored to his estates. Thus everything seemed to indicate that Mary had been exasperated into breaking with the party of moderation, the party of Murray and Lethington, and been driven into courses where her support, if any, must come from France and Rome. Yet she married without waiting for the necessary dispensation from the Pope. Her policy was henceforth influenced by her favour to Riccio, and by the jealous and arrogant temper of her husband. Mary well knew that Elizabeth had sent money to her rebels, whom she now pursued all through the south of Scotland; they fled from Edinburgh, where the valiant Brethren, brave enough in throwing stones at pilloried priests, refused to join them; and despite the feuds in her own camp, where Bothwell and Darnley were already on the worst terms, Mary drove the rebel lords across the Border at Carlisle on October 8.

Mary seemed triumphant, but the men with her—Lethington, and Morton the Chancellor—were disaffected; Darnley was mutinous: he thought himself neglected; he and his father resented Mary's leniency to Châtelherault, who had submitted and been sent to France; all parties hated Riccio. There was to be a Parliament early in March 1566. In February Mary sent the Bishop of Dunblane to Rome to ask for a subsidy; she intended to reintroduce the Spiritual Estate into the House as electors of the Lords of the Articles, "tending to have done some good anent the restoring of the old religion." The Nuncio who was to have brought the Pope's money later insisted that Mary should take the heads of Murray, Argyle, Morton, and Lethington! Whether she aimed at securing more than tolerance for Catholics is uncertain; but the Parliament, in which the exiled Lords were to be forfeited, was never held. The other nobles would never permit such a measure.

George Douglas, a stirring cadet of the great House was exciting Darnley's jealousy of Riccio, but already Randolph (February 5, 1566) had written to Cecil that "the wisest were aiming at putting all in hazard" to restore the exiled Lords. The nobles, in the last resort, would all stand by each other: there was now a Douglas plot of the old sort to bring back the exiles; and Darnley, with his jealous desire to murder Riccio, was but the cat's-paw to light the train and explode Mary and her Government. Ruthven, whom Mary had always distrusted, came into the conspiracy. Through Randolph all was known in England. "Bands" were drawn up, signed by Argyll (safe in his own hills), Murray, Glencairn, Rothes, Boyd, Ochiltree (the father of Knox's young wife), and Darnley. His name was put forward; his rights and succession were secured against the Hamiltons; Protestantism, too, was to be defended. Many Douglases, many of the Lothian gentry, were in the plot. Murray was to arrive from England as soon as Riccio had been slain and Mary had been seized.

Randolph knew all and reported to Elizabeth's ministers.

The plan worked with mechanical precision. On March 9 Morton and his company occupied Holyrood, going up the great staircase about eight at night; while Darnley and Ruthven, a dying man, entered the queen's supper-room by a privy stair. Morton's men burst in, Riccio was dragged forth, and died under forty daggers. Bothwell, Atholl, and Huntly, partisans of Mary, escaped from the palace; with them Mary managed to communicate on the morrow, when she also held talk with Murray, who had returned with the other exiles. She had worked on the fears and passions of Darnley; by promises of amnesty the Lords were induced to withdraw their guards next day, and in the following night, by a secret passage, and through the tombs of kings, Mary and Darnley reached the horses brought by Arthur Erskine.

It was a long dark ride to Dunbar, but there Mary was safe. She pardoned and won over Glencairn, whom she liked, and Rothes; Bothwell and Huntly joined her with a sufficient force, Ruthven and Morton fled to Berwick (Ruthven was to die in England), and Knox hastened into Kyle in Ayrshire. Darnley, who declared his own innocence and betrayed his accomplices, was now equally hated and despised by his late allies and by the queen and Murray,—indeed, by all men, chiefly by Morton and Argyll. Lethington was in hiding; but he was indispensable, and in September was reconciled to Mary.

On June 19, in Edinburgh Castle, she bore her child, later James VI; on her recovery Darnley was insolent, and was the more detested, while Bothwell was high in favour. In October most of the Lords signed, with Murray, a band for setting Darnley aside—*not* for his murder. He is said to have denounced Mary to Spain, France, and Rome for neglecting Catholic interests. In mid-October Mary was seriously ill at Jedburgh, where Bothwell, wounded in an encounter with a Border reiver, was welcomed, while Darnley, coldly received, went to his father's house on the Forth. On her recovery Mary resided in the last days of November at Craigmillar Castle, near Edinburgh. Here Murray, Argyll, Bothwell, Huntly, and Lethington held counsel with her as to Darnley. Lethington said that "a way would be found," a way that Parliament would approve, while Murray would "look through his fingers." Lennox believed that the plan was to arrest Darnley on some charge, and slay him if he resisted.

At Stirling (December 17), when the young prince was baptised with Catholic rites, Darnley did not appear; he sulked in his own rooms. A week later, the exiles guilty of Riccio's murder were recalled, among them Morton; and Darnley, finding all his enemies about to be united, went to Glasgow, where he fell ill of smallpox. Mary offered a visit (she had had the malady as a child), and was rudely rebuffed (January 1-13, 1567), but she was with him by January 21. From Glasgow, at this time, was written the long and fatal letter to Bothwell, which places Mary's guilt in luring Darnley to his death beyond doubt, if we accept the letters as authentic.[22]

Darnley was carried in a litter to the lonely house of Kirk o' Field, on the south wall of Edinburgh. Here Mary attended him in his sickness. On Sunday morning, February 9, Murray left Edinburgh for Fife. In the night of Sunday 9-Monday 10, the house where Darnley lay was blown up by gunpowder, and he, with an attendant, was found dead in the garden: how he was slain is not known.

That Bothwell, in accordance with a band signed by himself, Huntly, Argyll, and Lethington, and aided by some Border ruffians, laid and exploded the powder is certain. Morton was apprised by Lethington and Bothwell of the plot, but refused to join it without Mary's written commission, which he did not obtain. Against the queen there is no trustworthy direct evidence (if we distrust her alleged letters to Bothwell), but her conduct in protecting and marrying Bothwell (who was really in love with his wife) shows that she did not disapprove. The trial of Bothwell was a farce; Mary's abduction by him (April 24) and retreat with him to Dunbar was collusive. She married Bothwell on May 15. Her nobles, many of whom had signed a document urging her to marry Bothwell, rose against her; on June 15, 1567, she surrendered to them at Carberry Hill, while they, several of them deep in the murder plot, were not sorry to let Bothwell escape to Dunbar. After some piratical adventures, being pursued by Kirkcaldy he made his way to Denmark, where he died a prisoner.

Mary, first carried to Edinburgh and there insulted by the populace, was next hurried to Lochleven Castle. Her alleged letters to Bothwell were betrayed to the Lords (June 21), probably through Sir James

---

[22] I have no longer any personal doubt that Mary wrote the lost French original of this letter, usually numbered II in the Casket Letters (see my paper, "The Casket Letters," in 'The Scottish Historical Review,' vol. v., No. 17, pp. 1-12). The arguments tending to suggest that parts of the letter are forged (see my 'Mystery of Mary Stuart') are (I now believe) unavailing.

Balfour, who commanded in Edinburgh Castle. Perhaps Murray (who had left for France before the marriage to Bothwell), perhaps fear of Elizabeth, or human pity, induced her captors, contrary to the counsel of Lethington, to spare her life, when she had signed her abdication, while they crowned her infant son. Murray accepted the Regency; a Parliament in December established the Kirk; acquitted themselves of rebellion; and announced that they had proof of Mary's guilt in her own writing. Her romantic escape from Lochleven (May 2, 1568) gave her but an hour of freedom. Defeated on her march to Dumbarton Castle in the battle of Langside Hill, she lost heart and fled to the coast of Galloway; on May 16 crossed the Solway to Workington in Cumberland; and in a few days was Elizabeth's prisoner in Carlisle Castle.

Mary had hitherto been a convinced but not a very obedient daughter of the Church; for example, it appears that she married Darnley before the arrival of the Pope's dispensation. At this moment Philip of Spain, the French envoy to Scotland, and the French Court had no faith in her innocence of Darnley's death; and the Pope said "he knew not which of these ladies were the better"—Mary or Elizabeth. But from this time, while a captive in England, Mary was the centre of the hopes of English Catholics: in miniatures she appears as queen, quartering the English arms; she might further the ends of Spain, of France, of Rome, of English rebels, while her existence was a nightmare to the Protestants of Scotland and a peril to Elizabeth.

After Mary's flight, Murray was, as has been said, Regent for the crowned baby James. In his council were the sensual, brutal, but vigorous Morton, with Mar, later himself Regent, a man of milder nature; Glencairn; Ruthven, whom Mary detested—he had tried to make unwelcome love to her at Lochleven; and "the necessary evil," Lethington. How a man so wily became a party to the murder of Darnley cannot be known: now he began to perceive that, if Mary were restored, as he believed that she would be, his only safety lay in securing her gratitude by secret services.

On the other side were the Hamiltons with their ablest man, the Archbishop; the Border spears who were loyal to Bothwell; and two of the conspirators in the murder of Darnley, Argyll and Huntly; with Fleming and Herries, who were much attached to Mary. The two parties, influenced by Elizabeth, did not now come to blows, but awaited the results of English inquiries into Mary's guilt, and of Elizabeth's consequent action.

CHAPTER XXI

# Minority *of* James VI

"Let none of them escape" was Elizabeth's message to the gaolers of Mary and her companions at Carlisle. The unhappy queen prayed to see her in whose hospitality she had confided, or to be allowed to depart free. Elizabeth's policy was to lead her into consenting to reply to her subjects' accusations, and Mary drifted into the shuffling English inquiries at York in October, while she was lodged at Bolton Castle. Murray, George Buchanan, Lethington (now distrusted by Murray), and Morton produced, for Norfolk and other English Commissioners at York, copies, at least, of the incriminating letters which horrified the Duke of Norfolk. Yet, probably through the guile of Lethington, he changed his mind, and became a suitor for Mary's hand. He bade her refuse compromise, whereas compromise was Lethington's hope: a full and free inquiry would reveal his own guilt in Darnley's murder. The inquiry was shifted to London in December, Mary always being refused permission to appear and speak for herself; nay, she was not allowed even to see the letters which she was accused of having written. Her own Commissioners, Lord Herries and Bishop Lesley, who (as Mary knew in Herries's case) had no faith in her innocence, showed their want of confidence by proposing a compromise; this was not admitted. Morton explained how he got the silver casket with the fatal letters, poems to Bothwell, and other papers; they were read in translations, English and Scots; handwritings were compared, with no known result; evidence was heard, and Elizabeth, at last, merely decided—that she could not admit Mary to her presence. The English Lords agreed, "as the case does now stand," and presently many of them were supporting Norfolk in his desire to marry the accused. Murray was told (January 10, 1669) that he had proved nothing which could make Elizabeth "take any evil opinion of the queen, her good sister," nevertheless, Elizabeth would support him in his government of Scotland, while declining to recognise James VI as king.

All compromises Mary now utterly refused: she would live and die a queen. Henceforth the tangled intrigues cannot be disengaged in a work of this scope. Elizabeth made various proposals to Mary, all involving her resignation as queen, or at least the suspension of her rights. Mary refused to listen; her party in Scotland, led by Châtelherault, Herries, Huntly, and Argyll, did not venture to meet Murray and his party in war, and was counselled by Lethington, who still, in semblance, was of Murray's faction. Lethington was convinced that, sooner or later, Mary would return; and he did not wish to incur "her *particular* ill-will." He knew that Mary, as she said, "had that in black and white which would hang him" for the murder of Darnley. Now Lethington, Huntly, and Argyll were daunted, without stroke of sword, by Murray, and a Convention to discuss messages from Elizabeth and Mary met at Perth (July 25-28, 1569), and refused to allow the annulment of her marriage with Bothwell, though previously they had insisted on its annulment. Presently Lethington was publicly accused of Darnley's murder by Crawford, a retainer of Lennox; was imprisoned, but was released by Kirkcaldy, commander in Edinburgh Castle, which henceforth became the fortress of Mary's cause.

The secret of Norfolk's plan to marry the Scottish queen now reached Elizabeth, making her more hostile to Mary; an insurrection in the North broke out; the Earl of Northumberland was driven into Scotland, was betrayed by Hecky Armstrong, and imprisoned at Loch Leven. Murray offered to hand over Northumberland to Elizabeth in exchange for Mary, her life to be guaranteed by hostages, but, on January 23, 1570, Murray was shot by Hamilton of Bothwellhaugh from a window of a house in Linlithgow belonging to Archbishop Hamilton. The murderer escaped and joined his clan. During his brief regency, Murray had practically detached Huntly and Argyll from armed support of Mary's cause; he had reduced the Border to temporary quiet by the free use of the gibbet; but he had not ventured to face Lethington's friends and bring him to trial: if he had, many others would have been compromised. Murray was sly and avaricious, but, had he been legitimate, Scotland would have been well governed under his vigour and caution.

# Regencies *of* Lennox, Mar, *and* Morton

Randolph was now sent to Edinburgh to make peace between Mary's party and her foes impossible. He succeeded; the parties took up arms, and Sussex ravaged the Border in revenge of a raid by Buccleuch. On May 14, Lennox, with an English force, was sent north: he devastated the Hamilton country; was made Regent in July; and, in April 1571, had his revenge on Archbishop Hamilton, who was taken at the capture, by Crawford, of Dumbarton Castle, held by Lord Fleming, a post of vital moment to the Marians; and was hanged at Stirling for complicity in the slaying of Murray. George Buchanan, Mary's old tutor, took advantage of these facts to publish quite a fresh account of Darnley's murder: the guilt of the Hamiltons now made that of Bothwell almost invisible!

Edinburgh Castle, under Kirkcaldy with Lethington, held out; Knox reluctantly retired from Edinburgh to St Andrews, where he was unpopular; but many of Mary's Lords deserted her, and though Lennox was shot (September 4) in an attack by Buccleuch and Ker of Ferniehirst on Stirling Castle, where he was holding a Parliament, he was succeeded by Mar, who was inspired by Morton, a far stronger man. Presently the discovery of a plot between Mary, Norfolk, the English Catholics, and Spain, caused the Duke's execution, and more severe incarceration for Mary.

In Scotland there was no chance of peace. Morton and his associates would not resign the lands of the Hamiltons, Lethington, and Kirkcaldy; Lethington knew that no amnesty would cover his guilt (though he had been nominally cleared) in the slaying of Darnley. One after the other of Mary's adherents made their peace; but Kirkcaldy and Lethington, in Edinburgh Castle, seemed safe while money and supplies held out. Knox had prophesied that Kirkcaldy would be hanged, but did not live to see his desire on his enemy, or on Mary, whom Elizabeth was about to hand over to Mar for instant execution. Knox died on November 24, 1572; Mar, the Regent, had predeceased him by a month, leaving Morton in power. On May 28, 1573, the castle, attacked by guns and engineers from England, and cut off from water, struck its flag. The brave Kirkcaldy was hanged; Lethington, who had long been moribund, escaped by an opportune death. The best soldier in Scotland and the most modern of her wits thus perished together. Concerning Knox, the opinions of his contemporaries differed. By his own account the leaders of his party deemed him "too extreme," and David Hume finds his ferocious delight in chronicling the murders of his foes "rather amusing," though sad! Quarrels of religion apart, Knox was a very good-hearted man; but where religion was concerned, his temper was remote from the Christian. He was a perfect agitator; he knew no tolerance, he spared no violence of language, and in diplomacy, when he diplomatised, he was no more scrupulous than another. Admirably vigorous and personal as literature, his History needs constant correction from documents. While to his secretary, Bannatyne, Knox seemed "a man of God, the light of Scotland, the mirror of godliness"; many silent, douce folk among whom he laboured probably agreed in the allegation quoted by a diarist of the day, that Knox "had, as was alleged, the most part of the blame of all the sorrows of Scotland since the slaughter of the late Cardinal."

In these years of violence, of "the Douglas wars" as they were called, two new tendencies may be observed. In January 1572, Morton induced an assembly of preachers at Leith to accept one of his clan, John Douglas, as Archbishop of St Andrews: other bishops were appointed, called *Tulchan* bishops, from the *tulchan* or effigy of a calf employed to induce cows to yield their milk. The Church revenues were drawn through these unapostolic prelates, and came into the hands of the State, or at least of Morton. With these bishops, superintendents co-existed, but not for long. "The horns of the mitre" already began to peer above Presbyterian parity, and Morton is said to have remarked that there would never be peace in Scotland till some preachers were hanged. In fact, there never was peace between Kirk and State till a deplorable number of preachers were hanged by the Governments of Charles II and James II.

A meeting of preachers in Edinburgh, after the Bartholomew massacre, in the autumn of 1572, demanded that "it shall be lawful to all the subjects in this realm to invade them and every one of them to the death." The persons to be "invaded to the death" are recalcitrant Catholics, "grit or small," persisting in remaining in Scotland.[23]

The alarmed demands of the preachers were merely disregarded by the Privy Council. The ruling nobles, as Bishop Lesley says, would never gratify the preachers by carrying out the bloody penal Acts to their full extent against Catholics. There was no expulsion of all

---

[23] I can construe in no other sense the verbose "article." It may be read in Dr Hay Fleming's 'Reformation in Scotland,' pp. 449, 450, with sufficient commentary, pp. 450-453.

Catholics who dared to stay; no popular massacre of all who declined to go. While Morton was in power he kept the preachers well in hand. He did worse: he starved the ministers, and thrust into the best livings wanton young gentlemen, of whom his kinsman, Archibald Douglas, an accomplice in Darnley's death and a trebly-dyed traitor, was the worst. But in 1575, the great Andrew Melville, an erudite scholar and a most determined person, began to protest against the very name of bishop in the Kirk; and in Adamson, made by Morton successor of John Douglas at St Andrews, Melville found a mark and a victim. In economics, as an English diplomatist wrote to Cecil in November 1572, the country, despite the civil war, was thriving; "the noblemen's great credit decaying,… the ministry and religion increaseth, and the desire in them to prevent the practice of the Papists." The Englishman, in November, may refer to the petition for persecution of October 20, 1572.

The death of old Châtelherault now left the headship of the Hamiltons in more resolute hands; Morton was confronted by opposition from Argyll, Atholl, Buchan, and Mar; and Morton, in 1576-1577, made approaches to Mary. When the young James VI came to his majority Morton's enemies would charge him with his guilty foreknowledge, through Both well, of Darnley's murder, so he made advances to Mary in hope of an amnesty. She suspected a trap and held aloof.

# CHAPTER XXII

# Reign *of* James VI

On March 4, 1578, a strong band of nobles, led by Argyll, presented so firm a front that Morton resigned the Regency; but in April 1578, a Douglas plot, backed by Angus and Morton, secured for the Earl of Mar the command of Stirling Castle and custody of the King; in June 1578, after an appearance of civil war, Morton was as strong as ever. After dining with him, in April 1579, Atholl, the main hope of Mary in Scotland, died suddenly, and suspicion of poison fell on his host. But Morton's ensuing success in expelling from Scotland the Hamilton leaders, Lord Claude and Arbroath, brought down his own doom. With them Sir James Balfour, deep in the secrets of Darnley's death, was exiled; he opened a correspondence with Mary, and presently procured for her "a contented revenge" on Morton.

Two new characters in the long intrigue of vengeance now come on the scene. Both were Stewarts, and as such were concerned in the feud against the Hamiltons. The first was a cousin of Darnley, brought up in France, namely Esme Stuart d'Aubigny, son of John, a brother of Lennox. He had all the accomplishments likely to charm the boy king, now in his fourteenth year.

James had hitherto been sternly educated by George Buchanan, more mildly by Peter Young. Buchanan and others had not quite succeeded in bringing him to scorn and hate his mother; Lady Mar, who was very kind to him, had exercised a gentler influence. The boy had read much, had hunted yet more eagerly, and had learned dissimulation and distrust, so natural to a child weak and ungainly in body and the conscious centre of the intrigues of violent men. A favourite of his was James Stewart, son of Lord Ochiltree, and brother-in-law of John Knox. Stewart was Captain of the Guard, a man of learning, who had been in foreign service; he was skilled in all bodily feats, was ambitious, reckless, and resolute, and no friend of the preachers. The two Stewarts, d'Aubigny and the Captain, became allies.

In a Parliament at Edinburgh (November 1579) their foes, the chiefs of the Hamiltons, were forfeited (they had been driven to seek shelter with Elizabeth), while d'Aubigny got their lands and the key of Scotland, Dumbarton Castle, on the estuary of Clyde. The Kirk, regarding d'Aubigny, now Earl of Lennox, despite his Protestant professions, as a Papist or an atheist, had little joy in Morton, who was denounced in a printed placard as guilty in Darnley's murder: Sir James Balfour could show his signature to the band to slay Darnley, signed by Huntly, Bothwell, Argyll, and Lethington. This was not true. Balfour knew much, was himself involved, but had not the band to show, or did not dare to produce it.

To strengthen himself, Lennox was reconciled to the Kirk; to help the Hamiltons, Elizabeth sent Bowes to intrigue against Lennox, who was conspiring in Mary's interest, or in that of the Guises, or in his own. When Lennox succeeded in getting Dumbarton Castle, an open door for France, into his power, Bowes was urged by Elizabeth to join with Morton and "lay violent hands" on Lennox (August 31, 1580), but in a month Elizabeth cancelled her orders.

Bowes was recalled; Morton, to whom English aid had been promised, was left to take his chances. Morton had warning from Lord Robert Stewart, Mary's half-brother, to fly the country, for Sir James Balfour, with his information, had landed. On December 31, 1580, Captain Stewart accused Morton, in presence of the Council, of complicity in Darnley's murder. He was put in ward; Elizabeth threatened war; the preachers stormed against Lennox; a plot to murder him (a Douglas plot) and to seize James was discovered; Randolph, who now represented Elizabeth, was fired at, and fled to Berwick; James Stewart was created Earl of Arran. In March 1581 the king and Lennox tried to propitiate the preachers by signing a negative Covenant against Rome, later made into a precedent for the famous Covenant of 1638. On June 1 Morton was tried for guilty foreknowledge of Darnley's death. He was executed deservedly, and his head was stuck on a spike of the Tolbooth. The death of this avaricious, licentious, and resolute though unamiable Protestant was a heavy blow to the preachers and their party, and a crook in the lot of Elizabeth.

# The War *of* Kirk *and* King

The next twenty years were occupied with the strife of Kirk and King, whence arose "all the cumber of Scotland" till 1689. The preachers, led by the learned and turbulent Andrew Melville, had an ever-present terror of a restoration of Catholicism, the creed of a number of the nobles and of an unknown proportion of the people. The Reformation of 1559-1560 had been met by no Catholic resistance; we might suppose that the enormous majority of the people were Protestants, though the reverse has been asserted. But whatever the theological preferences of the country may have been, the justifiable fear of practical annexation by France had overpowered all other considerations. By 1580 it does not seem that there was any good reason for the Protestant nervousness, even if some northern counties and northern and Border peers preferred Catholicism. The king himself, a firm believer in his own theological learning and acuteness, was thoroughly Protestant.

But the preachers would scarcely allow him to remain a Protestant. Their claims, as formulated by Andrew Melville, were inconsistent with the right of the State to be mistress in her own house. In a General Assembly at Glasgow (1581) Presbyteries were established; Episcopacy was condemned; the Kirk claimed for herself a separate jurisdiction, uninvadable by the State. Elizabeth, though for State reasons she usually backed the Presbyterians against James, also warned him of "a sect of dangerous consequence, which would have no king but a presbytery." The Kirk, with her sword of excommunication, and with the inspired violence of the political sermons and prayers, invaded the secular authority whenever and wherever she pleased, and supported the preachers in their claims to be tried first, when accused of treasonable libels, in their own ecclesiastical courts. These were certain to acquit them.

James, if not pressed in this fashion, had no particular reason for desiring Episcopal government of the Kirk, but being so pressed he saw no refuge save in bishops. Meanwhile his chief advisers— d'Aubigny, now Duke of Lennox, and James Stewart, the destroyer of Morton, now, to the prejudice of the Hamiltons, Earl of Arran—were men whose private life, at least in Arran's case, was scandalous. If Arran were a Protestant, he was impatient of the rule of the pulpiteers; and Lennox was working, if not sincerely in Mary's interests, certainly in his own and for those of the Catholic House of Guise. At the same time he favoured the king's Episcopal schemes, and, late in 1581, appointed a preacher named Montgomery to the recently vacant Archbishopric of Glasgow, while he himself, like Morton, drew most of the revenues. Hence arose tumults, and, late in 1581 and in 1582, priestly and Jesuit emissaries went and came, intriguing for a Catholic rising, to be supported by a large foreign force which they had not the slightest chance of obtaining from any quarter. Archbishop Montgomery was excommunicated by the Kirk, and James, as we saw, had signed "A Negative Confession" (1581).

In 1582 Elizabeth was backing the exiled Presbyterian Earl of Angus and the Earl of Gowrie (Ruthven), while Lennox was contemplating a *coup d'état* in Edinburgh (August 27). Gowrie, with the connivance of England, struck the first blow. He, Mar, and their accomplices captured James at Ruthven Castle, near Perth (August 23, "the Raid of Ruthven"), with the approval of the General Assembly of the Kirk. It was a Douglas plot managed by Angus and Elizabeth. James Stewart of the Guard (now Earl of Arran) was made prisoner; Lennox fled the country. In October 1582, in a Parliament at Holyrood, the conspirators passed Acts indemnifying themselves, and the General Assembly approved them. These Acts were rescinded later, and James had learned for life his hatred of the Presbyterians who had treacherously seized and insulted their king.[24]

In May 1583 Lennox died in Paris, leaving an heir. On June 27 James made his escape, "a free king," to the castle of St Andrews: he proclaimed an amnesty and feigned reconciliation with his captor, the Earl of Gowrie, chief of the house so hateful to Mary—the Ruthvens. At the same time James placed himself in friendly relations with his kinsfolk, the Guises, the terror of Protestants. He had already been suspected, on account of Lennox, as inclined to Rome: in fact, he was always a Protestant, but baited on every side—by England, by the Kirk, by a faction of his nobles: he intrigued for allies in every direction.

---

[24] It appears that there was both a plot by Lennox, after the Raid of Ruthven, to seize James—"preaching will be of no avail to convert him," his mother wrote; and also an English plot, rejected by Gowrie, to poison both James and Mary! For the former, see Professor Hume Brown, 'History of Scotland,' vol. ii. p. 289; for the latter, see my 'History of Scotland,' vol. ii. pp. 286, 287, with the authorities in each case.

The secret history of his intrigues has never been written. We find the persecuted and astute lad either in communication with Rome, or represented by shady adventurers as employing them to establish such communications. At one time, as has been recently discovered, a young man giving himself out as James's bastard brother (a son of Darnley begotten in England) was professing to bear letters from James to the Pope. He was arrested on the Continent, and James could not be brought either to avow or disclaim his kinsman!

A new Lennox, son of the last, was created a duke; a new Bothwell, Francis Stewart (nephew of Mary's Bothwell), began to rival his uncle in turbulence. Knowing that Anglo-Scottish plots to capture him again were being woven daily by Angus and others, James, in February 1584, wrote a friendly and compromising letter to the Pope. In April, Arran (James Stewart) crushed a conspiracy by seizing Gowrie at Dundee, and then routing a force with which Mar and Angus had entered Scotland. Gowrie, confessing his guilt as a conspirator, was executed at Stirling (May 2, 1584), leaving, of course, his feud to his widow and son. The chief preachers fled; Andrew Melville was already in exile, with several others, in England. Melville, in February, had been charged with preaching seditious sermons, had brandished a Hebrew Bible at the Privy Council, had refused secular jurisdiction and appealed to a spiritual court, by which he was certain to be acquitted. Henceforward, when charged with uttering treasonable libels from the pulpit, the preachers were wont to appeal, in the first instance, to a court of their own cloth, and on this point James in the long-run triumphed over the Kirk.

In a Parliament of May 18, 1584, such declinature of royal jurisdiction was, by "The Black Acts," made treason: Episcopacy was established; the heirs of Gowrie were disinherited; Angus, Mar, and other rebels were forfeited. But such forfeitures never held long in Scotland.

In August 1584 a new turn was given to James's policy by Arran, who was Protestant, if anything, in belief, and hoped to win over Elizabeth, the harbourer of all enemies of James. Arran's instrument was the beautiful young Master of Gray, in France a Catholic, a partisan of Mary, and leagued with the Guises. He was sent to persuade Elizabeth to banish James's exiled rebels, but, like a Lethington on a smaller scale, he set himself to obtain the restoration of these lords as against Arran, while he gratified Elizabeth by betraying to her the secrets of Mary. This man was the adoring friend of the flower of chivalry, Sir Philip Sidney!

As against Arran the plot succeeded. Making Berwick, on English soil, their base, in November 1585 the exiles, lay and secular, backed by England, returned, captured James at Stirling, and drove Arran to lurk about the country, till, many years after, Douglas of Parkhead met and slew him, avenging Morton; and, when opportunity offered, Douglas was himself slain by an avenging Stewart at the Cross of Edinburgh. The age reeked with such blood feuds, of which the preachers could not cure their fiery flocks.

In December 1585 Parliament restored Gowrie's forfeited family to their own (henceforth they were constantly conspiring against James), and the exiled preachers returned to their manses and pulpits. But bishops were not abolished, though the Kirk, through the Synod of Fife, excommunicated the Archbishop of St Andrews, Adamson, who replied in kind. He was charged with witchcraft, and in the long-run was dragged down and reduced to poverty, being accused of dealings with witches—and hares!

In July 1586 England and Scotland formed an alliance, and Elizabeth promised to make James an allowance of £4000 a-year. This, it may be feared, was the blood-price of James's mother: from her son, and any hope of aid from her son, Mary was now cut off. Walsingham laid the snares into which she fell, deliberately providing for her means of communication with Babington and his company, and deciphering and copying the letters which passed through the channel which he had contrived. A trifle of forgery was also done by his agent, Phelipps. Mary, knowing herself deserted by her son, was determined, as James knew, to disinherit him. For this reason, and for the £4000, he made no strong protest against her trial. One of his agents in London—the wretched accomplice in his father's murder, Archibald Douglas—was consenting to her execution. James himself thought that strict imprisonment was the best course; but the Presbyterian Angus declared that Mary "could not be blamed if she had caused the Queen of England's throat to be cut for detaining her so unjustly imprisoned." The natural man within us entirely agrees with Angus!

A mission was sent from Holyrood, including James's handsome new favourite, the Master of Gray, with his cousin, Logan of Restalrig, who sold the Master to Walsingham. The envoys were to beg for Mary's life. The Master had previously betrayed her; but he was not wholly lost, and in London he did his best, contrary to what is commonly stated, to secure her life. He thus incurred the enmity of his former allies in the English Court, and, as he had foreseen, he was ruined in Scotland—his *previous* letters, hostile to Mary, being betrayed by his aforesaid cousin, Logan of Restalrig.

On February 8, 1567, ended the lifelong tragedy of Mary Stuart. The woman whom Elizabeth vainly moved Amyas Paulet to murder was publicly decapitated at Fotheringay. James vowed that he would not accept from Elizabeth "the price of his mother's blood." But despite the fury of his nobles James sat still and took the money, at most some £4000 annually,—when he could get it.

During the next fifteen years the reign of James, and his struggle for freedom from the Kirk, was perturbed by a long series of intrigues of which the details are too obscure and complex for presentation here. His chief Minister was now John Maitland, a brother of Lethington, and as versatile, unscrupulous, and intelligent as the rest of that House. Maitland had actually been present, as Lethington's representative, at the tragedy of the Kirk-o'-Field. He was Protestant, and favoured the party of England. In the State the chief parties were the Presbyterian nobles, the majority of the gentry or lairds, and the preachers on one side; and the great Catholic families of Huntly, Morton (the title being now held by a Maxwell), Errol, and Crawford on the other. Bothwell (a sister's son of Mary's Bothwell) flitted meteor-like, more Catholic than anything else, but always plotting to seize James's person; and in this he was backed by the widow of Gowrie and the preachers, and encouraged by Elizabeth. In her fear that James would join the Catholic nobles, whom the preachers eternally urged him to persecute, Elizabeth smiled on the Protestant plots—thereby, of course, fostering any inclination which James may have felt to seek Catholic aid at home and abroad. The plots of Mary were perpetually confused by intrigues of priestly emissaries, who interfered with the schemes of Spain and mixed in the interests of the Guises.

A fact which proved to be of the highest importance was the passing, in July 1587, of an Act by which much of the ecclesiastical property of the ancient Church was attached to the Crown, to be employed in providing for the maintenance of the clergy. But James used much of it in making temporal lordships: for example, at the time of the mysterious Gowrie Conspiracy (August 1600), we find that the Earl of Gowrie had obtained the Church lands of the Abbey of Scone, which his brother, the Master of Ruthven, desired. With the large revenues now at his disposal James could buy the support of the baronage, who, after the execution in 1584 of the Earl of Gowrie (the father of the Gowrie of the conspiracy of 1600), are not found leading and siding with the ministers in a resolute way. By 1600 young Gowrie was the only hope of the preachers, and probably James's ability to enrich the nobles helped to make them stand aloof. Meanwhile, fears and hopes of the success of the Spanish Armada held the minds of the Protestants and of the Catholic earls. "In this world-wolter," as James said, no Scot moved for Spain except that Lord Maxwell who had first received and then been deprived of the Earldom of Morton. James advanced against him in Dumfriesshire and caused his flight. As for the Armada, many ships drifted north round Scotland, and one great vessel, blown up in Tobermory Bay by Lachlan Maclean of Duart, still invites the attention of treasure-hunters (1911).

# The Catholic Earls

Early in 1589 Elizabeth became mistress of some letters which proved that the Catholic earls, Huntly and Errol, were intriguing with Spain. The offence was lightly passed over, but when the earls, with Crawford and Montrose, drew to a head in the north, James, with much more than his usual spirit, headed the army which advanced against them: they fled from him near Aberdeen, surrendered, and were for a brief time imprisoned. As nobody knows how Fortune's wheel may turn, and as James, hard pressed by the preachers, could neglect no chance of support, he would never gratify the Kirk by crushing the Catholic earls, by temperament he was no persecutor. His calculated leniency caused him years of trouble.

Meanwhile James, after issuing a grotesque proclamation about the causes of his spirited resolve, sailed in October to woo a sea-king's daughter over the foam, the Princess Anne of Denmark. After happy months passed, he wrote, "in drinking and driving ower," he returned with his bride in May 1590.

The General Assembly then ordered prayers for the Puritans oppressed in England; none the less Elizabeth, the oppressor, continued to patronise the plots of the Puritans of Scotland. They now lent their approval to the foe of James's minister, Maitland, namely, the wild Francis Stewart, Earl of Bothwell, a sister's son of Mary's Bothwell. This young man had the engaging quality of gay and absolute recklessness; he was dear to ladies and the wild young gentry of Lothian and the Borders; he broke prisons, released friends, dealt with wizards, aided by Lady Gowrie stole into Holyrood, his ruling ambition being to capture the king. The preachers prayed for "sanctified plagues" against James, and regarded Bothwell favourably as a sanctified plague.

A strange conspiracy within Clan Campbell, in which Huntly and Maitland were implicated, now led to the murder, among others, of the bonny Earl of Murray by Huntly in partnership with Maitland (February 1592).

James was accused of having instigated this crime, from suspicion of Murray as a partner in the wild enterprises of Bothwell, and was so hard pressed by sermons that, in the early summer of 1592, he allowed the Black Acts to be abrogated, and "the Charter of the liberties of the Kirk" to be passed. One of these liberties was to persecute Catholics in accordance with the penal Acts of 1560. The Kirk was almost an *imperium in imperio*, but was still prohibited from appointing the time and place of its own General Assemblies without Royal assent. This weak point in their defences enabled James to vanquish them, but, in June, Bothwell attacked him in the Palace of Falkland and put him in considerable peril.

The end of 1592 and the opening of 1593 were remarkable for the discovery of "The Spanish Blanks," papers addressed to Philip of Spain, signed by Huntly, the new Earl of Angus, and Errol, to be filled up with an oral message requesting military aid for Scottish Catholics. Such proceedings make our historians hold up obtesting hands against the perfidy of idolaters. But clearly, if Knox and the congregation were acting rightly when they besought the aid of England against Mary of Guise, then Errol and Huntly are not to blame for inviting Spain to free them from persecution. Some inkling of the scheme had reached James, and a paper in which he weighed the pros and cons is in existence. His suspected understanding with the Catholic earls, whom he merely did not wish to estrange hopelessly, was punished by a sanctified plague. On July 24, 1593, by aid of the late Earl Gowrie's daughter, Bothwell entered Holyrood, seized the king, extorted his own terms, went and amazed the Dean of Durham by his narrative of the adventure, and seemed to have the connivance of Elizabeth. But in September James found himself in a position to repudiate his forced engagement. Bothwell now allied himself with the Catholic earls, and, as a Catholic, had no longer the prayers of the preachers. James ordered levies to attack the earls, while Argyll led his clan and the Macleans against Huntly, only to be defeated by the Gordon horse at the battle of Glenrinnes (October 3). Huntly and his allies, however, dared not encounter King James and Andrew Melville, who marched together against them, and they were obliged to fly to the Continent. Bothwell, with his retainer, Colville, continued, with Cecil's connivance, to make desperate plots for seizing James; indeed, Cecil was intriguing with them and other desperadoes even after 1600. Throughout all the Tudor period, from Henry VII to 1601, England was engaged in a series of conspiracies against the persons of the princes of Scotland. The Catholics of the south of Scotland now lost Lord Maxwell, slain by a "Lockerby Lick" in a great clan battle with the Johnstones at Dryfe Sands.

In 1595, James's minister, John Maitland, brother of Lethington, died, and early in 1596 an organisation called "the Octavians" was made to regulate the distracted finance of the country. On April 13, 1596, Walter Scott of Buccleuch made himself an everlasting name by the bloodless rescue of Kinmont Willie, an Armstrong reiver, from the Castle of Carlisle, where he was illegally held by Lord Scrope. The period was notable for the endless raids by the clans on both sides of the Border, celebrated in ballads.

James had determined to recall the exiled Catholic earls, undeterred by the eloquence of "the last of all our sincere Assemblies," held with deep emotion in March 1596. The earls came home; in September at Falkland Palace Andrew Melville seized James by the sleeve, called him "God's silly vassal," and warned him that Christ and his Kirk were the king's overlords. Soon afterwards Mr David Black of St Andrews spoke against Elizabeth in a sermon which caused diplomatic remonstrances. Black would be tried, in the first instance, only by a Spiritual Court of his brethren. There was a long struggle, the ministers appointed a kind of standing Committee of Safety; James issued a proclamation dissolving it, and, on December 17, inflammatory sermons led a deputation to try to visit James, who was with the Lords of Session in the Tolbooth. Whether under an alarm of a Popish plot or not, the crowd became so fierce and menacing that the great Lachlan Maclean of Duart rode to Stirling to bring up Argyll in the king's defence with such forces as he could muster. The king retired to Linlithgow; the Rev. Mr Bruce, a famous preacher credited with powers of prophecy, in vain appealed to the Duke of Hamilton to lead the godly. By threatening to withdraw the Court and Courts of Justice from Edinburgh James brought the citizens to their knees, and was able to take order with the preachers.

CHAPTER XXIII

# The Gowrie Conspiracy

James, in reducing the Kirk, relied as much on his cunning and "kingcraft" as on his prerogative. He summoned a Convention of preachers and of the Estates to Perth at the end of February 1597, and thither he brought many ministers from the north, men unlike the zealots of Lothian and the Lowlands. He persuaded them to vote themselves a General Assembly; and they admitted his right to propose modifications in Church government, to forbid unusual convocations (as in Edinburgh during the autumn of 1596); they were not to preach against Acts of Parliament or of Council, nor appoint preachers in the great towns without the Royal assent, and were not to attack individuals from the pulpit. An attempt was to be made to convert the Catholic lords. A General Assembly at Dundee in May ratified these decisions, to the wrath of Andrew Melville, and the Catholic earls were more or less reconciled to the Kirk, which at this period had not one supporter among the nobility. James had made large grants of Church lands among the noblesse, and they abstained from their wonted conspiracies for a while. The king occupied himself much in encouraging the persecution of witches, but even that did not endear him to the preachers.

In the Assembly of March 1598 certain ministers were allowed to sit and vote in Parliament. In 1598-1599 a privately printed book by James, the 'Basilicon Doron,' came to the knowledge of the clergy: it revealed his opinions on the right of kings to rule the Church, and on the tendency of the preachers to introduce a democracy "with themselves as Tribunes of the People," a very fair definition of their policy. It was to stop them that he gradually introduced a bastard kind of bishops, police to keep the pulpiteers in order. They were refusing, in face of the king's licence, to permit a company of English players to act in Edinburgh, for they took various powers into their hands.

Meanwhile James's relations with England, where Elizabeth saw with dismay his victory over her allies, his clergy, were unfriendly. Plots were encouraged against him, but it is not probable that England was aware of the famous and mysterious conspiracy of the young Earl of Gowrie, who was warmly welcomed by Elizabeth on his return from Padua, by way of Paris. He had been summoned by Bruce, James's chief clerical adversary, and the Kirk had high hopes of the son of the man of the Raid of Ruthven. He led the opposition to taxation for national defence in a convention of June-July 1600. On August 5, in his own house at Perth, where James, summoned thither by Gowrie's younger brother, had dined with him, Gowrie and his brother were slain by John Ramsay, a page to the king.

This affair was mysterious. The preachers, and especially Bruce, refused to accept James's own account of the events, at first, and this was not surprising. Gowrie was their one hope among the peers, and the story which James told is so strange that nothing could be stranger or less credible except the various and manifestly mendacious versions of the Gowrie party.[25]

James's version of the occurrences must be as much as possible condensed, and there is no room for the corroborating evidence of Lennox and others. As the king was leaving Falkland to hunt a buck early on August 5, the Master of Ruthven, who had ridden over from his brother's house in Perth, accosted him. The Master declared that he had on the previous evening arrested a man carrying a pot of gold; had said nothing to Gowrie; had locked up the man and his gold in a room, and now wished James to come instantly and examine the fellow. The king's curiosity and cupidity were less powerful than his love of sport: he would first kill his buck. During the chase James told the story to Lennox, who corroborated. Ruthven sent a companion to inform his brother; none the less, when the king, with a considerable following, did appear at Gowrie's house, no preparation for his reception had been made.

---

[25] Of these versions, that long lost one which was sent to England has been published for the first time, with the previously unnoticed incident of Robert Oliphant, in the author's 'James VI and the Gowrie Mystery.' Here it is also demonstrated that all the treasonable letters attributed in 1606-1608 to Logan were forged by Logan's solicitor, George Sprot, though the principal letter seems to me to be a copy of an authentic original. That all, *as they stand*, are forgeries is the unanimous opinion of experts. See the whole of the documents in the author's 'Confessions of George Sprot.' Roxburghe Club.

The Master was now in a quandary: he had no prisoner and no pot of gold. During dinner Gowrie was very nervous; after it James and the Master slipped upstairs together while Gowrie took the gentlemen into the garden to eat cherries. Ruthven finally led James into a turret off the long gallery; he locked the door, and pointing to a man in armour with a dagger, said that he "had the king at his will." The man, however, fell a-trembling, James made a speech, and the Master went to seek Gowrie, locking the door behind him. At or about this moment, as was fully attested, Cranstoun, a retainer of Gowrie, reported to him and the gentlemen that the king had ridden away. They all rushed to the gate, where the porter, to whom Gowrie gave the lie, swore that the king had not left the place. The gentlemen going to the stables passed under the turret-window, whence appeared the king, red in the face, bellowing "treason!" The gentlemen, with Lennox, rushed upstairs, and through the gallery, but could not force open the door giving on the turret. But young Ramsay had run up a narrow stair in the tower, burst open the turret-door opening on the stair, found James struggling with the Master, wounded the Master, and pushed him downstairs. In the confusion, while the king's falcon flew wildly about the turret till James set his foot on its chain, the man with the dagger vanished. The Master was slain by two of James's attendants; the Earl, rushing with four or five men up the turret-stair, fell in fight by Ramsay's rapier.

Lennox and his company now broke through the door between the gallery and the turret, and all was over except a riotous assemblage of the town's folk. The man with the dagger had fled: he later came in and gave himself up; he was Gowrie's steward; his name was Henderson; it was he who rode with the Master to Falkland and back to Perth to warn Gowrie of James's approach. He confessed that Gowrie had then bidden him put on armour, on a false pretence, and the Master had stationed him in the turret. The fact that Henderson had arrived (from Falkland) at Gowrie's house by half-past ten was amply proved, yet Gowrie had made no preparations for the royal visit. If Henderson was not the man in the turret, his sudden and secret flight from Perth is unexplained. Moreover, Robert Oliphant, M.A., said, in private talk, that the part of the man in the turret had, some time earlier, been offered to him by Gowrie; he refused and left the Earl's service. It is manifest that James could not have arranged this set of circumstances: the thing is impossible. Therefore the two Ruthvens plotted to get him into their hands early in the day; and, when he arrived late, with a considerable train, they endeavoured to send these gentlemen after the king, by averring that he had ridden homewards. The dead Ruthvens with their house were forfeited.

Among the preachers who refused publicly to accept James's account of the events in Gowrie's house on August 5, Mr Bruce was the most eminent and the most obstinate. He had, on the day after the famous riot of December 1596, written to Hamilton asking him to countenance, as a chief nobleman, "the godly barons and others who had convened themselves," at that time, in the cause of the Kirk. Bruce admitted that he knew Hamilton to be ambitious, but Hamilton's ambition did not induce him to appear as captain of a new congregation. The chief need of the ministers' party was a leader among the great nobles. Now, in 1593, the young Earl of Gowrie had leagued himself with the madcap Bothwell. In April 1594, Gowrie, Bothwell, and Atholl had addressed the Kirk, asking her to favour and direct their enterprise. Bothwell made an armed demonstration and failed; Gowrie then went abroad, to Padua and Rome, and, apparently in 1600, Mr Bruce sailed to France, "for the calling," he says, "of the Master of Gowrie"—he clearly means "the Earl of Gowrie." The Earl came, wove his plot, and perished. Mr Bruce, therefore, was averse to accepting James's account of the affair at Gowrie House. After a long series of negotiations Bruce was exiled north of Tay.

# Union *of the* Crowns

In 1600 James imposed three bishops on the Kirk. Early in 1601 broke out Essex's rebellion of one day against Elizabeth, a futile attempt to imitate Scottish methods as exhibited in the many raids against James. Essex had been intriguing with the Scottish king, but to what extent James knew of and encouraged his enterprise is unknown. He was on ill terms with Cecil, who, in 1601, was dealing with several men that intended no good to James. Cecil is said to have received a sufficient warning as to how James, on ascending the English throne, would treat him; and he came to terms, secretly, with Mar and Kinloss, the king's envoys to Elizabeth. Their correspondence is extant, and proves that Cecil, at last, was "running the Scottish course," and making smooth the way for James's accession. (The correspondence begins in June 1601.)

Very early on Thursday, March 24, 1603, Elizabeth went to her account, and James received the news from Sir Robert Carey, who reached Holyrood on the Saturday night, March 26. James entered London on May 6, and England was free from the fear of many years concerning a war for the succession. The Catholics hoped for lenient usage: disappointment led some desperate men to engage in the Gunpowder Plot. James was not more satisfactory to the Puritans.

Encouraged by the fulsome adulation which grew up under the Tudor dynasty, and free from dread of personal danger, James henceforth governed Scotland "with the pen," as he said, through the Privy Council. This method of ruling the ancient kingdom endured till the Union of 1707, and was fraught with many dangers. The king was no longer in touch with his subjects. His best action was the establishment of a small force of mounted constabulary which did more to put down the eternal homicides, robberies, and family feuds than all the sermons could achieve.

The persons most notable in the Privy Council were Seton (later Lord Dunfermline), Hume, created Earl of Dunbar, and the king's advocate, Thomas Hamilton, later Earl of Haddington. Bishops, with Spottiswoode, the historian, Archbishop of Glasgow, sat in the Privy Council, and their progressive elevation, as hateful to the nobles as to the Kirk, was among the causes of the civil war under Charles I. By craft and by illegal measures James continued to depress the Kirk. A General Assembly, proclaimed by James for July 1604 in Aberdeen, was prorogued; again, unconstitutionally, it was prorogued in July

1605. Nineteen ministers, disobeying a royal order, appeared and constituted the Assembly. Joined by ten others, they kept open the right of way. James insisted that the Council should prosecute them: they, by fixing a new date for an Assembly, without royal consent; and James, by letting years pass without an Assembly, broke the charter of the Kirk of 1592.

The preachers, when summoned to the trial, declined the jurisdiction. This was violently construed as treason, and a jury, threatened by the legal officers with secular, and by the preachers with future spiritual punishment, by a small majority condemned some of the ministers (January 1606). This roused the wrath of all classes. James wished for more prosecutions; the Council, in terror, prevailed on him to desist. He continued to grant no Assemblies till 1608, and would not allow "caveats" (limiting the powers of Bishops) to be enforced. He summoned (1606) the two Melvilles, Andrew and his nephew James, to London, where Andrew bullied in his own violent style, and was, quite illegally, first imprisoned and then banished to France.

In December 1606 a convention of preachers was persuaded to allow the appointment of "constant Moderators" to keep the presbyteries in order; and then James recognised the convention as a General Assembly. Suspected ministers were confined to their parishes or locked up in Blackness Castle. In 1608 a General Assembly was permitted the pleasure of excommunicating Huntly. In 1610 an Assembly established Episcopacy, and no excommunications not ratified by the Bishop were allowed: the only comfort of the godly was the violent persecution of Catholics, who were nosed out by the "constant Moderators," excommunicated if they refused to conform, confiscated, and banished.

James could succeed in these measures, but his plan for uniting the two kingdoms into one, Great Britain, though supported by the wisdom and eloquence of Bacon, was frustrated by the jealousies of both peoples. Persons born after James's accession (the *post nati*) were, however, admitted to equal privileges in either kingdom (1608). In 1610 James had two of his bishops, and Spottiswoode, consecrated by three English bishops, but he did not yet venture to interfere with the forms of Presbyterian public worship.

In 1610 James established two Courts of High Commission (in 1615 united in one Court) to try offences in morals and religion. The Archbishops presided, laity and clergy formed the body of the Court, and it was regarded as vexatious and tyrannical. The same terms, to be sure, would now be applied to the interference of preachers and presbyteries with private life and opinion. By 1612 the king had established Episcopacy, which, for one reason or another, became equally hateful to the nobles, the gentry, and the populace. James's motives were motives of police. Long experience had taught him the inconveniences of presbyterial government as it then existed in Scotland.

To a Church organised in the presbyterian manner, as it has been practised since 1689, James had, originally at least, no objection. But the combination of "presbyterian Hildebrandism" with factions of the turbulent *noblesse*; the alliance of the Power of the Keys with the sword and lance, was inconsistent with the freedom of the State and of the individual. "The absolutism of James," says Professor Hume Brown, "was forced upon him in large degree by the excessive claims of the Presbyterian clergy."

Meanwhile the thievish Border clans, especially the Armstrongs, were assailed by hangings and banishments, and Ulster was planted by Scottish settlers, willing or reluctant, attracted by promise of lands, or planted out, that they might not give trouble on the Border.

Persecution of Catholics was violent, and in spring 1615 Father Ogilvie was hanged after very cruel treatment directed by Archbishop Spottiswoode. In this year the two ecclesiastical Courts of High Commission were fused into one, and an Assembly was coerced into passing what James called "Hotch-potch resolutions" about changes in public worship. James wanted greater changes, but deferred them till he visited Scotland in 1617, when he was attended by the luckless figure of Laud, who went to a funeral—in a surplice! James had many personal bickerings with preachers, but his five main points, "The Articles of Perth" (of these the most detested were: (1) Communicants must kneel, not sit, at the Communion; (4) Christmas, Easter, and Pentecost must be observed; and (5) Confirmation must be introduced), were accepted by an Assembly in 1618. They could not be enforced, but were sanctioned by Parliament in 1621. The day was called Black Saturday, and omens were drawn by both parties from a thunderstorm which occurred at the time of the ratification of the Articles of Perth by Parliament in Edinburgh (August 4, 1621).

By enforcing these Articles James passed the limit of his subjects' endurance. In their opinion, as in Knox's, to kneel at the celebration of the Holy Communion was an act of idolatry, was "Baal worship," and no pressure could compel them to kneel. The three great festivals of the Christian Church, whether Roman, Genevan, or Lutheran, had no certain warrant in Holy Scripture, but were rather repugnant to the Word of God. The king did not live to see the bloodshed and misery caused by his reckless assault on the liberties and consciences of his subjects; he died on March 27, 1625, just before the Easter season in which it was intended to enforce his decrees.

The ungainliness of James's person, his lack of courage on certain occasions (he was by no means a constant coward), and the feebleness of his limbs might be attributed to pre-natal influences; he was injured before he was born by the sufferings of his mother at the time of Riccio's murder. His deep dissimulation he learnt in his bitter childhood and harassed youth. His ingenious mind was trained to pedantry; he did nothing worse, and nothing more congenial to the cruel superstitions of his age, than in his encouragement of witch trials and witch burnings promoted by the Scottish clergy down to the early part of the eighteenth century.

His plantation of Ulster by Scottish settlers has greatly affected history down to our own times, while the most permanent result of the awards by which he stimulated the colonisation of Nova Scotia has been the creation of hereditary knighthoods or baronetcies.

His encouragement of learning left its mark in the foundation of the Town's College of Edinburgh, on the site of Kirk-o'-Field, the scene of his father's murder.

The south-western Highlands, from Lochaber to Islay and Cantyre, were, in his reign, the scene of constant clan feuds and repressions, resulting in the fall of the Macdonalds, and the rise of the Campbell chief, Argyll, to the perilous power later wielded by the Marquis against Charles I. Many of the sons of the dispossessed Macdonalds, driven into Ireland, were to constitute the nucleus of the army of Montrose. In the Orkneys and Shetlands the constant turbulence of Earl Patrick and his family ended in the annexation of the islands to the Crown (1612), and the Earl's execution (1615).

# CHAPTER XXIV

# Charles I

The reign of Charles I opened with every sign of the tempests which were to follow. England and Scotland were both seething with religious fears and hatreds. Both parties in England, Puritans and Anglicans, could be satisfied with nothing less than complete domination. In England the extreme Puritans, with their yearning after the Genevan presbyterian discipline, had been threatening civil war even under Elizabeth. James had treated them with a high hand and a proud heart. Under Charles, wedded to a "Jezebel," a Catholic wife, Henrietta Maria, the Puritan hatred of such prelates as Laud expressed itself in threats of murder; while heavy fines and cruel mutilations were inflicted by the party in power. The Protestant panic, the fear of a violent restoration of Catholicism in Scotland, never slumbered. In Scotland, Catholics were at this time bitterly persecuted, and believed that a presbyterian general massacre of them all was being organised. By the people the Anglican bishops and the prayer-book were as much detested as priests and the Mass. When Charles placed six prelates on his Privy Council, and recognised the Archbishop of St Andrews, Spottiswoode, as first in precedence among his subjects, the nobles were angry and jealous. Charles would not do away with the infatuated Articles of Perth. James, as he used to say, had "governed Scotland by the pen" through his Privy Council. Charles knew much less than James of the temper of the Scots, among whom he had never come since his infancy, and *his* Privy Council with six bishops was apt to be even more than commonly subservient.

In Scotland as in England the expenses of national defence were a cause of anger; and the mismanagement of military affairs by the king's favourite, Buckingham, increased the irritation. It was brought to a head in Scotland by the "Act of Revocation," under which all Church lands and Crown lands bestowed since 1542 were to be restored to the Crown. This Act once more united in opposition the nobles and the preachers; since 1596 they had not been in harmony. In 1587, as we saw, James VI had annexed much of the old ecclesiastical property to the Crown; but he had granted most of it to nobles and barons as "temporal lordships." Now, by Charles, the temporal lords who held such lands were menaced, the judges ("Lords of Session") who would have defended their interests were removed from the Privy Council (March 1626), and, in August, the temporal lords remonstrated with the king through deputations.

In fact, they took little harm—redeeming their holdings at the rate of ten years' purchase. The main result was that landowners were empowered to buy the tithes on their own lands from the multitude of "titulars of tithes" (1629) who had rapaciously and oppressively extorted these tenths of the harvest every year. The ministers had a safe provision at last, secured on the tithes, in Scotland styled "teinds," but this did not reconcile most of them to bishops and to the Articles of Perth. Several of the bishops were, in fact, "latitudinarian" or "Arminian" in doctrine, wanderers from the severity of Knox and Calvin. With them began, perhaps, the "Moderatism" which later invaded the Kirk; though their ideal slumbered during the civil war, to awaken again, with the teaching of Archbishop Leighton, under the Restoration. Meanwhile the nobles and gentry had been alarmed and mulcted, and were ready to join hands with the Kirk in its day of resistance.

In June 1633 Charles at last visited his ancient kingdom, accompanied by Laud. His subjects were alarmed and horrified by the sight of prelates in lawn sleeves, candles in chapel, and even a tapestry showing the crucifixion. To this the bishops are said to have bowed,— plain idolatry. In the Parliament of June 18 the eight representatives of each Estate, who were practically all-powerful as Lords of the Articles, were chosen, not from each Estate by its own members, but on a method instituted, or rather revived, by James VI in 1609. The nobles made the choice from the bishops, the bishops from the nobles, and the elected sixteen from the barons and burghers. The twenty-four were all thus episcopally minded: they drew up the bills, and the bills were voted on without debate. The grant of supply made in these circumstances was liberal, and James's ecclesiastical legislation, including the sanction of the "rags of Rome" worn by the bishops, was ratified. Remonstrances from the ministers of the old Kirk party were disregarded; and—the thin end of the wedge—the English Liturgy was introduced in the Royal Chapel of Holyrood and in that of St

Salvator's College, St Andrews, where it has been read once, on a funeral occasion, in recent years.

In 1634-35, on the information of Archbishop Spottiswoode, Lord Balmerino was tried for treason because he possessed a supplication or petition which the Lords of the minority, in the late Parliament, had drawn up but had not presented. He was found guilty, but spared: the proceeding showed of what nature the bishops were, and alienated and alarmed the populace and the nobles and gentry. A remonstrance in a manly spirit by Drummond of Hawthornden, the poet, was disregarded.

In 1635 Charles authorised a Book of Canons, heralding the imposition of a Liturgy, which scarcely varied, and when it varied was thought to differ for the worse, from that of the Church of England. By these canons, the most nakedly despotic of innovations, the preachers could not use their sword of excommunication without the assent of the Bishops. James VI had ever regarded with horror and dread the licence of "conceived prayers," spoken by the minister, and believed to be extemporary or directly inspired. There is an old story that one minister prayed that James might break his leg: certainly prayers for "sanctified plagues" on that prince were publicly offered, at the will of the minister. Even a very firm Presbyterian, the Laird of Brodie, when he had once heard the Anglican service in London, confided to his journal that he had suffered much from the nonsense of "conceived prayers." They were a dangerous weapon, in Charles's opinion: he was determined to abolish them, rather that he might be free from the agitation of the pulpit than for reasons of ritual, and to proclaim his own headship of the Kirk of "King Christ."

This, in the opinion of the great majority of the preachers and populace, was flat blasphemy, an assumption of "the Crown Honours of Christ." The Liturgy was "an ill-mumbled Mass," the Mass was idolatry, and idolatry was a capital offence. However strange these convictions may appear, they were essential parts of the national belief. Yet, with the most extreme folly, Charles, acting like Henry VIII as his own Pope, thrust the canons and this Liturgy upon the Kirk and country. No sentimental arguments can palliate such open tyranny.

The Liturgy was to be used in St Giles' Church, the town kirk of Edinburgh (cleansed and restored by Charles himself), on July 23, 1637. The result was a furious brawl, begun by the women, of all presbyterians the fiercest, and, it was said, by men disguised as women. A gentleman was struck on the ear by a woman for the offence of saying "Amen," and the famous Jenny Geddes is traditionally reported to have thrown her stool at the Dean's head. The service was interrupted, the Bishop was the mark of stones, and "the Bishops' War," the Civil War, began in this brawl. James VI, being on the spot, had thoroughly quieted Edinburgh after a more serious riot, on December 17, 1596. But Charles was far away; the city had not to fear the loss of the Court and its custom, as on the earlier occasion (the removal of the Council to Linlithgow in October 1637 was a trifle), and the Council had to face a storm of petitions from all classes of the community. Their prayer was that the Liturgy should be withdrawn. From the country, multitudes of all classes flocked into Edinburgh and formed themselves into a committee of public safety, "The Four Tables," containing sixteen persons.

The Tables now demanded the removal of the bishops from the Privy Council (December 21, 1637). The question was: Who were to govern the country, the Council or the Tables? The logic of the Presbyterians was not always consistent. The king must not force the Liturgy on them, but later, their quarrel with him was that he would not, at their desire, force the absence of the Liturgy on England. If the king had the right to inflict Presbyterianism on England, he had the right to thrust the Liturgy on Scotland: of course he had neither one right nor the other. On February 19, 1638, Charles's proclamation, refusing the prayers of the supplication of December, was read at Stirling. Nobles and people replied with protestations to every royal proclamation. Foremost on the popular side was the young Earl of Montrose: "you will not rest," said Rothes, a more sober leader, "till you be lifted up above the lave in three fathoms of rope." Rothes was a true prophet; but Montrose did not die for the cause that did "his green unknowing youth engage."

The Presbyterians now desired yearly General Assemblies (of which James VI had unlawfully robbed the Kirk); the enforcement of an old brief-lived system of restrictions (*caveats*) on the bishops; the abolition of the Articles of Perth; and, as always, of the Liturgy. If he granted all this Charles might have had trouble with the preachers, as James VI had of old. Yet the demands were constitutional; and in Charles's position he would have done well to assent. He was obstinate in refusal.

The Scots now "fell upon the consideration of a band of union to be made legally," says Rothes, their leader, the chief of the House of Leslie (the family of Norman Leslie, the slayer of Cardinal Beaton). Now a "band" of this kind could not, by old Scots law, be legally made; such bands, like those for the murder of Riccio and of Darnley, and for many other enterprises, were not smiled upon by the law. But, in 1581, as we saw, James VI had signed a covenant against popery; its tenor was imitated in that of 1638, and there was added "a general band for the maintenance of true religion" (Presbyterianism) "*and of the King's person.*" That part of the band was scarcely kept when the Covenanting army surrendered Charles to the English. They had vowed, in their band, to "stand to the defence of our dread Sovereign the King's Majesty, his person and authority." They kept this vow by hanging men who held the king's commission. The words as to defending the king's authority were followed by "in the defence and preservation of the aforesaid true religion." This appears to mean that only a presbyterian king is to be defended. In any case the preachers assumed the right to interpret the Covenant, which finally led to the conquest of Scotland by Cromwell. As the Covenant was made between God and the Covenanters, on ancient Hebrew precedent it was declared to be binding on all succeeding generations. Had Scotland resisted tyranny without this would-be biblical pettifogging Covenant, her condition would have been the more gracious. The signing of the band began at Edinburgh in Greyfriars' Churchyard on February 28, 1638.

This Covenant was a most potent instrument for the day, but the fruits thereof were blood and tears and desolation: for fifty-one years common-sense did not come to her own again. In 1689 the Covenant was silently dropped, when the Kirk was restored.

This two-edged insatiable sword was drawn: great multitudes signed with enthusiasm, and they who would not sign were, of course, persecuted. As they said, "it looked not like a thing approved of God, which was begun and carried on with fury and madness, and obtruded on people with threatenings, tearing of clothes, and drawing of blood." Resistance to the king—if need were, armed resistance—was necessary, was laudable, but the terms of the Covenant were, in the highest degree impolitic and unstatesmanlike. The country was handed over to the preachers; the Scots, as their great leader Argyll was to discover, were "distracted men in distracted times."

Charles wavered and sent down the Marquis of Hamilton to represent his waverings. The Marquis was as unsettled as his predecessor, Arran, in the minority of Queen Mary. He dared not promulgate the proclamations; he dared not risk civil war; he knew that Charles, who said he was ready, was unprepared in his mutinous English kingdom. He granted, at last, a General Assembly and a free

Parliament, and produced another Covenant, "the King's Covenant," which of course failed to thwart that of the country.

The Assembly, at Glasgow (November 21, 1638), including noblemen and gentlemen as elders, was necessarily revolutionary, and needlessly riotous and profane. It arraigned and condemned the bishops in their absence. Hamilton, as Royal Commissioner, dissolved the Assembly, which continued to sit. The meeting was in the Cathedral, where, says a sincere Covenanter, Baillie, whose letters are a valuable source, "our rascals, without shame, in great numbers, made din and clamour." All the unconstitutional ecclesiastical legislation of the last forty years was rescinded,—as all the new presbyterian legislation was to be rescinded at the Restoration. Some bishops were excommunicated, the rest were deposed. The press was put under the censorship of the fanatical lawyer, Johnston of Waristoun, clerk of the Assembly.

On December 20 the Assembly, which sat on after Hamilton dissolved it, broke up. Among the Covenanters were to be reckoned the Earl of Argyll (later the only Marquis of his House), and the Earl, later Marquis, of Montrose. They did not stand long together. The Scottish Revolution produced no man at once great and successful, but, in Montrose, it had one man of genius who gave his life for honour's sake; in Argyll, an astute man, not physically courageous, whose "timidity in the field was equalled by his timidity in the Council," says Mr Gardiner.

In spring (1639) war began. Charles was to move in force on the Border; the fleet was to watch the coasts; Hamilton, with some 5000 men, was to join hands with Huntly (both men were wavering and incompetent); Antrim, from north Ireland, was to attack and contain Argyll; Ruthven was to hold Edinburgh Castle. But Alexander Leslie took that castle for the Covenanters; they took Dumbarton; they fortified Leith; Argyll ravaged Huntly's lands; Montrose and Leslie occupied Aberdeen; and their party, in circumstances supposed to be discreditable to Montrose, carried Huntly to Edinburgh. (The evidence is confused. Was Huntly unwilling to go? Charles (York, April 23, 1639) calls him "feeble and false." Mr Gardiner says that, in this case, and in this alone, Montrose stooped to a mean action.) Hamilton merely dawdled and did nothing: Montrose had entered Aberdeen (June 19), and then came news of negotiations between the king and the Covenanters.

As Charles approached from the south, Alexander Leslie, a Continental veteran (very many of the Covenant's officers were

Dugald Dalgettys from the foreign wars), occupied Dunse Law, with a numerous army in great difficulties as to supplies. "A natural mind might despair," wrote Waristoun, who "was brought low before God indeed." Leslie was in a strait; but, on the other side, so was Charles, for a reconnaissance of Leslie's position was repulsed; the king lacked money and supplies; neither side was of a high fighting heart; and offers to negotiate came from the king, informally. The Scots sent in "a supplication," and on June 18 signed a treaty which was a mere futile truce. There were to be a new Assembly, and a new Parliament in August and September.

Charles should have fought: if he fell he would fall with honour; and if he survived defeat "all England behoved to have risen in revenge," says the Covenanting letter-writer, Baillie, later Principal of Glasgow University. The Covenanters at this time could not have invaded England, could not have supported themselves if they did, and were far from being harmonious among themselves. The defeat of Charles at this moment would have aroused English pride and united the country. Charles set out from Berwick for London on July 29, leaving many fresh causes of quarrel behind him.

Charles supposed that he was merely "giving way for the present" when he accepted the ratification by the new Assembly of all the Acts of that of 1638. He never had a later chance to recover his ground. The new Assembly made the Privy Council pass an Act rendering signature of the Covenant compulsory on all men: "the new freedom is worse than the old slavery," a looker-on remarked. The Parliament discussed the method of electing the Lords of the Articles—a method which, in fact, though of prime importance, had varied and continued to vary in practice. Argyll protested that the constitutional course was for each Estate to elect its own members. Montrose was already suspected of being influenced by Charles. Charles refused to call Episcopacy unlawful, or to rescind the old Acts establishing it. Traquair, as Commissioner, dissolved the Parliament; later Charles refused to meet envoys sent from Scotland, who were actually trying, as their party also tried, to gain French mediation or assistance,—help from "idolaters"!

In spring 1640 the Scots, by an instrument called "The Blind Band," imposed taxation for military purposes; while Charles in England called The Short Parliament to provide Supply. The Parliament refused and was prorogued; words used by Strafford about the use of the army in Ireland to suppress Scotland were hoarded up against him. The Scots Parliament, though the king had prorogued it, met in June, despite the opposition of Montrose. The Parliament, when it ceased to meet, appointed a Standing Committee of some forty members of all ranks, including Montrose and his friends Lord Napier and Stirling of Keir. Argyll refused to be a member, but acted on a commission of fire and sword "to root out of the country" the northern recusants against the Covenant. It was now that Argyll burned Lord Ogilvy's Bonny House of Airlie and Forthes; the cattle were driven into his own country; all this against, and perhaps in consequence of, the intercession of Ogilvy's friend and neighbour, Montrose.

Meanwhile the Scots were intriguing with discontented English peers, who could only give sympathy; Saville, however, forged a letter from six of them inviting a Scottish invasion. There was a movement for making Argyll practically Dictator in the North; Montrose thwarted it, and in August, while Charles with a reluctant and disorderly force was marching on York Montrose at Cumbernauld, the house of the Earl of Wigtoun made a secret band with the Earls Marischal, Wigtoun, Home, Atholl, Mar, Perth, Boyd, Galloway, and others, for their mutual defence against the scheme of dictatorship for Argyll. On August 20 Montrose, the foremost, forded Tweed, and led his regiment into England. On August 30, almost unopposed, the Scots entered Newcastle, having routed a force which met them at Newburn-on-Tyne.

They again pressed their demands on the king; simultaneously twelve English peers petitioned for a parliament and the trial of the king's Ministers. Charles gave way. At Ripon Scottish and English commissioners met; the Scots received "brotherly assistance" in money and supplies (a daily £850), and stayed where they were; while the Long Parliament met in November, and in April 1641 condemned the great Strafford: Laud soon shared his doom. On August 10 the demands of the Scots were granted: as a sympathetic historian writes, they had lived for a year at free quarters, "and recrossed the Border with the handsome sum of £200,000 to their credit."

During the absence of the army the Kirk exhibited symptoms not favourable to its own peace. Amateur theologians held private religious gatherings, which, it was feared, tended towards the heresy of the English Independents and to the "break up of the whole Kirk," some of whose representatives forbade these conventicles, while "the rigid sort" asserted that the conventiclers "were esteemed the godly of the land." An Act of the General Assembly was passed against the meetings; we observe that here are the beginnings of strife between the most godly and the rather moderately pious.

The secret of Montrose's Cumbernauld band had come to light after November 1640: nothing worse, at the moment, befell than the burning of the band by the Committee of Estates, to whom Argyll referred the matter. On May 21, 1641, the Committee was disturbed, for Montrose was collecting evidence as to the words and deeds of Argyll when he used his commission of fire and sword at the Bonny House of Airlie and in other places. Montrose had spoken of the matter to a preacher, he to another, and the news reached the Committee. Montrose had learned from a prisoner of Argyll, Stewart the younger of Ladywell, that Argyll had held counsels to discuss the deposition of the king. Ladywell produced to the Committee his written statement that Argyll had spoken before him of these consultations of lawyers and divines. He was placed in the castle, and was so worked on that he "cleared" Argyll and confessed that, advised by Montrose, he had reported Argyll's remarks to the king. Papers with hints and names in cypher were found in possession of the messenger.

The whole affair is enigmatic; in any case Ladywell was hanged for "leasing-making" (spreading false reports), an offence not previously capital, and Montrose with his friends was imprisoned in the castle. Doubtless he had meant to accuse Argyll before Parliament of treason. On July 27, 1641, being arraigned before Parliament, he said, "My resolution is to carry with me fidelity and honour to the grave." He lay in prison when the king, vainly hoping for support against the English Parliament, visited Edinburgh (August 14-November 17, 1641).

Charles was now servile to his Scottish Parliament, accepting an Act by which it must consent to his nominations of officers of State. Hamilton with his brother, Lanark, had courted the alliance and lived in the intimacy of Argyll. On October 12 Charles told the House "a very strange story." On the previous day Hamilton had asked leave to retire from Court, in fear of his enemies. On the day of the king's speaking, Hamilton, Argyll, and Lanark had actually retired. On October 22, from their retreat, the brothers said that they had heard of a conspiracy, by nobles and others in the king's favour, to cut their throats. The evidence is very confused and contradictory: Hamilton and Argyll were said to have collected a force of 5000 men in the town, and, on October 5, such a gathering was denounced in a proclamation. Charles in vain asked for a public inquiry into the affair before the whole House. He now raised some of his opponents a step in the peerage: Argyll became a marquis, and Montrose was released from prison. On October 28 Charles announced the untoward news of an Irish rising and massacre. He was, of course, accused of having caused it, and the massacre was in turn the cause of, or pretext for, the shooting and hanging of Irish prisoners—men and women—in Scotland during the civil war. On November 18 he left Scotland forever.

The events in England of the spring in 1642, the attempted arrest of the five members (January 4), the retreat of the queen to France, Charles's retiral to York, indicated civil war, and the king set up his standard at Nottingham on August 22. The Covenanters had received from Charles all that they asked; they had no quarrel with him, but they argued that if he were victorious in England he would use his strength and withdraw his concessions to Scotland.

Sir Walter Scott "leaves it to casuists to decide whether one contracting party is justified in breaking a solemn treaty upon the suspicion that in future contingencies it might be infringed by the other." He suggests that to the needy nobles and Dugald Dalgettys of the Covenant "the good pay and free quarters" and "handsome sums" of England were an irresistible temptation, while the preachers thought they would be allowed to set up "the golden candlestick" of presbytery in England ('Legend of Montrose,' chapter I) Of the two the preachers were the more grievously disappointed.

A General Assembly of July-August 1642 was, as usual, concerned with politics, for politics and religion were inextricably intermixed. The Assembly appointed a Standing Commission to represent it, and the powers of the Commission were of so high a strain that "to some it is terrible already," says the Covenanting letter-writer Baillie. A letter from the Kirk was carried to the English Parliament which acquiesced in the abolition of Episcopacy. In November 1642 the English Parliament, unsuccessful in war, appealed to Scotland for armed aid; in December Charles took the same course.

The Commission of the General Assembly, and the body of administrators called Conservators of the Peace, overpowered the Privy Council, put down a petition of Montrose's party (who declared that they were bound by the Covenant to defend the king), and would obviously arm on the side of the English Parliament if England would adopt Presbyterian government. They held a Convention of the Estates (June 22, 1643); they discovered a Popish plot for an attack on Argyll's country by the Macdonalds in Ireland, once driven from Kintyre by the Campbells, and now to be led by young Colkitto. While thus excited, they received in the General Assembly (August 7) a deputation from the English Parliament; and now was framed a new band between the English Parliament and Scotland. It was an alliance, "The Solemn League and Covenant," by which Episcopacy was to be abolished and religion established "according to the Word of God." To the Covenanters this phrase meant that England would establish Presbyterianism, but they were disappointed. The ideas of the Independents, such as Cromwell, were almost as much opposed to presbytery as to episcopacy, and though the Covenanters took the pay and fought the battles of the Parliament against their king, they never received what they had meant to stipulate for,—the establishment of presbytery in England. Far from that, Cromwell, like James VI, was to deprive them of their ecclesiastical palladium, the General Assembly.

Foreseeing nothing, the Scots were delighted when the English accepted the new band. Their army, under Alexander Leslie (Earl of Leven), now too old for his post, crossed Tweed in January 1644. They might never have crossed had Charles, in the autumn of 1643, listened to Montrose and allowed him to attack the Covenanters in Scotland. In December 1643, Hamilton and Lanark, who had opposed Montrose's views and confirmed the king in his waverings, came to him at Oxford. Montrose refused to serve with them, rather he would go abroad; and Hamilton was imprisoned on charges of treason: in fact, he had been double-minded, inconstant, and incompetent. Montrose's scheme implied clan warfare, the use of exiled Macdonalds, who were Catholics, against the Campbells. The obvious objections were very strong; but "needs must when the devil drives": the Hanoverian kings employed foreign soldiers against their subjects in 1715 and 1745; but the Macdonalds were subjects of King Charles.

Hamilton's brother, Lanark, escaped, and now frankly joined the Covenanters. Montrose was promoted to a Marquisate, and received the Royal Commission as Lieutenant-General (February 1644), which alienated old Huntly, chief of the Gordons, who now and again divided and paralysed that gallant clan. Montrose rode north, where, in February 1644, old Leslie, with twenty regiments of foot, three thousand horse, and many guns, was besieging Newcastle. With him was the prototype of Scott's Dugald Dalgetty, Sir James Turner, who records examples of Leslie's senile incompetency. Leslie, at least, forced the Marquis of Newcastle to a retreat, and a movement of Montrose on Dumfries was paralysed by the cowardice or imbecility of the Scottish magnates on the western Border. He returned, took Morpeth, was summoned by Prince Rupert, and reached him the day after the disaster of Marston Moor (July 2, 1644), from which Buccleuch's Covenanting regiment ran without stroke of sword, while Alexander Leslie also fled, carrying news of his own defeat. It appears that the Scottish horse, under David Leslie, were at Marston Moor, as always, the pick of their army.

Rupert took over Montrose's men, and the great Marquis, disguised as a groom, rode hard to the house of a kinsman, near Tay, between Perth and Dunkeld. Alone and comfortless, in a little wood, Montrose met a man who was carrying the Fiery Cross, and summoning the country to resist the Irish Scots of Alastair Macdonald (Colkitto), who had landed with a force of 1500 musketeers in Argyll, and was believed to be descending on Atholl, pursued by Seaforth and Argyll, and faced by the men of Badenoch. The two armies[26] were confronting each other when Montrose, in plaid and kilt, approached Colkitto and showed him his commission. Instantly the two opposed forces combined into one, and with 2500 men, some armed with bows and arrows, and others having only one charge for each musket, Montrose began his year of victories.

The temptation to describe in detail his extraordinary series of successes and of unexampled marches over snow-clad and pathless mountains must be resisted. The mobility and daring of Montrose's irregular and capricious levies, with his own versatile military genius and the heroic valour of Colkitto, enabled him to defeat a large Covenanting force at Tippermuir, near Perth: here he had but his 2500 men (September 1); to repeat his victory at Aberdeen[27] (September 13), to evade and discourage Argyll, who retired to Inveraray; to winter in and ravage Argyll's country, and to turn on his tracks from a northern retreat and destroy the Campbells at Inverlochy, where Argyll looked on from his galley (February 2, 1645).

---

[26] Colkitto's men and the Badenoch contingent.

[27] Much has been made of cruelties at Aberdeen. Montrose sent in a drummer, asking the Provost to remove the old men, women, and children. The drummer was shot, as, at Perth, Montrose's friend, Kilpont, had been murdered. The enemy were pursued through the town. Spalding names 115 townsmen slain in the whole battle and pursuit. Women were slain if they were heard to mourn their men—not a very probable story. Not one woman is named. The Burgh Records mention no women slain. Baillie says "the town was well plundered." Jaffray, who fled from the fight as fast as his horse could carry him, says that women and children were slain. See my 'History of Scotland,' vol. iii. pp. 126-128.

General Baillie, a trained soldier, took the command of the Covenanting levies and regular troops ("Red coats"), and nearly surprised Montrose in Dundee. By a retreat showing even more genius than his victories, he escaped, appeared on the north-east coast, and scattered a Covenanting force under Hurry, at Auldearn, near Inverness (May 9, 1645).

Such victories as Montrose's were more than counterbalanced by Cromwell's defeat of Rupert and Charles at Naseby (June 14, 1645); while presbytery suffered a blow from Cromwell's demand, that the English Parliament should grant "freedom of conscience," not for Anglican or Catholic, of course, but for religions non-Presbyterian. The "bloody sectaries," as the Presbyterians called Cromwell's Independents, were now masters of the field: never would the blue banner of the Covenant be set up south of Tweed.

Meanwhile General Baillie marched against Montrose, who outmanœuvred him all over the eastern Highlands, and finally gave him battle at Alford on the Don. Montrose had not here Colkitto and the western clans, but his Gordon horse, his Irish, the Farquharsons, and the Badenoch men were triumphantly successful. Unfortunately, Lord Gordon was slain: he alone could bring out and lead the clan of Huntly. Only by joining hands with Charles could Montrose do anything decisive. The king, hoping for no more than a death in the field "with honour and a good conscience," pushed as far north as Doncaster, where he was between Poyntz's army and a great cavalry force, led by David Leslie, from Hereford, to launch against Montrose. The hero snatched a final victory. He had but a hundred horse, but he had Colkitto and the flower of the fighting clans, including the invincible Macleans. Baillie, in command of new levies of some 10,000 men, was thwarted by a committee of Argyll and other noble amateurs. He met the enemy south of Forth, at Kilsyth, between Stirling and Glasgow. The fiery Argyll made Baillie desert an admirable position— Montrose was on the plain, Baillie was on the heights—and expose his flank by a march across Montrose's front. The Macleans and Macdonalds, on the lower slope of the hill, without orders, saw their chance, and racing up a difficult glen, plunged into the Covenanting flank. Meanwhile the more advanced part of the Covenanting force were driving back some Gordons from a hill on Montrose's left, who were rescued by a desperate charge of Aboyne's handful of horse among the red coats; Airlie charged with the Ogilvies; the advanced force of the Covenant was routed, and the Macleans and Macdonalds completed the work they had begun (August 15). Few of the unmounted Covenanters escaped from Kilsyth; and Argyll, taking boat in the Forth, hurried to Newcastle, where David Leslie, coming north, obtained infantry regiments to back his 4000 cavalry.

In a year Montrose, with forces so irregular and so apt to go home after every battle, had actually cleared militant Covenanters out of Scotland. But the end had come. He would not permit the sack of Glasgow. Three thousand clansmen left him; Colkitto went away to harry Kintyre. Aboyne and the Gordons rode home on some private pique; and Montrose relied on men whom he had already proved to be broken reeds, the Homes and Kers (Roxburgh) of the Border, and the futile and timid Traquair. When he came among them they forsook him and fled; on September 10, at Kelso, Sir Robert Spottiswoode recognised the desertion and the danger.

Meanwhile Leslie, with an overpowering force of seasoned soldiers, horse and foot, marched with Argyll, not to Edinburgh, but down Gala to Tweed; while Montrose had withdrawn from Kelso, up Ettrick to Philiphaugh, on the left of Ettrick, within a mile of Selkirk. He had but 500 Irish, who entrenched themselves, and an uncertain number of mounted Border lairds with their servants and tenants. Charteris of Hempsfield, who had been scouting, reported that Leslie was but two or three miles distant, at Sunderland Hall, where Tweed and Ettrick meet; but the news was not carried to Montrose, who lay at Selkirk. At breakfast, on September 13, Montrose learned that Leslie was attacking. What followed is uncertain in its details. A so-called "contemporary ballad" is incredibly impossible in its anachronisms, and is modern. In this egregious doggerel we are told that a veteran who had fought at Solway Moss a century earlier, and at "cursed Dunbar" a few years later (or under Edward I?), advised Leslie to make a turning movement behind Linglie Hill. This is not evidence. Though Leslie may have made such a movement, he describes his victory as very easy: and so it should have been, as Montrose had only the remnant of his Antrim men and a rabble of reluctant Border recruits.

A news letter from Haddington, of September 16, represents the Cavaliers as making a good fight. The mounted Border lairds galloped away. Most of the Irish fell fighting: the rest were massacred, whether after promise of quarter or not is disputed. *Their captured women were hanged in cold blood some months later.* Montrose, the Napiers, and some forty horse either cut their way through or evaded Leslie's overpowering cavalry, and galloped across the hills of Yarrow to the

Tweed. He had lost only the remnant of his Scoto-Irish; but the Gordons, when Montrose was presently menacing Glasgow, were held back by Huntly, and Colkitto pursued his private adventures. Montrose had been deserted by the clans, and lured to ruin by the perfidious promises of the Border lords and lairds. The aim of his strategy had been to relieve the Royalists of England by a diversion that would deprive the Parliamentarians of their paid Scottish allies, and what man might do Montrose had done.

After his first victory Montrose, an excommunicated man, fought under an offer of £1500 for his murder, and the Covenanters welcomed the assassin of his friend, Lord Kilpont.

The result of Montrose's victories was hostility between the Covenanting army in England and the English, who regarded them as expensive and inefficient. Indeed, they seldom, save for the command of David Leslie, displayed military qualities, and later, were invariably defeated when they encountered the English under Cromwell and Lambert.

Montrose never slew a prisoner, but the Convention at St Andrews, in November 1645, sentenced to death their Cavalier prisoners (Lord Ogilvy escaped disguised in his sister's dress), and they ordered the hanging of captives and of the women who had accompanied the Irish. "It was certain of the clergy who pressed for the extremest measures."[28] They had revived the barbarous belief, retained in the law of ancient Greece, that the land had been polluted by, and must be cleansed by, blood, under penalty of divine wrath. As even the Covenanting Baillie wrote, "to this day no man in England has been executed for bearing arms against the Parliament." The preachers argued that to keep the promises of quarter which had been given to the prisoners was *"to violate the oath of the Covenant."*[29]

The prime object of the English opponents of the king was now "to hustle the Scots out of England."[30] Meanwhile Charles, not captured but hopeless, was negotiating with all the parties, and ready to yield on every point except that of forcing presbytery on England—a matter which, said Montereuil, the French ambassador, "did not concern them but their neighbours." Charles finally trusted the Scots with his person, and the question is, had he or had he not assurance

---

[28] Craig-Brown, 'History of Selkirkshire,' vol. i. pp. 190, 193. 'Act. Parl. Scot.,' vol. vi. pt. i. p. 492.
[29] 'Act. Parl. Scot.,' vol. vi. pt. i. p. 514.
[30] Hume Brown, vol. ii. p. 339.

that he would be well received? If he had any assurance it was merely verbal, "a shadow of a security," wrote Montereuil. Charles was valuable to the Scots only as a pledge for the payment of their arrears of wages. There was much chicanery and shuffling on both sides, and probably there were misconceptions on both sides. A letter of Montereuil (April 26, 1646) convinced Charles that he might trust the Scots; they verbally promised "safety, honour, and conscience," but refused to sign a copy of their words. Charles trusted them, rode out of Oxford, joined them at Southwell, and, says Sir James Turner, who was present, was commanded by Lothian to sign the Covenant, and "barbarously used." They took Charles to Newcastle, denying their assurance to him. "With unblushing falsehood," says Mr Gardiner, they in other respects lied to the English Parliament. On May 19 Charles bade Montrose leave the country, which he succeeded in doing, despite the treacherous endeavours of his enemies to detain him till his day of safety (August 31) was passed.

The Scots of the army were in a quandary. The preachers, their masters, would not permit them to bring to Scotland an uncovenanted king. They could not stay penniless in England. For £200,000 down and a promise, never kept, of a similar sum later, they left Charles in English hands, with some assurances for his safety, and early in February 1647 crossed Tweed with their thirty-six cartloads of money. The act was hateful to very many Scots, but the Estates, under the command of the preachers, had refused to let the king, while uncovenanted, cross into his native kingdom, and to bring him meant war with England. But *that* must ensue in any case. The hope of making England presbyterian, as under the Solemn League and Covenant, had already perished.

Leslie, with the part of the army still kept up, chased Colkitto, and, at Dunavertie, under the influence of Nevoy, a preacher, put 300 Irish prisoners to the sword.

The parties in Scotland were now: (1) the Kirk, Argyll, the two Leslies, and most of the Commons; (2) Hamilton, Lanark, and Lauderdale, who had no longer anything to fear, as regards their estates, from Charles or from bishops, and who were ashamed of his surrender to the English; (3) Royalists in general. With Charles (December 27, 1647) in his prison at Carisbrooke, Lauderdale, Loudoun, and Lanark made a secret treaty, *The Engagement*, which they buried in the garden, for if it were discovered the Independents of the army would have attacked Scotland.

An Assembly of the Scots Estates on March 3, 1648, had a large majority of nobles, gentry, and many burgesses in favour of aiding the captive king; on the other side Argyll was backed by the omnipotent Commission of the General Assembly, and by the full force of prayers and sermons. The letter-writer, Baillie, now deemed "that it were for the good of the world that churchmen did meddle with ecclesiastical affairs only." The Engagers insisted on establishing presbytery in England, which neither satisfied the Kirk nor the Cavaliers and Independents. Nothing more futile could have been devised.

The Estates, in May, began to raise an army; the preachers denounced them: there was a battle between armed communicants of the preachers' party and the soldiers of the State at Mauchline. Invading England on July 8, Hamilton had Lambert and Cromwell to face him, and left Argyll, the preachers, and their "slashing communicants" in his rear. Lanark had vainly urged that the west country fanatics should be crushed before the Border was crossed. By a march worthy of Montrose across the fells into Lanarkshire, Cromwell reached Preston; cut in between the northern parts of Hamilton's army; defeated the English Royalists and Langdale, and cut to pieces or captured the Scots, disunited as their generals were, at Wigan and Warrington (August 17-19). Hamilton was taken and was decapitated later. The force that recrossed the Border consisted of such mounted men as escaped, with the detachment of Monro which had not joined Hamilton.

The godly in Scotland rejoiced at the defeat of their army: the levies of the western shires of Ayr, Renfrew, and Lanark occupied Edinburgh: Argyll and the Kirk party were masters, and when Cromwell arrived in Edinburgh early in October he was entertained at dinner by Argyll. The left wing of the Covenant was now allied with the Independents—the deadly foes of presbytery! To the ordinary mind this looks like a new breach of the Covenant, that impossible treaty with Omnipotence. Charles had written that the divisions of parties were probably "God's way to punish them for their many rebellions and perfidies." The punishment was now beginning in earnest, and the alliance of extreme Covenanters with "bloody sectaries" could not be maintained. Yet historians admire the statesmanship of Argyll!

If the edge which the sword of the Covenant turned against the English enemies of presbytery were blunted, the edge that smote Covenanters less extreme than Argyll and the preachers was whetted afresh. In the Estates of January 5, 1649, Argyll, whose party had a large majority, and the fanatical Johnston of Waristoun (who made private covenants with Jehovah) demanded disenabling Acts against all who had in any degree been tainted by the *Engagement* for the rescue of the king. The Engagers were divided into four "Classes," who were rendered incapable by "The Act of Classes" of holding any office, civil or military. This Act deprived the country of the services of thousands of men, just at the moment when the English army, the Independents, Argyll's allies, were holding the Trial of Charles I; and, in defiance of timid remonstrances from the Scottish Commissioners in England, cut off "that comely head" (January 30, 1649), which meant war with Scotland.

# Scotland & Charles II

This was certain, for, on February 5, on the news of the deed done at Whitehall, the Estates proclaimed Charles II as Scottish King—if he took the Covenant. By an ingenious intrigue Argyll allowed Lauderdale and Lanark, whom the Estates had intended to arrest, to escape to Holland, where Charles was residing, and their business was to bring that uncovenanted prince to sign the Covenant, and to overcome the influence of Montrose, who, with Clarendon, of course resisted such a trebly dishonourable act of perjured hypocrisy. During the whole struggle, since Montrose took the king's side, he had been thwarted by the Hamiltons. They invariably wavered: now they were for a futile policy of dishonour, in which they involved their young king, Argyll, and Scotland. Montrose stood for honour and no Covenant; Argyll, the Hamiltons, Lauderdale, and the majority of the preachers stood for the Covenant with dishonour and perjury; the left wing of the preachers stood for the Covenant, but not for its dishonourable and foresworn acceptance by Charles.

As a Covenanter, Charles II would be the official foe of the English Independents and army; Scotland would need every sword in the kingdom, and the kingdom's best general, Montrose, yet the Act of Classes, under the dictation of the preachers, rejected every man tainted with participation in or approval of the Engagement—or of neglecting family prayers!

Charles, in fact, began (February 22) by appointing Montrose his Lieutenant-Governor and Captain-General in Scotland, though Lauderdale and Lanark "abate not an ace of their damned Covenant in all their discourses," wrote Hyde. The dispute between Montrose, on the side of honour, and that of Lanark, Lauderdale, and other Scottish envoys, ended as—given the character of Charles II and his destitution—it must end. Charles (January 22, 1650) despatched Montrose to fight for him in Scotland, and sent him the Garter. Montrose knew his doom: he replied, "With the more alacrity shall I abandon still my life to search my death for the interests of your Majesty's honour and service." He searched his death, and soon he found it.

On May 1, Charles, by the Treaty of Breda, vowed to sign the Covenant; a week earlier Montrose, not joined by the Mackenzies, had been defeated by Strachan at Carbisdale, on the south of the Kyle, opposite Invershin, in Sutherlandshire. He was presently captured, and crowned a glorious life of honour by a more glorious death on the gibbet (May 21). He had kept his promise; he had searched his death; he had loyally defended, like Jeanne d'Arc, a disloyal king; he had "carried fidelity and honour with him to the grave." His body was mutilated, his limbs were exposed,—they now lie in St Giles' Church, Edinburgh, where is his beautiful monument.

Montrose's last words to Charles (March 26, from Kirkwall) implored that Prince "to be just to himself,"—not to perjure himself by signing the Covenant. The voice of honour is not always that of worldly wisdom, but events proved that Charles and Scotland could have lost nothing and must have gained much had the king listened to Montrose. He submitted, we saw, to commissioners sent to him from Scotland. Says one of these gentlemen, "*He... sinfully complied with what we most sinfully pressed upon him,... our sin was more than his.*"

While his subjects in Scotland were executing his loyal servants taken prisoners in Montrose's last defeat, Charles crossed the sea, signing the Covenants on board ship, and landed at the mouth of Spey. What he gained by his dishonour was the guilt of perjury; and the consequent distrust of the wilder but more honest Covenanters, who knew that he had perjured himself, and deemed his reception a cause of divine wrath and disastrous judgments. Next he was separated from most of his false friends, who had urged him to his guilt, and from all Royalists; and he was not allowed to be with his army, which the preachers kept "purging" of all who did not come up to their standard of sanctity.

Their hopeful scheme was to propitiate the Deity and avert wrath by purging out officers of experience, while filling up their places with godly but incompetent novices in war, "ministers' sons, clerks, and such other sanctified creatures." This final and fatal absurdity was the result of playing at being the Israel described in the early historic books of the Old Testament, a policy initiated by Knox in spite of the humorous protests of Lethington.

For the surer purging of that Achan, Charles, and to conciliate the party who deemed him the greatest cause of wrath of all, the king had to sign a false and disgraceful declaration that he was "afflicted in spirit before God because of the impieties of his father and mother"! He was helpless in the hands of Argyll, David Leslie, and the rest: he knew they would desert him if he did not sign, and he yielded (August 16). Meanwhile Cromwell, with Lambert, Monk, 16,000 foot and horse, and a victualling fleet, had reached Musselburgh, near Edinburgh, by July 28.

David Leslie very artfully evaded every attempt to force a fight, but hung about him in all his movements. Cromwell was obliged to retreat for lack of supplies in a devastated country, and on September 1 reached Dunbar by the coast road. Leslie, marching parallel along the hill-ridges, occupied Doonhill and secured a long, deep, and steep ravine, "the Peaths," near Cockburnspath, barring Cromwell's line of march. On September 2 the controlling clerical Committee was still busily purging and depleting the Scottish army. The night of September 2-3 was very wet, the officers deserted their regiments to take shelter. Says Leslie himself, "We might as easily have beaten them as we did James Graham at Philiphaugh, if the officers had stayed by their own troops and regiments." Several witnesses, and Cromwell himself, asserted that, owing to the insistence of the preachers, Leslie moved his men to the lower slopes on the afternoon of September 2. "The Lord hath delivered them into our hands," Cromwell is reported to have said. They now occupied a position where the banks of the lower Broxburn were flat and assailable, not steep and forming a strong natural moat, as on the higher level. All night Cromwell rode along and among his regiments of horse, biting his lip till the blood ran down his chin. Leslie thought to surprise Cromwell; Cromwell surprised Leslie, crossed the Broxburn on the low level, before dawn, and drove into the Scots who were all unready, the matches of their muskets being wet and unlighted. The centre made a good stand, but a flank charge by English cavalry cut up the Scots foot, and Leslie fled with the nobles, gentry, and mounted men. In killed, wounded, and prisoners the Scots are said to have lost 14,000 men, a manifest exaggeration. It was an utter defeat.

"Surely," wrote Cromwell, "it is probable the Kirk has done her do." The Kirk thought not; purging must go on, "nobody must blame the Covenant." Neglect of family prayers was selected as one cause of the defeat! Strachan and Ker, two extreme whigamores of the left wing of the godly, went to raise a western force that would neither acknowledge Charles nor join Cromwell, who now took Edinburgh Castle. Charles was reduced by Argyll to make to him the most slavish promises, including the payment of £40,000, the part of the price of Charles I which Argyll had not yet touched.

On October 4 Charles made "the Start"; he fled to the Royalists of Angus,—Ogilvy and Airlie: he was caught, brought back, and preached at. Then came fighting between the Royalists and the Estates. Middleton, a good soldier, Atholl, and others, declared that they must and would fight for Scotland, though they were purged out by the preachers. The Estates (November 4) gave them an indemnity. On this point the Kirk split into twain: the wilder men, led by the Rev. James Guthrie, refused reconciliation (the Remonstrants); the less fanatical would consent to it, on terms (the Resolutioners). The Committee of Estates dared to resist the Remonstrants: even the Commissioners of the General Assembly "cannot be against the raising of all fencible persons,"—and at last adopted the attitude of all sensible persons. By May 21, 1651, the Estates rescinded the insane Act of Classes, but the strife between clerical Remonstrants and Resolutioners persisted till after the Restoration, the *Remonstrants* being later named *Protesters*.

Charles had been crowned at Scone on January 1, again signing the Covenants. Leslie now occupied Stirling, avoiding an engagement. In July, while a General Assembly saw the strife of the two sects, came news that Lambert had crossed the Forth at Queensferry, and defeated a Scots force at Inverkeithing, where the Macleans fell almost to a man; Monk captured a number of the General Assembly, and, as Cromwell, moving to Perth, could now assail Leslie and the main Scottish force at Stirling, they, by a desperate resolution, with 4000 horse and 9000 foot, invaded England by the west marches, "laughing," says one of them, "at the ridiculousness of our own condition." On September 1 Monk stormed and sacked Dundee as Montrose sacked Aberdeen, but if he made a massacre like that by Edward I at Berwick, history is lenient to the crime.

On August 22 Charles, with his army, reached Worcester, whither Cromwell marched with a force twice as great as that of the king. Worcester was a Sedan: Charles could neither hold it nor, though he charged gallantly, could he break through Cromwell's lines. Before nightfall on September 3 Charles was a fugitive: he had no army; Hamilton was slain, Middleton and David Leslie with thousands more were prisoners. Monk had already captured, at Alyth (August 28), the whole of the Government, the Committee of Estates, and had also caught some preachers, including James Sharp, later Archbishop of St Andrews. England had conquered Scotland at last, after twelve years of government by preachers acting as interpreters of the Covenant between Scotland and Jehovah.

# CHAPTER XXV

# Conquered Scotland

**D**uring the nine years of the English military occupation of Scotland everything was merely provisional; nothing decisive could occur. In the first place (October 1651), eight English Commissioners, including three soldiers, Monk, Lambert, and Deane, undertook the administration of the conquered country. They announced tolerance in religion (except for Catholicism and Anglicanism, of course), and during their occupation the English never wavered on a point so odious to the Kirk. The English rulers also, as much as they could, protected the women and men whom the lairds and preachers smelled out and tortured and burned for witchcraft. By way of compensation for the expenses of war all the estates of men who had sided with Charles were confiscated. Taxation also was heavy. On four several occasions attempts were made to establish the Union of the two countries; Scotland, finally, was to return thirty members to sit in the English Parliament. But as that Parliament, under Cromwell, was subject to strange and sudden changes, and as the Scottish representatives were usually men sold to the English side, the experiment was not promising. In its first stage it collapsed with Cromwell's dismissal of the Long Parliament on April 20, 1653. Argyll meanwhile had submitted, retaining his estates (August 1652); but of five garrisons in his country three were recaptured, not without his goodwill, by the Highlanders; and in these events began Monk's aversion, finally fatal, to the Marquis as a man whom none could trust, and in whom finally nobody trusted.

An English Commission of Justice, established in May 1652, was confessedly more fair and impartial than any Scotland had known, which was explained by the fact that the English judges "were kinless loons." Northern cavaliers were relieved by Monk's forbidding civil magistrates to outlaw and plunder persons lying under Presbyterian excommunication, and sanitary measures did something to remove from Edinburgh the ancient reproach of filth, for the time. While the Protesters and Resolutioners kept up their quarrel, the Protesters claiming to be the only genuine representatives of Kirk and Covenant, the General Assembly of the Resolutioners was broken up (July 21, 1653) by Lilburne, with a few soldiers, and henceforth the Kirk, having no General Assembly, was less capable of promoting civil broils. Lilburne suspected that the Assembly was in touch with new stirrings towards a rising in the Highlands, to lead which Charles had, in 1652, promised to send Middleton, who had escaped from an English prison, as general. It was always hard to find anyone under whom the great chiefs would serve, and Glencairn, with Kenmure, was unable to check their jealousies.

Charles heard that Argyll would appear in arms for the Crown, when he deemed the occasion good; meanwhile his heir, Lord Lorne, would join the rising. He did so in July 1653, under the curse of Argyll, who, by letters to Lilburne and Monk, and by giving useful information to the English, fatally committed himself as treasonable to the Royal cause. Examples of his conduct were known to Glencairn, who communicated them to Charles.

At the end of February 1654 Middleton arrived in Sutherland to head the insurrection: but Monk chased the small and disunited force from county to county, and in July Morgan defeated and scattered its remnants at Loch Garry, just south of Dalnaspidal. The Armstrongs and other Border clans, who had been moss-trooping in their ancient way, were also reduced, and new fortresses and garrisons bridled the fighting clans of the west. With Cromwell as protector in 1654, Free Trade with England was offered to the Scots with reduced taxation: an attempt to legislate for the Union failed. In 1655-1656 a Council of State and a Commission of Justice included two or three Scottish members, and burghs were allowed to elect magistrates who would swear loyalty to Cromwell. Cromwell died on the day of his fortunate star (September 3, 1658), and twenty-one members for Scotland sat in Richard Cromwell's Parliament. When that was dissolved, and when the Rump was reinstated, a new Bill of Union was introduced, and, by reason of the provisions for religious toleration (a thing absolutely impious in Presbyterian eyes), was delayed till (October 1659) the Rump was sent to its account. Conventions of Burghs and Shires were now held by Monk, who, leading his army of occupation south in January 1660, left the Resolutioners and Protesters standing at gaze, as hostile as ever, awaiting what thing should befall. Both parties still cherished the Covenants, and so long as these documents were held to be forever binding on all generations, so long as the king's authority was to be resisted in defence of these treaties with Omnipotence, it was plain that in Scotland there could neither be content nor peace. For twenty-eight years, during a generation of profligacy and turmoil, cruelty and corruption, the Kirk and country were to reap what they had sown in 1638.

# CHAPTER XXVI

# The Restoration

There was "dancing and derray" in Scotland among the laity when the king came to his own again. The darkest page in the national history seemed to have been turned; the conquering English were gone with their abominable tolerance, their craze for soap and water, their aversion to witch-burnings. The nobles and gentry would recover their lands and compensation for their losses; there would be offices to win, and "the spoils of office."

It seems that in Scotland none of the lessons of misfortune had been learned. Since January the chiefs of the milder party of preachers, the Resolutioners,—they who had been reconciled with the Engagers,—were employing the Rev. James Sharp, who had been a prisoner in England, as their agent with Monk, with Lauderdale, in April, with Charles in Holland and, again, in London. Sharp was no fanatic. From the first he assured his brethren, Douglas of Edinburgh, Baillie, and the rest, that there was no chance for "rigid Presbyterianism." They could conceive of no Presbyterianism which was not rigid, in the manner of Andrew Melville, to whom his king was "Christ's silly vassal." Sharp warned them early that in face of the irreconcilable Protesters, "moderate Episcopacy" would be preferred; and Douglas himself assured Sharp that the new generation in Scotland "bore a heart-hatred to the Covenant," and are "wearied of the yoke of presbyterial government."

This was true: the ruling classes had seen too much of presbyterial government, and would prefer bishops as long as they were not pampered and all-powerful. On the other hand the lesser gentry, still more their godly wives, the farmers and burgesses, and the preachers, regarded the very shadow of Episcopacy as a breach of the Covenant and an insult to the Almighty. The Covenanters had forced the

Covenant on the consciences of thousands, from the king downwards, who in soul and conscience loathed it. They were to drink of the same cup—Episcopacy was to be forced on them by fines and imprisonments. Scotland, her people and rulers were moving in a vicious circle. The Resolutioners admitted that to allow the Protesters to have any hand in affairs was "to breed continual distemper and disorders," and Baillie was for banishing the leaders of the Protesters, irreconcilables like the Rev. James Guthrie, to the Orkney islands. But the Resolutioners, on the other hand, were no less eager to stop the use of the liturgy in Charles's own household, and to persecute every sort of Catholic, Dissenter, Sectary, and Quaker in Scotland. Meanwhile Argyll, in debt, despised on all sides, and yet dreaded, was holding a great open-air Communion meeting of Protesters at Paisley, in the heart of the wildest Covenanting region (May 27, 1660). He was still dangerous; he was trying to make himself trusted by the Protesters, who were opposed to Charles. It may be doubted if any great potentate in Scotland except the Marquis wished to revive the constitutional triumphs of Argyll's party in the last Parliament of Charles I. Charles now named his Privy Council and Ministers without waiting for parliamentary assent—though his first Parliament would have assented to anything. He chose only his late supporters: Glencairn who raised his standard in 1653; Rothes, a humorous and not a cruel voluptuary; and, as Secretary for Scotland in London, Lauderdale, who had urged him to take the Covenant, and who for twenty years was to be his buffoon, his favourite, and his wavering and unscrupulous adviser. Among these greedy and treacherous profligates there would, had he survived, have been no place for Montrose.

In defiance of warnings from omens, second-sighted men, and sensible men, Argyll left the safe sanctuary of his mountains and sea-straits, and betook himself to London, "a fey man." Most of his past was covered by an Act of Indemnity, but not his doings in 1653. He was arrested before he saw the king's face (July 8, 1660), and lay in the Tower till, in December, he was taken to be tried for treason in Scotland.

Sharp's friends were anxious to interfere in favour of establishing Presbyterianism in England; he told them that the hope was vain; he repeatedly asked for leave to return home, and, while an English preacher assured Charles that the rout of Worcester had been God's vengeance for his taking of the Covenant, Sharp (June 25) told his Resolutioners that "the Protesters' doom is dight."

Administration in Scotland was intrusted to the Committee of Estates whom Monk (1650) had captured at Alyth, and with them Glencairn, as Chancellor, entered Edinburgh on August 22. Next day, while the Committee was busy, James Guthrie and some Protester preachers met, and, in the old way, drew up a "supplication." They denounced religious toleration, and asked for the establishment of Presbytery in England, and the filling of all offices with Covenanters. They were all arrested and accused of attempting to "rekindle civil war," which would assuredly have followed had their prayer been accepted. Next year Guthrie was hanged. But ten days after his arrest Sharp had brought down a letter of Charles to the Edinburgh Presbytery, promising to "protect and preserve the government of the Church of Scotland as it is established by law." Had the words run "as it may be established by law" (in Parliament) it would not have been a dishonourable quibble—as it was.

Parliament opened on New Year's Day 1661, with Middleton as Commissioner. In the words of Sir George Mackenzie, then a very young advocate and man of letters, "never was Parliament so obsequious." The king was declared "supreme Governor over all persons and in all causes" (a blow at Kirk judicature), and all Acts between 1633 and 1661 were rescinded, just as thirty years of ecclesiastical legislation had been rescinded by the Covenanters. A sum of £40,000 yearly was settled on the king. Argyll was tried, was defended by young George Mackenzie, and, when he seemed safe, his doom was fixed by the arrival of a Campbell from London bearing some of his letters to Lilburne and Monk (1653-1655) which the Indemnity of 1651 did not cover. He died, by the axe (not the rope, like Montrose), with dignity and courage.

The question of Church government in Scotland was left to Charles and his advisers. The problem presented to the Government of the Restoration by the Kirk was much more difficult and complicated than historians usually suppose. The pretensions which the preachers had inherited from Knox and Andrew Melville were practically incompatible, as had been proved, with the existence of the State. In the southern and western shires,—such as those of Dumfries, Galloway, Ayr, Renfrew, and Lanark,—the forces which attacked the Engagers had been mustered; these shires had backed Strachan and Ker and Guthrie in the agitation against the king, the Estates, and the less violent clergy, after Dunbar. But without Argyll, and with no probable noble leaders, they could do little harm; they had done none under the English occupation, which abolished the General Assembly. To have restored the Assembly, or rather two Assemblies—that of the Protesters and that of the Resolutionists,—would certainly have been perilous. Probably the wisest plan would have been to grant a General Assembly, to meet *after* the session of Parliament; not, as had been the custom, to meet before it and influence or coerce the Estates. Had that measure proved perilous to peace it need not have been repeated,—the Kirk might have been left in the state to which the English had reduced it.

This measure would not have so much infuriated the devout as did the introduction of "black prelacy," and the ejection of some 300 adored ministers, chiefly in the south-west, and "the making of a desert first, and then peopling it with owls and satyrs" (the curates), as Archbishop Leighton described the action of 1663. There ensued the finings of all who would not attend the ministrations of "owls and satyrs,"—a grievance which produced two rebellions (1666 and 1679) and a doctrine of anarchism, and was only worn down by eternal and cruel persecutions.

By violence the Restoration achieved its aim: the Revolution of 1688 entered into the results; it was a bitter moment in the evolution of Scotland—a moment that need never have existed. Episcopacy was restored, four bishops were consecrated, and Sharp accepted (as might have long been foreseen) the See of St Andrews. He was henceforth reckoned a Judas, and assuredly he had ruined his character for honour: he became a puppet of Government, despised by his masters, loathed by the rest of Scotland.

In May-September 1662, Parliament ratified the change to Episcopacy. It seems to have been thought that few preachers except the Protesters would be recalcitrant, refuse collation from bishops, and leave their manses. In point of fact, though they were allowed to consult their consciences till February 1663, nearly 300 ministers preferred their consciences to their livings. They remained centres of the devotion of their flocks, and the "curates," hastily gathered, who took their places, were stigmatised as ignorant and profligate, while, as they were resisted, rabbled, and daily insulted, the country was full of disorder.

The Government thus mortally offended the devout classes, though no attempt was made to introduce a liturgy. In the churches the services were exactly, or almost exactly, what they had been; but excommunications could now only be done by sanction of the bishops. Witch-burnings, in spite of the opposition of George

Mackenzie and the Council, were soon as common as under the Covenant. Oaths declaring it unlawful to enter into Covenants or take up arms against the king were imposed on all persons in office.

Middleton, of his own authority, now proposed the ostracism, by parliamentary ballot, of twelve persons reckoned dangerous. Lauderdale was mainly aimed at (it is a pity that the bullet did not find its billet), with Crawford, Cassilis, Tweeddale, Lothian, and other peers who did not approve of the recent measures. But Lauderdale, in London, seeing Charles daily, won his favour; Middleton was recalled (March 1663), and Lauderdale entered freely on his wavering, unscrupulous, corrupt, and disastrous period of power.

The Parliament of June 1663, meeting under Rothes, was packed by the least constitutional method of choosing the Lords of the Articles. Waristoun was brought from France, tried, and hanged, "expressing more fear than I ever saw," wrote Lauderdale, whose Act "against Separation and Disobedience to Ecclesiastical Authority" fined abstainers from services in their parish churches. In 1664, Sharp, who was despised by Lauderdale and Glencairn, obtained the erection of that old grievance—a Court of High Commission, including bishops, to punish nonconformists. Sir James Turner was intrusted with the task of dragooning them, by fining and the quartering of soldiers on those who would not attend the curates and would keep conventicles. Turner was naturally clement and good-natured, but wine often deprived him of his wits, and his soldiery behaved brutally. Their excesses increased discontent, and war with Holland (1664) gave them hopes of a Dutch ally. Conventicles became common; they had an organisation of scouts and sentinels. The malcontents intrigued with Holland in 1666, and schemed to capture the three Keys of the Kingdom—the castles of Stirling, Dumbarton, and Edinburgh. The States-General promised, when this was done, to send ammunition and 150,000 gulden (July 1666).

When rebellion did break out it had no foreign aid, and a casual origin. In the south-west Turner commanded but seventy soldiers, scattered all about the country. On November 14 some of them mishandled an old man in the clachan of Dalry, on the Ken. A soldier was shot in revenge (Mackenzie speaks as if a conventicle was going on in the neighbourhood); people gathered in arms, with the Laird of Corsack, young Maxwell of Monreith, and M'Lennan; caught Turner, undressed, in Dumfries, and carried him with them as they "went conventicling about," as Mackenzie writes, holding prayer-meetings, led by Wallace, an old soldier of the Covenant. At Lanark they renewed the Covenant. Dalziel of Binns, who had learned war in Russia, led a pursuing force. The rebels were disappointed in hopes of Dutch or native help at Edinburgh; they turned, when within three miles of the town, into the passes of the Pentland Hills, and at Bullion Green, on November 28, displayed fine soldierly qualities and courage, but fled, broken, at nightfall. The soldiers and countryfolk, who were unsympathetic, took a number of prisoners, preachers and laymen, on whom the Council, under the presidency of Sharp, exercised a cruelty bred of terror. The prisoners were defended by George Mackenzie: it has been strangely stated that he was Lord Advocate, and persecuted them! Fifteen rebels were hanged: the use of torture to extract information was a return, under Fletcher, the King's Advocate, to a practice of Scottish law which had been almost in abeyance since 1638—except, of course, in the case of witches. Turner vainly tried to save from the Boot[31] the Laird of Corsack, who had protected his life from the fanatics. "The executioner favoured Mr Mackail," says the Rev. Mr Kirkton, himself a sufferer later. This Mr Mackail, when a lad of twenty-one (1662), had already denounced the rulers, in a sermon, as on the moral level of Haman and Judas.

It is entirely untrue that Sharp concealed a letter from the king commanding that no blood should be shed (Charles detested hanging people). If anyone concealed his letter, it was Burnet, Archbishop of Glasgow. Dalziel now sent Ballantyne to supersede Turner and to exceed him in ferocity; and Bellenden and Tweeddale wrote to Lauderdale deprecating the cruelties and rapacity of the reaction, and avowing contempt of Sharp. He was "snibbed," confined to his diocese, and "cast down, yea, lower than the dust," wrote Rothes to Lauderdale. He was held to have exaggerated in his reports the forces of the spirit of revolt; but Tweeddale, Sir Robert Murray, and Kincardine found when in power that matters were really much more serious than they had supposed. In the disturbed districts—mainly the old Strathclyde and Pictish Galloway—the conformist ministers were perpetually threatened, insulted, and robbed.

According to a sympathetic historian, "on the day when Charles should abolish bishops and permit free General Assemblies, the western Whigs would become his law-abiding subjects; but till that day they would be irreconcilable." But a Government is not always well

---

[31] The Boot was an old French and Scottish implement. It was a framework into which the human leg was inserted; wedges were then driven between the leg and the framework.

advised in yielding to violence. Moreover, when Government had deserted its clergy, and had granted free General Assemblies, the two Covenants would re-arise, and the pretensions of the clergy to dominate the State would be revived. Lauderdale drifted into a policy of alternate "Indulgences" or tolerations, and of repression, which had the desired effect, at the maximum of cost to justice and decency. Before England drove James II from the throne, but a small remnant of fanatics were in active resistance, and the Covenants had ceased to be dangerous.

A scheme of partial toleration was mooted in 1667, and Rothes was removed from his practical dictatorship, while Turner was made the scapegoat of Rothes, Sharp, and Dalziel. The result of the scheme of toleration was an increase in disorder. Bishop Leighton had a plan for abolishing all but a shadow of Episcopacy; but the temper of the recalcitrants displayed itself in a book, 'Naphtali,' advocating the right of the godly to murder their oppressors. This work contained provocations to anarchism, and, in Knox's spirit, encouraged any Phinehas conscious of a "call" from Heaven to do justice on such persons as he found guilty of troubling the godly.

Fired by such Christian doctrines, on July 11, 1668, one Mitchell—"a preacher of the Gospel, and a youth of much zeal and piety," says Wodrow the historian—shot at Sharp, wounded the Bishop of Orkney in the street of Edinburgh, and escaped. This event delayed the project of conciliation, but in July 1669 the first Indulgence was promulgated. On making certain concessions, outed ministers were to be restored. Two-and-forty came in, including the Resolutioner Douglas, in 1660 the correspondent of Sharp. The Indulgence allowed the indulged to reject Episcopal collation; but while brethren exiled in Holland denounced the scheme (these brethren, led by Mr MacWard, opposed all attempts at reconciliation), it also offended the Archbishops, who issued a Remonstrance. Sharp was silenced; Burnet of Glasgow was superseded, and the see was given to the saintly but unpractical Leighton. By 1670 conventiclers met in arms, and "a clanking Act," as Lauderdale called it, menaced them with death: Charles II resented but did not rescind it. In fact, the disorders and attacks on conformist ministers were of a violence much overlooked by our historians. In 1672 a second Indulgence split the Kirk into factions—the exiles in Holland maintaining that preachers who accepted it should be held men unholy, false brethren. But the Indulged increased in numbers, and finally in influence.

To such a man as Leighton the whole quarrel seemed "a scuffle of drunken men in the dark." An Englishman entering a Scottish church at this time found no sort of liturgy; prayers and sermons were what the minister chose to make them—in fact, there was no persecution for religion, says Sir George Mackenzie. But if men thought even a shadow of Episcopacy an offence to Omnipotence, and the king's authority in ecclesiastical cases a usurping of "the Crown Honours of Christ"; if they consequently broke the law by attending armed conventicles and assailing conformist preachers, and then were fined or imprisoned,—from their point of view they were being persecuted for their religion. Meanwhile they bullied and "rabbled" the "curates" for *their* religion: such was Leighton's "drunken scuffle in the dark."

In 1672 Lauderdale married the rapacious and tyrannical daughter of Will Murray—of old the whipping-boy of Charles I, later a disreputable intriguer. Lauderdale's own ferocity of temper and his greed had created so much dislike that in the Parliament of 1673 he was met by a constitutional opposition headed by the Duke of Hamilton, and with Sir George Mackenzie as its orator. Lauderdale consented to withdraw monopolies on salt, tobacco, and brandy; to other grievances he would not listen (the distresses of the Kirk were not brought forward), and he dissolved the Parliament. The opposition tried to get at him through the English Commons, who brought against him charges like those which were fatal to Strafford. They failed; and Lauderdale, holding seven offices himself, while his brother Haltoun was Master of the Mint, ruled through a kind of clique of kinsmen and creatures.

Leighton, in despair, resigned his see: the irreconcilables of the Kirk had crowned him with insults. The Kirk, he said, "abounded in furious zeal and endless debates about the empty name and shadow of a difference in government, in the meanwhile not having of solemn and orderly public worship as much as a shadow."

Wodrow, the historian of the sufferings of the Kirk, declares that through the riotous proceedings of the religious malcontents "the country resembled war as much as peace." But an Act of Council of 1677 bidding landowners sign a bond for the peaceable behaviour of all on their lands was refused obedience by many western lairds. They could not enforce order, they said: hence it seemed to follow that there was much disorder. Those who refused were, by a stretch of the law of "law-burrows," bound over to keep the peace of the Government. Lauderdale, having nothing that we would call a police, little money, and a small insufficient force of regulars, called in "the Highland Host," the retainers of Atholl, Glenorchy, Mar, Moray, and Airlie, and other northern lords, and quartered them on the disturbed districts for a month. They were then sent home bearing their spoils (February 1678). Atholl and Perth (later to be the Catholic minister of James II) now went over to "the Party," the opposition, Hamilton's party; Hamilton and others rode to London to complain against Lauderdale, but he, aided by the silver tongue of Mackenzie, who had changed sides, won over Charles, and Lauderdale's assailants were helpless.

Great unpopularity and disgrace were achieved by the treatment of the pious Mitchell, who, we have seen, missed Sharp and shot the Bishop of Orkney in 1668. In 1674 he was taken, and confessed before the Council, after receiving from Rothes, then Chancellor, assurance of his life: this with Lauderdale's consent. But when brought before the judges, he retracted his confession. He was kept a prisoner on the Bass Rock; in 1676 was tortured; in January 1678 was again tried. Haltoun (who in a letter of 1674 had mentioned the assurance of life), Rothes, Sharp, and Lauderdale, all swore that, to their memory, no assurance had been given in 1674. Mitchell's counsel asked to be allowed to examine the Register of the Council, but, for some invisible technical reasons, the Lords of the Justiciary refused; the request, they said, came too late. Mackenzie prosecuted; he had been Mitchell's counsel in 1674, and it is impossible to follow the reasoning by which he justifies the condemnation and hanging of Mitchell in January 1678. Sharp was supposed to have urged Mitchell's trial, and to have perjured himself, which is far from certain. Though Mitchell was guilty, the manner of his taking off was flagrantly unjust and most discreditable to all concerned.

Huge armed conventicles, and others led by Welsh, a preacher, marched about through the country in December 1678 to May 1679. In April 1679 two soldiers were murdered while in bed; next day John Graham of Claverhouse, who had served under the Prince of Orange with credit, and now comes upon the scene, reported that Welsh was organising an armed rebellion, and that the peasants were seizing the weapons of the militia. Balfour of Kinloch (Burley) and Robert Hamilton, a laird in Fife, were the leaders of that extreme sect which was feared as much by the indulged preachers as by the curates, and, on May 2, 1679, Balfour, with Hackstoun of Rathillet (who merely looked on), and other pious desperadoes, passed half an hour in clumsily hacking Sharp to death, in the presence of his daughter, at Magus Moor near St Andrews.

The slayers, says one of them, thanked the Lord "for leading them by His Holy Spirit in every step they stepped in that matter," and it is obvious that mere argument was unavailing with gentlemen who cherished such opinions. In the portraits of Sharp we see a face of refined goodness which makes the physiognomist distrust his art. From very early times Cromwell had styled Sharp "Sharp of that ilk." He was subtle, he had no fanaticism, he warned his brethren in 1660 of the impossibility of restoring their old authority and discipline. But when he accepted an archbishopric he sold his honour; his servility to Charles and Lauderdale was disgusting; fear made him cruel; his conduct at Mitchell's last trial is, at best, ambiguous; and the hatred in which he was held is proved by the falsehoods which his enemies told about his private life and his sorceries.

The murderers crossed the country, joined the armed fanatics of the west, under Robert Hamilton, and on Restoration Day (May 29) burned Acts of the Government at Rutherglen. Claverhouse rode out of Glasgow with a small force, to inquire into this proceeding; met the armed insurgents in a strong position defended by marshes and small lochs; sent to Lord Ross at Glasgow for reinforcements which did not arrive; and has himself told how he was defeated, pursued, and driven back into Glasgow. "This may be accounted the beginning of the rebellion in my opinion."

Hamilton shot with his own hand one of the prisoners, and reckoned the sparing of the others "one of our first steppings aside." Men so conscientious as Hamilton were rare in his party, which was ruined presently by its own distracted counsels.

The forces of the victors of Drumclog were swollen by their success, but they were repulsed with loss in an attack on Glasgow. The commands of Ross and Claverhouse were then withdrawn to Stirling, and when Livingstone joined them at Larbert, the whole army mustered but 1800 men—so weak were the regulars. The militia was raised, and the king sent down his illegitimate son, Monmouth, husband of the heiress of Buccleuch, at the head of several regiments of redcoats. Argyll was not of service; he was engaged in private war with the Macleans, who refused an appeal for help from the rebels. They, in Glasgow and at Hamilton, were quarrelling over the Indulgence: the extremists called Mr Welsh's party "rotten-hearted"— Welsh would not reject the king's authority—the Welshites were the more numerous. On June 22 the Clyde, at Bothwell Bridge, separated the rebels—whose preachers were inveighing against each other— from Monmouth's army. Monmouth refused to negotiate till the others laid down their arms, and after a brief artillery duel, the Royal infantry carried the bridge, and the rest of the affair was pursuit by the cavalry. The rival Covenanting leaders, Russel, one of Sharp's murderers, and Ure, give varying accounts of the affair, and each party blames the other. The rebel force is reckoned at from five to seven thousand, the Royal army was of 2300 according to Russel. "Some hundreds" of the Covenanters fell, and "many hundreds," the Privy Council reported, were taken.

The battle of Bothwell Bridge severed the extremists, Robert Hamilton, Richard Cameron and Cargill, the famous preachers, and the rest, from the majority of the Covenanters. They dwindled to the "Remnant," growing the fiercer as their numbers decreased. Only two ministers were hanged; hundreds of prisoners were banished, like Cromwell's prisoners after Dunbar, to the American colonies. Of these some two hundred were drowned in the wreck of their vessel off the Orkneys. The main body were penned up in Greyfriars Churchyard; many escaped; more signed a promise to remain peaceful, and shun conventicles. There was more of cruel carelessness than of the deliberate cruelty displayed in the massacres and hangings of women after Philiphaugh and Dunaverty. But the avaricious and corrupt rulers, after 1679, headed by James, Duke of York (Lauderdale being removed), made the rising of Bothwell Bridge the pretext for fining and ruining hundreds of persons, especially lairds, who were accused of helping or harbouring rebels. The officials were rapacious for their own profit. The records of scores of trials prosecuted for the sake of spoil, and disgraced by torture and injustice, make miserable reading. Between the trials of the accused and the struggle with the small minority of extremists led by Richard Cameron and the aged Mr Cargill, the history of the country is monotonously wretched. It was in prosecuting lairds and peasants and preachers that Sir George Mackenzie, by nature a lenient man and a lover of literature, gained the name of "the bluidy advocate."

Cameron and his followers rode about after issuing the wildest manifestoes, as at Sanquhar in the shire of Dumfries (June 22, 1680). Bruce of Earlshall was sent with a party of horse to pursue, and, in the wild marshes of Airs Moss, in Ayrshire, Cameron "fell praying and fighting"; while Hackstoun of Rathillet, less fortunate, was taken, and the murder of Sharp was avenged on him with unspeakable cruelties. The Remnant now formed itself into organised and armed societies; their conduct made them feared and detested by the majority of the preachers, who longed for a quiet life, not for the establishment of a

Mosaic commonwealth, and "the execution of righteous judgments" on "malignants." Cargill was now the leader of the Remnant, and Cargill, in a conventicle at Torwood, of his own authority excommunicated the king, the Duke of York, Lauderdale, Rothes, Dalziel, and Mackenzie, whom he accused of leniency to witches, among other sins. The Government apparently thought that excommunication, to the mind of Cargill and his adherents, meant outlawry, and that outlawry might mean the assassination of the excommunicated. Cargill was hunted, and (July 12, 1681) was captured by "wild Bonshaw." It was believed by his party that the decision to execute Cargill was carried by the vote of Argyll, in the Privy Council, and that Cargill told Rothes (who had signed the Covenant with him in their youth) that Rothes would be the first to die. Rothes died on July 26, Cargill was hanged on July 27.

On the following day James, Duke of York, as Royal Commissioner, opened the first Parliament since 1673-74. James secured an Act making the right of succession to the Crown independent of differences of religion; he, of course, was a Catholic. The Test Act was also passed, a thing so self-contradictory in its terms that any man might take it whose sense of humour overcame his sense of honour. Many refused, including a number of the conformist ministers. Argyll took the Test "as far as it is consistent with itself and with the Protestant religion."

Argyll, the son of the executed Marquis, had recovered his lands, and acquired the title of Earl mainly through the help of Lauderdale. During the religious troubles from 1660 onwards he had taken no great part, but had sided with the Government, and approved of the torture of preachers. But what ruined him now (though the facts have been little noticed) was his disregard of the claims of his creditors, and his obtaining the lands of the Macleans in Mull and Morven, in discharge of an enormous debt of the Maclean chief to the Marquis, executed in 1661. The Macleans had vainly attempted to prove that the debt was vastly inflated by familiar processes, and had resisted in arms the invasion of the Campbells. They had friends in Seaforth, the Mackenzies, and in the Earl of Errol and other nobles.

These men, especially Mackenzie of Tarbet, an astute intriguer, seized their chance when Argyll took the Test "with a qualification," and though, at first, he satisfied and was reconciled to the Duke of York, they won over the Duke, accused Argyll to the king, brought him before a jury, and had him condemned of treason and incarcerated. The object may have been to intimidate him, and destroy his almost royal power in the west and the islands. In any case, after a trial for treason, in which one vote settled his doom, he escaped in disguise as a footman (perhaps by collusion, as was suspected), fled to England, conspired there with Scottish exiles and a Covenanting refugee, Mr Veitch, and, as Charles would not allow him to be searched for, he easily escaped to Holland. (For details, see my book, 'Sir George Mackenzie.')

It was, in fact, clan hatred that dragged down Argyll. His condemnation was an infamous perversion of justice, but as Charles would not allow him to be captured in London, it is most improbable that he would have permitted the unjust capital sentence to be carried out. The escape was probably collusive, and the sole result of these intricate iniquities was to create for the Government an enemy who would have been dangerous if he had been trusted by the extreme Presbyterians. In England no less than in Scotland the supreme and odious injustice of Argyll's trial excited general indignation. The Earl of Aberdeen (Gordon of Haddo) was now Chancellor, and Queensberry was Treasurer for a while; both were intrigued against at Court by the Earl of Perth and his brother, later Lord Melfort, and probably by far the worst of all the knaves of the Restoration.

Increasing outrages by the Remnant, now headed by the Rev. Mr James Renwick, a very young man, led to more furious repression, especially as in 1683 Government detected a double plot—the wilder English aim being to raise the rabble and to take or slay Charles and his brother at the Rye House; while the more respectable conspirators, English and Scots, were believed to be acquainted with, though not engaged in, this design. The Rev. Mr Carstares was going and coming between Argyll and the exiles in Holland and the intriguers at home. They intended as usual first to surprise Edinburgh Castle. In England Algernon Sidney, Lord Russell, and others were arrested, while Baillie of Jerviswoode and Carstares were apprehended—Carstares in England. He was sent to Scotland, where he could be tortured. The trial of Jerviswoode was if possible more unjust than even the common run of these affairs, and he was executed (December 24, 1684).

The conspiracy was, in fact, a very serious affair: Carstares was confessedly aware of its criminal aspect, and was in the closest confidence of the ministers of William of Orange. What his dealings were with them in later years he would never divulge. But it is clear that if the plotters slew Charles and James, the hour had struck for the Dutch deliverer's appearance. If we describe the Rye House Plot as aiming merely at "the exclusion of the Duke of York from the throne," we shut our eyes to evidence and make ourselves incapable of understanding the events. There were plotters of every degree and rank, and they were intriguing with Argyll, and, through Carstares who knew, though he refused a part in the murder plot, were in touch at once with Argyll and the intimates of William of Orange.

Meanwhile "the hill men," the adherents of Renwick, in October 1684, declared a war of assassination against their opponents, and announced that they would try malignants in courts of their own. Their manifesto ("The Apologetical Declaration") caused an extraordinary measure of repression. A test—the abjuration of the *criminal* parts of Renwick's declaration—was to be offered by military authority to all and sundry. Refusal to abjure entailed military execution. The test was only obnoxious to sincere fanatics; but among them must have been hundreds of persons who had no criminal designs, and merely deemed it a point of honour not to "homologate" any act of a Government which was corrupt, prelatic, and unholy.

Later victims of this view of duty were Margaret Lauchleson and Margaret Wilson—an old woman and a young girl—cruelly drowned by the local authorities at Wigtown (May 1685). A myth represents Claverhouse as having been present. The shooting of John Brown, "the Christian Carrier," by Claverhouse in the previous week was an affair of another character. Claverhouse did not exceed his orders, and ammunition and treasonable papers were in Brown's possession; he was also sheltering a red-handed rebel. Brown was not shot merely "because he was a Nonconformist," nor was he shot by the hand of Claverhouse.

These incidents of "the killing time" were in the reign of James II; Charles II had died, to the sincere grief of most of his subjects, on February 2, 1685. "Lecherous and treacherous" as he was, he was humorous and good-humoured. The expected invasion of Scotland by Argyll, of England by Monmouth, did not encourage the Government to use respective lenity in the Covenanting region, from Lanarkshire to Galloway.

Argyll, who sailed from Holland on May 2, had a council of Lowlanders who thwarted him. His interests were in his own principality, but he found it occupied by Atholl and his clansmen, and the cadets of his own House as a rule would not rally to him. The Lowlanders with him, Sir Patrick Hume, Sir John Cochrane, and the rest, wished to move south and join hands with the Remnant in the west and in Galloway; but the Remnant distrusted the sudden religious zeal of Argyll, and were cowed by Claverhouse. The coasts were watched by Government vessels of war, and when, after vain movements round about his own castle, Inveraray, Argyll was obliged by his Lowlanders to move on Glasgow, he was checked at every turn; the leaders, weary and lost in the marshes, scattered from Kilpatrick on Clyde; Argyll crossed the river, and was captured by servants of Sir John Shaw of Greenock. He was not put to trial nor to torture; he was executed on the verdict of 1681. About 200 suspected persons were lodged by Government in Dunottar Castle at the time and treated with abominable cruelty.

The Covenanters were now effectually put down, though Renwick was not taken and hanged till 1688. The preachers were anxious for peace and quiet, and were bitterly hostile to Renwick. The Covenant was a dead letter as far as power to do mischief was concerned. It was not persecution of the Kirk, but demand for toleration of Catholics and a manifest desire to restore the Church, that in two years lost James his kingdoms.

On April 29, 1686, James's message to the Scots Parliament asked toleration for "our innocent subjects" the Catholics. He had substituted Perth's brother, now entitled Earl of Melfort, for Queensberry; Perth was now Chancellor; both men had adopted their king's religion, and the infamous Melfort can hardly be supposed to have done so honestly. Their families lost all in the event except their faith. With the request for toleration James sent promises of free trade with England, and he asked for no supplies. Perth had introduced Catholic vestments and furnishings in Holyrood chapel, which provoked a No Popery riot. Parliament would not permit toleration; James removed many of the Council and filled their places with Catholics. Sir George Mackenzie's conscience "dirled"; he refused to vote for toleration and he lost the Lord Advocateship, being superseded by Sir James Dalrymple, an old Covenanting opponent of Claverhouse in Galloway.

In August James, by prerogative, did what the Estates would not do, and he deprived the Archbishop of Glasgow and the Bishop of Dunkeld of their Sees: though a Catholic, he was the king-pope of a Protestant church! In a decree of July 1687 he extended toleration to the Kirk, and a meeting of preachers at Edinburgh expressed "a deep sense of your Majesty's gracious and surprising favour." The Kirk was indeed broken, and, when the Revolution came, was at last ready for a compromise from which the Covenants were omitted. On February 17, 1688, Mr Renwick was hanged at Edinburgh: he had been prosecuted by Dalrymple. On the same day Mackenzie superseded Dalrymple as Lord Advocate.

After the birth of the White Rose Prince of Wales (June 10, 1688), Scotland, like England, apprehended that a Catholic king would be followed by a Catholic son. The various contradictory lies about the child's birth flourished, all the more because James ventured to select the magistrates of the royal burghs. It became certain that the Prince of Orange would invade, and Melfort madly withdrew the regular troops, with Claverhouse (now Viscount Dundee) to aid in resisting William in England, though Balcarres proposed a safer way of holding down the English northern counties by volunteers, the Highland clans, and new levies. Thus the Privy Council in Scotland were left at the mercy of the populace.

Of the Scottish army in England all were disbanded when James fled to France, except a handful of cavalry, whom Dundee kept with him. Perth fled from Edinburgh, but was taken and held a prisoner for four years; the town train-band, with the mob and some Cameronians, took Holyrood, slaying such of the guard as they did not imprison; "many died of their wounds and hunger." The chapel and Catholic houses were sacked, and gangs of the armed Cameronian societies went about in the south-west, rabbling, robbing, and driving away ministers of the Episcopalian sort. Atholl was in power in Edinburgh; in London, where James's Scots friends met, the Duke of Hamilton was made President of Council, and power was left till the assembling of a Convention at Edinburgh (March 1689) in the hands of William.

In Edinburgh Castle the wavering Duke of Gordon was induced to remain by Dundee and Balcarres; while Dundee proposed to call a Jacobite convention in Stirling. Melfort induced James to send a letter contrary to the desires of his party; Atholl, who had promised to join them, broke away; the life of Dundee was threatened by the fanatics, and on March 18, seeing his party headless and heartless, Dundee rode north, going "wherever might lead him the shade of Montrose."

Mackay now brought to Edinburgh regiments from Holland, which overawed the Jacobites, and he secured for William the key of the north, the castle of Stirling. With Hamilton as President, the Convention, with only four adverse votes, declared against James and his son; and Hamilton (April 3) proclaimed at the cross the reign of William and Mary. The claim of rights was passed and declared Episcopacy intolerable. Balcarres was thrown into prison: on May 11 William took the Coronation oath for Scotland, merely protesting that he would not "root out heretics," as the oath enjoined.

This was "the end o' an auld sang," the end of the Stuart dynasty, and of the equally "divine rights" of kings and of preachers.

In a sketch it is impossible to convey any idea of the sufferings of Scotland, at least of Covenanting Scotland, under the Restoration. There was contest, unrest, and dragoonings, and the quartering of a brutal and licentious soldiery on suspected persons. Law, especially since 1679, had been twisted for the conviction of persons whom the administration desired to rob. The greed and corruption of the rulers, from Lauderdale, his wife, and his brother Haltoun, to Perth and his brother, the Earl of Melfort, whose very title was the name of an unjustly confiscated estate, is almost inconceivable.[32] Few of the foremost men in power, except Sir George Mackenzie and Claverhouse, were free from personal profligacy of every sort. Claverhouse has left on record his aversion to severities against the peasantry; he was for prosecuting such gentry as the Dalrymples. As constable of Dundee he refused to inflict capital punishment on petty offenders, and Mackenzie went as far as he dared in opposing the ferocities of the inquisition of witches. But in cases of alleged treason Mackenzie knew no mercy.

Torture, legal in Scotland, was used with barbarism unprecedented there after each plot or rising, to extract secrets which, save in one or two cases like that of Carstares, the victims did not possess. They were peasants, preachers, and a few country gentlemen: the nobles had no inclination to suffer for the cause of the Covenants. The Covenants continued to be the idols of the societies of Cameronians, and of many preachers who were no longer inclined to die for these documents,— the expression of such strange doctrines, the causes of so many sorrows and of so many martyrdoms. However little we may sympathise with the doctrines, none the less the sufferers were idealists, and, no less than Montrose, preferred honour to life.

With all its sins, the Restoration so far pulverised the pretensions which, since 1560, the preachers had made, that William of Orange was not obliged to renew the conflict with the spiritual sons of Knox and Andrew Melville.

This fact is not so generally recognised as it might be. It is therefore proper to quote the corroborative opinion of the learned Historiographer-Royal of Scotland, Professor Hume Brown. "By concession and repression the once mighty force of Scottish

---

[32] Many disgusting details may be read in the author's 'Life of Sir George Mackenzie.'

Presbyterianism had been broken. Most deadly of the weapons in the accomplishment of this result had been the three Acts of Indulgence which had successively cut so deep into the ranks of uniformity. In succumbing to the threats and promises of the Government, the Indulged ministers had undoubtedly compromised the fundamental principles of Presbyterianism... The compliance of these ministers was, in truth, the first and necessary step towards that religious and political compromise which the force of circumstances was gradually imposing on the Scottish people," and "the example of the Indulged ministers, who composed the great mass of the Presbyterian clergy, was of the most potent effect in substituting the idea of toleration for that of the religious absolutism of Knox and Melville."[33]

It may be added that the pretensions of Knox and Melville and all their followers were no essential part of Presbyterial Church government, but were merely the continuation or survival of the clerical claims of apostolic authority, as enforced by such popes as Hildebrand and such martyrs as St Thomas of Canterbury.

---

[33] Hume Brown, ii. 414, 415.

CHAPTER XXVII

# William *and* Mary

hile Claverhouse hovered in the north the Convention
(declared to be a Parliament by William on June 5) took on, for the
first time in Scotland since the reign of Charles I, the aspect of an
English Parliament, and demanded English constitutional freedom of
debate. The Secretary in Scotland was William, Earl of Melville; that
hereditary waverer, the Duke of Hamilton, was Royal Commissioner;
but some official supporters of William, especially Sir James and Sir
John Dalrymple, were criticised and thwarted by "the club" of more
extreme Liberals. They were led by the Lowland ally who had vexed
Argyll, Hume of Polwarth; and by Montgomery of Skelmorley, who,
disappointed in his desire of place, soon engaged in a Jacobite plot.

The club wished to hasten the grant of Parliamentary liberties
which William was anxious not to give; and to take vengeance on
officials such as Sir James Dalrymple, and his son, Sir John, now Lord
Advocate, as he had been under James II. To these two men, foes of
Claverhouse, William clung while he could. The council obtained, but
did not need to use, permission to torture Jacobite prisoners,
"Cavaliers" as at this time they were styled; but Chieseley of Dalry,
who murdered Sir George Lockhart, President of the College of
Justice, was tortured.

The advanced Liberal Acts which were passed did not receive the
touch of the sceptre from Hamilton, William's Commissioner: thus
they were "vetoed," and of no effect. The old packed committee, "The
Lords of the Articles," was denounced as a grievance; the king was to
be permitted to appoint no officers of State without Parliament's
approbation. Hamilton offered compromises, for William clung to
"the Articles"; but he abandoned them in the following year, and
thenceforth till the Union (1707) the Scottish was "a Free Parliament."

Various measures of legislation for the Kirk——some to emancipate it as in its palmy days, some to keep it from meddling in politics——were proposed; some measures to abolish, some to retain lay patronage of livings, were mooted. The advanced party for a while put a stop to the appointment of judges, but in August came news of the Viscount Dundee in the north which terrified parliamentary politicians.

Edinburgh Castle had been tamely yielded by the Duke of Gordon; Balcarres, the associate of Dundee, had been imprisoned; but Dundee himself, after being declared a rebel, in April raised the standard of King James. As against him the Whigs relied on Mackay, a brave officer who had been in Dutch service, and now commanded regiments of the Scots Brigade of Holland. Mackay pursued Dundee, as Baillie had pursued Montrose, through the north: at Inverness, Dundee picked up some Macdonalds under Keppoch, but Keppoch was not satisfactory, being something of a freebooter. The Viscount now rode to the centre of his hopes, to the Macdonalds of Glengarry, the Camerons of Lochiel, and the Macleans who had been robbed of their lands by the Earl of Argyll, executed in 1685. Dundee summoned them to Lochiel's house on Loch Arkaig for May 18; he visited Atholl and Badenoch; found a few mounted men as recruits at Dundee; returned through the wilds to Lochaber, and sent round that old summons to a rising, the Fiery Cross, charred and dipped in a goat's blood.

Much time was spent in preliminary manœuvring and sparring between Mackay, now reinforced by English regulars, and Dundee, who for a time disbanded his levies, while Mackay went to receive fresh forces and to consult the Government at Edinburgh. He decided to march to the west and bridle the clans by erecting a strong fort at Inverlochy, where Montrose routed Argyll. A stronghold at Inverlochy menaced the Macdonalds to the north, and the Camerons in Lochaber, and, southwards, the Stewarts in Appin. But to reach Inverlochy Mackay had to march up the Tay, past Blair Atholl, and so westward through very wild mountainous country. To oppose him Dundee had collected 4000 of the clansmen, and awaited ammunition and men from James, then in Ireland. By the advice of the great Lochiel, a man over seventy but miraculously athletic, Dundee decided to let the clans fight in their old way,——a rush, a volley at close quarters, and then the claymore. By June 28 Dundee had received no aid from James,——of money "we have not twenty pounds"; and he was between the Earl of Argyll (son of the martyr of 1685) and Mackay with his 4000 foot and eight troops of horse.

On July 23 Dundee seized the castle of Blair Atholl, which had been the base of Montrose in his campaigns, and was the key of the country between the Tay and Lochaber. The Atholl clans, Murrays and Stewarts, breaking away from the son of their chief, the fickle Marquis of Atholl, were led by Stewart of Ballechin, but did not swell Dundee's force at the moment. From James Dundee now received but a battalion of half-starved Irishmen, under the futile General Cannon.

On July 27, at Blair, Dundee learned that Mackay's force had already entered the steep and narrow pass of Killiecrankie, where the road skirted the brawling waters of the Garry. Dundee had not time to defend the pass; he marched his men from Blair, keeping the heights, while Mackay emerged from the gorge, and let his forces rest on the wide level haugh beside the Garry, under the house of Runraurie, now called Urrard, with the deep and rapid river in their rear. On this haugh the tourist sees the tall standing stone which, since 1735 at least, has been known as "Dundee's stone." From the haugh rises a steep acclivity, leading to the plateau where the house of Runraurie stood. Mackay feared that Dundee would occupy this plateau, and that the fire thence would break up his own men on the haugh below. He therefore seized the plateau, which was an unfortunate manœuvre. He was so superior in numbers that both of his wings extended beyond Dundee's, who had but forty ill-horsed gentlemen by way of cavalry. After distracting Mackay by movements along the heights, as if to cut off his communications with the south, Dundee, who had resisted the prayers of the chiefs that he would be sparing of his person, gave the word to charge as the sun sank behind the western hills. Rushing downhill, under heavy fire and losing many men, the clans, when they came to the shock, swept the enemy from the plateau, drove them over the declivity, forced many to attempt crossing the Garry, where they were drowned, and followed, slaying, through the pass. Half of Hastings' regiment, untouched by the Highland charge, and all of Leven's men, stood their ground, and were standing there when sixteen of Dundee's horse returned from the pursuit. Mackay, who had lost his army, stole across the Garry with this remnant and made for Stirling. He knew not that Dundee lay on the field, dying in the arms of Victory. Precisely when and in what manner Dundee was slain is unknown; there is even a fair presumption, from letters of the English Government, that he was murdered by two men sent from England on some very secret mission. When last seen by his men, Dundee was plunged in the battle smoke, sword in hand, in advance of his horse.

When the Whigs—terrified by the defeat and expecting Dundee at Stirling with the clans and the cavaliers of the Lowlands—heard of his fall, their sorrow was changed into rejoicing. The cause of King James was mortally wounded by the death of "the glory of the Grahams," who alone could lead and keep together a Highland host. Deprived of his leadership and distrustful of his successor, General Cannon, the clans gradually left the Royal Standard. The Cameronian regiment, recruited from the young men of the organised societies, had been ordered to occupy Dunkeld. Here they were left isolated, "in the air," by Mackay or his subordinates, and on August 21 these raw recruits, under Colonel Cleland, who had fought at Drumclog, had to receive the attack of the Highlanders. Cleland had fortified the Abbey church and the "castle," and his Cameronians fired from behind walls and from loopholes with such success that Cannon called off the clansmen, or could not bring them to a second attack: both versions are given. Cleland fell in the fight; the clans disbanded, and Mackay occupied the castle of Blair.

Three weeks later the Cameronians, being unpaid, mutinied; and Ross, Annandale, and Polwarth, urging their demands for constitutional rights, threw the Lowlands into a ferment. Crawford, whose manner of speech was sanctimonious, was evicting from their parishes ministers who remained true to Episcopacy, and would not pray for William and Mary. Polwarth now went to London with an address to these Sovereigns framed by "the Club," the party of liberty. But the other leaders of that party, Annandale, Ross, and Montgomery of Skelmorley, all of them eager for place and office, entered into a conspiracy of intrigue with the Jacobites for James's restoration. In February 1690 the Club was distracted; and to Melville, as Commissioner in the Scottish Parliament, William gave orders that the Acts for re-establishing Presbytery and abolishing lay patronage of livings were to be passed. Montgomery was obliged to bid yet higher for the favour of the more extreme preachers and devotees,—but he failed. In April the Lords of the Articles were abolished at last, and freedom of parliamentary debate was thus secured. The Westminster Confession was reinstated, and in May, after the last remnants of a Jacobite force in the north had been surprised and scattered or captured by Sir Thomas Livingstone at Cromdale Haugh (May 1), the alliance of Jacobites and of the Club broke down, and the leaders of the Club saved themselves by playing the part of informers.

The new Act regarding the Kirk permitted the holding of Synods and General Assemblies, to be summoned by permission of William or of the Privy Council, with a Royal Commissioner present to restrain the preachers from meddling, as a body, with secular politics. The Kirk was to be organised by the "Sixty Bishops," the survivors of the ministers ejected in 1663. The benefices of ejected Episcopalian conformists were declared to be vacant. Lay patronage was annulled: the congregations had the right to approve or disapprove of presentees. But the Kirk was deprived of her old weapon, the attachment of civil penalties (that is practical outlawry) to her sentences of excommunication (July 19, 1690). The Covenant was silently dropped.

Thus ended, practically, the war between Kirk and State which had raged for nearly a hundred and twenty years. The cruel torturing of Nevile Payne, an English Jacobite taken in Scotland, showed that the new sovereigns and Privy Council retained the passions and methods of the old, but this was the last occasion of judicial torture for political offences in Scotland. Payne was silent, but was illegally imprisoned till his death.

The proceedings of the restored General Assembly were awaited with anxiety by the Government. The extremists of the Remnant, the "Cameronians," sent deputies to the Kirk. They were opposed to acknowledging sovereigns who were "the head of the Prelatics" in England, and they, not being supported by the Assembly, remained apart from the Kirk and true to the Covenants.

Much had passed which William disliked—the abolition of patronage, the persecution of Episcopalians—and Melville, in 1691, was removed by the king from the Commissionership.

The Highlands were still unsettled. In June 1691 Breadalbane, at heart a Jacobite, attempted to appease the chiefs by promises of money in settlement of various feuds, especially that of the dispossessed Macleans against the occupant of their lands, Argyll. Breadalbane was known by Hill, the commander of Fort William at Inverlochy, to be dealing between the clans and James, as well as between William and the clans. William, then campaigning in Flanders, was informed of this fact, thought it of no importance, and accepted a truce from July 1 to October 1 with Buchan, who commanded such feeble forces as still stood for James in the north. At the same time William threatened the clans, in the usual terms, with "fire and sword," if the chiefs did not take the oaths to his Government by January 1, 1692. Money and titles under the rank of earldoms were to be offered to Macdonald of Sleat, Maclean of Dowart, Lochiel, Glengarry, and Clanranald, if they would come in. All declined the bait—if

Breadalbane really fished with it. It is plain, contrary to Lord Macaulay's statement, that Sir John Dalrymple, William's trusted man for Scotland, at this time hoped for Breadalbane's success in pacifying the clans. But Dalrymple, by December 1691, wrote, "I think the Clan Donell must be rooted out, and Lochiel." He could not mean that he hoped to massacre so large a part of the population. He probably meant by "punitive expeditions" in the modern phrase—by "fire and sword," in the style current then—to break up the recalcitrants. Meanwhile it was Dalrymple's hope to settle ancient quarrels about the "superiorities" of Argyll over the Camerons, and the question of compensation for the lands reft by the Argyll family from the Macleans.

Before December 31, in fear of "fire and sword," the chiefs submitted, except the greatest, Glengarry, and the least in power, MacIan or Macdonald, with his narrow realm of Glencoe, whence his men were used to plunder the cattle of their powerful neighbour, Breadalbane. Dalrymple now desired not peace, but the sword. By January 9, 1692, Dalrymple, in London, heard that Glencoe had come in (he had accidentally failed to come in by January 1), and Dalrymple was "sorry." By January 11 Dalrymple knew that Glencoe had not taken the oath before January 1, and rejoiced in the chance to "root out that damnable sect." In fact, in the end of December Glencoe had gone to Fort William to take the oaths before Colonel Hill, but found that he must do so before the Sheriff of the shire at remote Inveraray. Various accidents of weather delayed him; the Sheriff also was not at Inveraray when Glencoe arrived, but administered the oaths on January 6. The document was taken to Edinburgh, where Lord Stair, Dalrymple's father, and others caused it to be deleted. Glengarry was still unsworn, but Glengarry was too strong to be "rooted out"; William ordered his commanding officer, Livingstone, "to extirpate that sect of thieves," the Glencoe men (January 16). On the same day Dalrymple sent down orders to him in the MacIans, and to guard all the passes, by land or water, from their glen. Of the actual *method* of massacre employed Dalrymple may have been ignorant; but orders "from Court" to "spare none," and to take no prisoners, were received by Livingstone on January 23.

On February 1, Campbell of Glenlyon, with 120 men, was hospitably received by MacIan, whose son, Alexander, had married Glenlyon's niece. On February 12, Hill sent 400 of his Inverlochy garrison to Glencoe to join hands with 400 of Argyll's regiment, under

Major Duncanson. These troops were to guard the southern passes out of Glencoe, while Hamilton was to sweep the passes from the north.

At 5 A.M. on February 13 the soldier-guests of MacIan began to slay and plunder. Men, women, and children were shot or bayoneted, 1000 head of cattle were driven away; but Hamilton arrived too late. Though the aged chief had been shot at once, his sons took to the hills, and the greater part of the population escaped with their lives, thanks to Hamilton's dilatoriness. "All I regret is that any of the sect got away," wrote Dalrymple on March 5, "and there is necessity to prosecute them to the utmost." News had already reached London "that they are murdered in their beds." The newspapers, however, were silenced, and the story was first given to Europe in April by the 'Paris Gazette.' The crime was unprecedented: it had no precedent, admits of no apology. Many an expedition of "fire and sword" had occurred, but never had there been a midnight massacre "under trust" of hosts by guests. King William, on March 6, went off to his glorious wars on the Continent, probably hoping to hear that the fugitive MacIans were still being "prosecuted"—if, indeed, he thought of them at all. But by October they were received into his peace.

William was more troubled by the General Assembly, which refused to take oaths of allegiance to him and his wife, and actually appointed a date for an Assembly without his consent. When he gave it, it was on condition that the members should take the oaths of allegiance. They refused: it was the old deadlock, but William at the last moment withdrew from the imposition of oaths of allegiance— moved, it is said, by Mr Carstares, "Cardinal Carstares," who had been privy to the Rye House Plot. Under Queen Anne, however, the conscientious preachers were compelled to take the oaths like mere laymen.

CHAPTER XXVIII

# Darien

The Scottish Parliament of May-July 1695, held while William was abroad, saw the beginning of evils for Scotland. The affair of Glencoe was examined into by a Commission, headed by Tweeddale, William's Commissioner: several Judges sat in it. Their report cleared William himself: Dalrymple, it was found, had "exceeded his instructions." Hill was exonerated. Hamilton, who commanded the detachment that arrived too late, fled the country. William was asked to send home for trial Duncanson and other butchers who were with his army. The king was also invited to deal with Dalrymple as he thought fit. He thought fit to give Dalrymple an indemnity, and made him Viscount Stair, with a grant of money, but did not retain him in office. He did not send the subaltern butchers home for trial. Many years later, in 1745, the MacIans insisted on acting as guards of the house and family of the descendant of Campbell of Glenlyon, the guest and murderer of the chief of Glencoe.

Perhaps by way of a sop to the Scots, William allowed an Act for the Establishment of a Scottish East India Company to be passed on June 20, 1695. He afterwards protested that in this matter he had been "badly served," probably meaning "misinformed." The result was the Darien Expedition, a great financial disaster for Scotland, and a terrible grievance. Hitherto since the Union of the Crowns all Scottish efforts to found trading companies, as in England, had been wrecked on English jealousy: there had always been, and to this new East India Company there was, a rival, a pre-existing English company. Scottish Acts for protection of home industries were met by English retaliation in a war of tariffs. Scotland had prohibited the exportation of her raw materials, such as wool, but was cut off from English and other foreign markets for her cloths. The Scots were more successful in secret and unlegalised trading with their kinsmen in the American colonies.

The Scottish East India Company's aim was to sell Scottish goods in many places, India for example; and it was secretly meant to found a factory and central mart on the isthmus of Panama. For these ends capital was withdrawn from the new and unsuccessful manufacturing companies. The great scheme was the idea of William Paterson (born 1658), the far-travelled and financially-speculative son of a farmer in Dumfriesshire. He was the "projector," or one of the projectors, of the Bank of England of 1694, investing £2000. He kept the Darien part of his scheme for an East India Company in the background, and it seems that William, when he granted a patent to that company, knew nothing of this design to settle in or near the Panama isthmus, which was quite clearly within the Spanish sphere of influence. When the philosopher John Locke heard of the scheme, he wished England to steal the idea and seize a port in Darien: it thus appears that he too was unaware that to do so was to inflict an insult and injury on Spain. There is reason to suppose that the grant of the patent to the East India Company was obtained by bribing some Scottish politician or politicians unnamed, though one name is not beyond probable conjecture.

In any case Paterson admitted English capitalists, who took up half of the shares, as the Act of Patent permitted them to do. By December William was writing that he "had been ill-served by some of my Ministers." He had no notice of the details of the Act of Patent till he had returned to England, and found English capitalists and the English Parliament in a fury. The Act committed William to interposing his authority if the ships of the company were detained by foreign powers, and gave the adventurers leave to take "reparation" by force from their assailants (this they later did when they captured in the Firth of Forth an English vessel, the *Worcester*).

On the opening of the books of the new company in London (October 1695) there had been a panic, and a fall of twenty points in the shares of the English East India Company. The English Parliament had addressed William in opposition to the Scots Company. The English subscribers of half the paid up capital were terrorised, and sold out. Later, Hamburg investments were cancelled through William's influence. All lowland Scotland hurried to invest—in the dark—for the Darien part of the scheme was practically a secret: it was vaguely announced that there was to be a settlement somewhere, "in Africa or the Indies, or both." Materials of trade, such as wigs, combs, Bibles, fish-hooks, and kid-gloves, were accumulated. Offices were built—later used as an asylum for pauper lunatics.

When, in July 1697, the secret of Panama came out, the English Council of Trade examined Dampier, the voyager, and (September) announced that the territory had never been Spain's, and that England ought to anticipate Scotland by seizing Golden Island and the port on the mainland.

In July 1698 the Council of the intended Scots colony was elected, bought three ships and two tenders, and despatched 1200 settlers with two preachers, but with most inadequate provisions, and flour as bad as that paid to Assynt for the person of Montrose. On October 30, in the Gulf of Darien they found natives who spoke Spanish; they learned that the nearest gold mines were in Spanish hands, and that the chiefs were carrying Spanish insignia of office. By February 1699 the Scots and Spaniards were exchanging shots. Presently a Scottish ship, cruising in search of supplies, was seized by the Spanish at Carthagena; the men lay in irons at Seville till 1700. Spain complained to William, and the Scots seized a merchant ship. The English Governor of Jamaica forbade his people, by virtue of a letter addressed by the English Government to all the colonies, to grant supplies to the starving Scots, most of whom sailed away from the colony in June, and suffered terrible things by sea and land. Paterson returned to Scotland. A new expedition which left Leith on May 12, 1699, found at Darien some Scots in two ships, and remained on the scene, distracted by quarrels, till February 1700, when Campbell of Fonab, sent with provisions in the *Speedy Return* from Scotland, arrived to find the Spaniards assailing the adventurers. He cleared the Spaniards out of their fort in fifteen minutes, but the Colonial Council learned that Spain was launching a small but adequate armada against them. After an honourable resistance the garrison capitulated, and marched out with colours flying (March 30). This occurred just when Scotland was celebrating the arrival of the news of Fonab's gallant feat of arms.

At home the country was full of discontent: William's agent at Hamburg had prevented foreigners from investing in the Scots company. English colonists had been forbidden to aid the Scottish adventurers. Two hundred thousand pounds, several ships, and many lives had been lost. "It is very like 1641," wrote an onlooker, so fierce were the passions that raged against William. The news of the surrender of the colonists increased the indignation. The king refused (November 1700) to gratify the Estates by regarding the Darien colony as a legal enterprise. To do so was to incur war with Spain and the anger of his English subjects. Yet the colony had been legally founded in accordance with the terms of the Act of Patent. While the Scots dwelt on this fact, William replied that the colony being extinct, circumstances were altered. The Estates voted that Darien *was* a lawful colony, and (1701) in an address to the Crown demanded compensation for the nation's financial losses. William replied with expressions of sympathy and hopes that the two kingdoms would consider a scheme of Union. A Bill for Union brought in through the English Lords was rejected by the English Commons.

There was hardly an alternative between Union and War between the two nations. War there would have been had the exiled Prince of Wales been brought up as a Presbyterian. His father James VII died a few months before William III passed away on March 7, 1702. Louis XIV acknowledged James, Prince of Wales, as James III of England and Ireland and VIII, of Scotland; and Anne, the boy's aunt, ascended the throne. As a Stuart she was not unwelcome to the Jacobites, who hoped for various chances, as Anne was believed to be friendly to her nephew.

In 1701 was passed an Act for preventing wrongous imprisonment and against undue delay in trials. But Nevile Payne continued to be untried and illegally imprisoned. Offenders, generally, could "run their letters" and protest, if kept in durance untried for sixty days.

The Revolution of 1688-89, with William's very reluctant concessions, had placed Scotland in entirely new relations with England. Scotland could now no longer be "governed by the pen" from London; Parliament could no longer be bridled and led, at English will, by the Lords of the Articles. As the religious mainspring of Scottish political life, the domination of the preachers had been weakened by the new settlement of the Kirk; as the country was now set on commercial enterprises, which England everywhere thwarted, it was plain that the two kingdoms could not live together on the existing terms. Union there must be, or conquest, as under Cromwell; yet an English war of conquest was impossible, because it was impossible for Scotland to resist. Never would the country renew, as in the old days, the alliance of France, for a French alliance meant the acceptance by Scotland of a Catholic king.

England, on her side, if Union came, was accepting a partner with very poor material resources. As regards agriculture, for example, vast regions were untilled, or tilled only in the straths and fertile spots by the hardy clansmen, who could not raise oats enough for their own subsistence, and periodically endured famines. In "the ill years" of

William, years of untoward weather, distress had been extreme. In the fertile Lowlands that old grievance, insecurity of tenure, and the raising of rents in proportion to improvements made by the tenants, had baffled agriculture. Enclosures were necessary for the protection of the crops, but even if tenants or landlords had the energy or capital to make enclosures, the neighbours destroyed them under cloud of night. The old labour-services were still extorted; the tenant's time and strength were not his own. Land was exhausted by absence of fallows and lack of manure. The country was undrained, lochs and morasses covered what is now fertile land, and hillsides now in pasture were under the plough. The once prosperous linen trade had suffered from the war of tariffs.

The life of the burghs, political and municipal and trading, was little advanced on the mediæval model. The independent Scot steadily resisted instruction from foreign and English craftsmen in most of the mechanical arts. Laws for the encouragement of trades were passed and bore little fruit. Companies were founded and were ruined by English tariffs and English competition. The most energetic of the population went abroad, here they prospered in commerce and in military service, while an enormous class of beggars lived on the hospitality of their neighbours at home. In such conditions of inequality it was plain that, if there was to be a Union, the adjustment of proportions of taxation and of representation in Parliament would require very delicate handling, while the differences of Church Government were certain to cause jealousies and opposition.

# CHAPTER XXIX

# Preliminaries *to the* Union

The Scottish Parliament was not dissolved at William's death, nor did it meet at the time when, legally, it ought to have met. Anne, in a message, expressed hopes that it would assent to Union, and promised to concur in any reasonable scheme for compensating the losers by the Darien scheme. When Parliament met, Queensberry, being Commissioner, soon found it necessary (June 30, 1702) to adjourn. New officers of State were then appointed, and there was a futile meeting between English and Scottish Commissioners chosen by the Queen to consider the Union.

Then came a General Election (1703), which gave birth to the last Scottish Parliament. The Commissioner, Queensberry, and the other officers of State, "the Court party," were of course for Union; among them was prominent that wavering Earl of Mar who was so active in promoting the Union, and later precipitated the Jacobite rising of 1715. There were in Parliament the party of Courtiers, friends of England and Union; the party of Cavaliers, that is Jacobites; and the Country party, led by the Duke of Hamilton, who was in touch with the Jacobites, but was quite untrustworthy, and much suspected of desiring the Crown of Scotland for himself.

Queensberry cozened the Cavaliers—by promises of tolerating their Episcopalian religion—into voting a Bill recognising Anne, and then broke his promise. The Bill for tolerating worship as practised by the Episcopalians was dropped; for the Commissioner of the General Assembly of the Kirk declared that such toleration was "the establishment of iniquity by law."

Queensberry's one aim was to get Supply voted, for war with France had begun. But the Country and the Cavalier parties refused Supply till an Act of Security for religion, liberty, law, and trade should be passed. The majority decided that, on the death of Anne, the

Estates should name as king of Scotland a Protestant representative of the House of Stewart, who should not be the successor to the English crown, save under conditions guaranteeing Scotland as a sovereign state, with frequent Parliaments, and security for Scottish navigation, colonies, trade, and religion (the Act of Security).

It was also decided that landholders and the burghs should drill and arm their tenants and dependants—if Protestant. Queensberry refused to pass this Act of Security; Supply, on the other side, was denied, and after a stormy scene Queensberry prorogued Parliament (September 16, 1703).

In the excitement, Atholl had deserted the Court party and voted with the majority. He had a great Highland following, he might throw it on the Jacobite side, and the infamous intriguer, Simon Frazer (the Lord Lovat of 1745), came over from France and betrayed to Queensberry a real or a feigned intrigue of Atholl with France and with the Ministers of James VIII, called "The Pretender."

Atholl was the enemy of Frazer, a canting, astute, and unscrupulous ruffian. Queensberry conceived that in a letter given to him by Lovat he had irrefutable evidence against Atholl as a conspirator, and he allowed Lovat to return to France, where he was promptly imprisoned as a traitor. Atholl convinced Anne of his own innocence, and Queensberry fell under ridicule and suspicion, lost his office of Commissioner, and was superseded by Tweeddale. In England the whole complex affair of Lovat's revelations was known as "The Scottish Plot"; Hamilton was involved, or feared he might be involved, and therefore favoured the new proposals of the Courtiers and English party for placing limits on the prerogative of Anne's successor, whoever he might be.

In the Estates (July 1704), after months passed in constitutional chicanery, the last year's Act of Security was passed and touched with the sceptre; and the House voted Supply for six months. But owing to a fierce dispute on private business—namely, the raising of the question, "Who were the persons accused in England of being engaged in the 'Scottish Plot'?"—no hint of listening to proposals for Union was uttered. Who could propose, as Commissioners to arrange Union, men who were involved—or in England had been accused of being involved—in the plot? Scotland had not yet consented that whoever succeeded Anne in England should also succeed in Scotland. They retained a means of putting pressure on England, the threat of having a separate king; they had made and were making military preparations (drill once a-month!), and England took up the gauntlet.

The menacing attitude of Scotland was debated on with much heat in the English Upper House (November 29), and a Bill passed by the Commons declared the retaliatory measures which England was ready to adopt.

It was at once proved that England could put a much harder pinch on Scotland than Scotland could inflict on England. Scottish drovers were no longer to sell cattle south of the Border, Scottish ships trading with France were to be seized, Scottish coals and linen were to be excluded, and regiments of regular troops were to be sent to the Border if Scotland did not accept the Hanoverian succession before Christmas 1705. If it came to war, Scotland could expect no help from her ancient ally, France, unless she raised the standard of King James. As he was a Catholic, the Kirk would prohibit this measure, so it was perfectly clear to every plain man that Scotland must accept the Union and make the best bargain she could.

In spring 1705 the new Duke of Argyll, "Red John of the Battles," a man of the sword and an accomplished orator, was made Commissioner, and, of course, favoured the Union, as did Queensberry and the other officers of State. Friction between the two countries arose in spring, when an Edinburgh jury convicted, and the mob insisted on the execution of, an English Captain Green, whose ship, the *Worcester*, had been seized in the Forth by Roderick Mackenzie, Secretary of the Scottish East India Company. Green was supposed to have captured and destroyed a ship of the Company's, the *Speedy Return*, which never did return. It was not proved that this ship had been Green's victim, but that he had committed acts of piracy is certain. The hanging of Green increased the animosity of the sister kingdoms.

When Parliament met, June 28, 1705, it was a parliament of groups. Tweeddale and others, turned out of office in favour of Argyll's Government, formed the Flying Squadron (*Squadrone volante*), voting in whatever way would most annoy the Government. Argyll opened by proposing, as did the Queen's Message, the instant discussion of the Union (July 3). The House preferred to deliberate on anything else, and the leader of the Jacobites or Cavaliers, Lockhart of Carnwath, a very able sardonic man, saw that this was, for Jacobite ends, a tactical error. The more time was expended the more chance had Queensberry to win votes for the Union. Fletcher of Saltoun, an independent and eloquent patriot and republican, wasted time by impossible proposals. Hamilton brought forward, and by only two votes lost, a proposal which England would never have dreamed of accepting. Canny

Jacobites, however, abstained from voting, and thence Lockhart dates the ruin of his country. Supply, at all events, was granted, and on that Argyll adjourned. The queen was to select Commissioners of both countries to negotiate the Treaty of Union; among the Commissioners Lockhart was the only Cavalier, and he was merely to watch the case in the Jacobite interest.

The meetings of the two sets of Commissioners began at Whitehall on April 16. It was arranged that all proposals, modifications, and results should pass in writing, and secrecy was to be complete.

The Scots desired Union with Home Rule, with a separate Parliament. The English would negotiate only on the lines that the Union was to be complete, "incorporating," with one Parliament for both peoples. By April 25, 1706, the Scots Commissioners saw that on this point they must acquiesce; the defeat of the French at Ramilies (May 23) proved that, even if they could have leaned on the French, France was a broken reed. International reciprocity in trade, complete freedom of trade at home and abroad, they did obtain.

As England, thanks to William III with his incessant Continental wars, had already a great National debt, of which Scotland owed nothing, and as taxation in England was high, while Scottish taxes under the Union would rise to the same level, and to compensate for the Darien losses, the English granted a pecuniary "Equivalent" (May 10). They also did not raise the Scottish taxes on windows, lights, coal, malt, and salt to the English level, that of war-taxation. The Equivalent was to purchase the Scottish shares in the East India Company, with interest at five per cent up to May 1, 1707. That grievance of the shareholders was thus healed, what public debt Scotland owed was to be paid (the Equivalent was about £400,000), and any part of the money unspent was to be given to improve fisheries and manufactures.

The number of Scottish members of the British Parliament was fixed at forty-five. On this point the Scots felt that they were hardly used; the number of their elected representatives of peers in the Lords was sixteen. Scotland retained her Courts of Law; the feudal jurisdictions which gave to Argyll and others almost princely powers were retained, and Scottish procedure in trials continued to vary much from the English model. Appeals from the Court of Session had previously been brought before the Parliament of Scotland; henceforth they were to be heard by the Judges, Scots and English, in the British House of Lords. On July 23, 1706, the treaty was completed; on October 3 the Scottish Parliament met to debate on it, with

Queensberry as Commissioner. Harley, the English Minister, sent down the author of 'Robinson Crusoe' to watch, spy, argue, persuade, and secretly report, and De Foe's letters contain the history of the session.

The parties in Parliament were thus variously disposed: the Cavaliers, including Hamilton, had been approached by Louis XIV and King James (the Pretender), but had not committed themselves. Queensberry always knew every risky step taken by Hamilton, who began to take several, but in each case received a friendly warning which he dared not disregard. At the opposite pole, the Cameronians and other extreme Presbyterians loathed the Union, and at last (November-December) a scheme for the Cameronians and the clans of Angus and Perthshire to meet in arms in Edinburgh and clear out the Parliament caused much alarm. But Hamilton, before the arrangement came to a head, was terrorised, and the intentions of the Cameronians, as far as their records prove, had never been officially ratified by their leaders.[34] There was plenty of popular rioting during the session, but Argyll rode into Edinburgh at the head of the Horse Guards, and Leven held all the gates with drafts from the garrison of the castle. The Commissioners of the General Assembly made protests on various points, but were pacified after the security of the Kirk had been guaranteed. Finally, Hamilton prepared a parliamentary mine, which would have blown the Treaty of Union sky-high, but on the night when he should have appeared in the House and set the match to his petard—he had toothache! This was the third occasion on which he had deserted the Cavaliers; the Opposition fell to pieces. The *Squadrone volante* and the majority of the peers supported the Bill, which was passed. On January 16, 1707, the Treaty of Union was touched with the sceptre, "and there is the end of an auld sang," said Seafield. In May 1707 a solemn service was held at St Paul's to commemorate the Union.

There was much friction in the first year of the Union over excisemen and tax-collectors: smuggling began to be a recognised profession. Meanwhile, since 1707, a Colonel Hooke had been acting in Scotland, nominally in Jacobite, really rather in French interests. Hooke's intrigues were in part betrayed by De Foe's agent, Ker of Kersland, an amusingly impudent knave, and were thwarted by jealousies of Argyll and Hamilton. By deceptive promises (for he was

---

[34] Dr Hay Fleming finds no mention of this affair in the Minutes of the Societies.

himself deceived into expecting the aid of the Ulster Protestants) Hooke induced Louis XIV to send five men-of-war, twenty-one frigates, and only two transports, to land James in Scotland (March 1708). The equinoctial gales and the severe illness of James, who insisted on sailing, delayed the start; the men on the outlook for the fleet were intoxicated, and Forbin, the French commander, observing English ships of war coming towards the Firth of Forth, fled, refusing James's urgent entreaties to be landed anywhere on the coast (March 24). It was believed that had he landed only with a valet the discontented country would have risen for their native king.

In Parliament (1710-1711) the Cavalier Scottish members, by Tory support, secured the release from prison of a Rev. Mr Greenshields, an Episcopalian who prayed for Queen Anne, indeed, but had used the liturgy. The preachers were also galled by the imposition on them of an abjuration oath, compelling them to pray for prelatical Queen Anne. Lay patronage of livings was also restored (1712) after many vicissitudes, and this thorn rankled in the Kirk, causing ever-widening strife for more than a century.

The imposition of a malt tax produced so much discontent that even Argyll, with all the Scottish members of Parliament, was eager for the repeal of the Act of Union, and proposed it in the House of Peers, when it was defeated by a small majority. In 1712, when about to start on a mission to France, Hamilton was slain in a duel by Lord Mohun. According to a statement of Lockhart's, "Cavaliers were to look for the best" from Hamilton's mission: it is fairly clear that he was to bring over James in disguise to England, as in Thackeray's novel, 'Esmond.' But the sword of Mohun broke the Jacobite plans. Other hopes expired when Bolingbroke and Harley quarrelled, and Queen Anne died (August 1, 1714). "The best cause in Europe was lost," cried Bishop Atterbury, "for want of spirit." He would have proclaimed James as king, but no man supported him, and the Elector of Hanover, George I, peacefully accepted the throne.

CHAPTER XXX

# George I

For a year the Scottish Jacobites, and Bolingbroke, who fled to France and became James's Minister, mismanaged the affairs of that most unfortunate of princes. By February 1715 the Earl of Mar, who had been distrusted and disgraced by George I, was arranging with the clans for a rising, while aid from Charles XII of Sweden was expected from March to August 1715. It is notable that Charles had invited Dean Swift to visit his Court, when Swift was allied with Bolingbroke and Oxford. From the author of 'Gulliver' Charles no doubt hoped to get a trustworthy account of their policy. The fated rising of 1715 was occasioned by the Duke of Berwick's advice to James that he must set forth to Scotland or lose his honour. The prince therefore, acting hastily on news which, two or three days later, proved to be false, in a letter to Mar fixed August 10 for a rising. The orders were at once countermanded, when news proving their futility was received, but James's messenger, Allan Cameron, was detained on the road, and Mar, not waiting for James's answer to his own last despatch advising delay, left London for Scotland without a commission; on August 27 held an Assembly of the chiefs, and, *still without a commission from James*, raised the standard of the king on September 6.[35]

The folly of Mar was consummate. He knew that Ormonde, the hope of the English Jacobites, had deserted his post and had fled to France.

Meanwhile Louis XIV was dying; he died on August 30, and the Regent d'Orléans, at the utmost, would only connive at, not assist, James's enterprise.

---

[35] All this is made clear from the letters of the date in the Stuart Papers (Historical Manuscript Commission).

Everything was contrary, everywhere was ignorance and confusion. Lord John Drummond's hopeful scheme for seizing Edinburgh Castle (September 8) was quieted *pulveris exigui jactu*, "the gentlemen were powdering their hair"—drinking at a tavern—and bungled the business. The folly of Government offered a chance: in Scotland they had but 2000 regulars at Stirling, where "Forth bridles the wild Highlandman." Mar, who promptly occupied Perth, though he had some 12,000 broadswords, continued till the end to make Perth his headquarters. A Montrose, a Dundee, even a Prince Charles, would have "masked" Argyll at Stirling and seized Edinburgh. In October 21-November 3, Berwick, while urging James to sail, absolutely refused to accompany him. The plans of Ormonde for a descent on England were betrayed by Colonel Maclean, in French service (November 4). In disguise and narrowly escaping from murderous agents of Stair (British ambassador to France) on his road,[36] James journeyed to St Malo (November 8).

In Scotland the Macgregors made a futile attempt on Dumbarton Castle, while Glengarry and the Macleans advanced on Inveraray Castle, negotiated with Argyll's brother, the Earl of Islay, and marched back to Strathfillan. In Northumberland Forster and Derwentwater, with some Catholic fox-hunters, in Galloway the pacific Viscount Kenmure, cruised vaguely about and joined forces. Mackintosh of Borlum, by a well-concealed movement, carried a Highland detachment of 1600 men across the Firth of Forth by boats (October 12-13), with orders to join Forster and Kenmure and arouse the Border. But on approaching Edinburgh Mackintosh found Argyll with 500 dragoons ready to welcome him; Mar took no advantage of Argyll's absence from Stirling, and Mackintosh, when Argyll returned thither, joined Kenmure and Forster, occupied Kelso, and marched into Lancashire. The Jacobite forces were pitifully ill-supplied, they had very little ammunition (the great charge against Bolingbroke was that he sent none from France), they seem to have had no idea that powder could be made by the art of man; they were torn by jealousies, and dispirited by their observation of Mar's incompetence.

We cannot pursue in detail the story of the futile campaign. On November 12 the mixed Highland, Lowland, and English command found itself cooped up in Preston, and after a very gallant defence of the town the English leaders surrendered to the king's mercy, after

---

[36] In addition to Saint Simon's narrative we have the documentary evidence taken in a French inquiry.

arranging an armistice which made it impossible for Mackintosh to cut his way through the English ranks and retreat to the north. About 1600 prisoners were taken. Derwentwater and Kenmure were later executed. Forster and Nithsdale made escapes; Charles Wogan, a kinsman of the chivalrous Wogan of 1650, and Mackintosh, with six others, forced their way out of Newgate prison on the night before their trial. Wogan was to make himself heard of again. Mar had thrown away his Highlanders, with little ammunition and without orders, on a perfectly aimless and hopeless enterprise.

Meanwhile he himself, at Perth, had been doing nothing, while in the north, Simon Frazer (Lord Lovat) escaped from his French prison, raised his clan and took the castle of Inverness for King George. He thus earned a pardon for his private and public crimes, and he lived to ruin the Jacobite cause and lose his own head in 1745-46.

While the north, Ross-shire and Inverness, were daunted and thwarted by the success of Lovat, Mar led his whole force from Perth to Dunblane, apparently in search of a ford over Forth. His Frazers and many of his Gordons deserted on November 11; on November 12 Mar, at Ardoch (the site of an old Roman camp), learned that Argyll was marching through Dunblane to meet him. Next day Mar's force occupied the crest of rising ground on the wide swell of Sheriffmuir: his left was all disorderly; horse mixed with foot; his right, with the fighting clans, was well ordered, but the nature of the ground hid the two wings of the army from each other. On the right the Macdonalds and Macleans saw Clanranald fall, and on Glengarry's cry, "Vengeance to-day!" they charged with the claymore and swept away the regulars of Argyll as at Killiecrankie and Prestonpans. But, as the clans pursued and slew, their officers whispered that their own centre and left were broken and flying. Argyll had driven them to Allan Water; his force, returning, came within close range of the victorious right of Mar. "Oh, for one hour of Dundee!" cried Gordon of Glenbucket, but neither party advanced to the shock. Argyll retired safely to Dunblane, while Mar deserted his guns and powder-carts, and hurried to Perth. He had lost the gallant young Earl of Strathmore and the brave Clanranald; on Argyll's side his brother Islay was wounded, and the Earl of Forfar was slain. Though it was a drawn battle, it proved that Mar could not move: his forces began to scatter; Huntly was said to have behaved ill. It was known that Dutch auxiliaries were to reinforce Argyll, and men began to try to make terms of surrender. Huntly rode off to his own country, and on December 22 (old style) James landed at Peterhead.

James had no lack of personal courage. He had charged again and again at Malplaquet with the Household cavalry of Louis XIV, and he had encountered great dangers of assassination on his way to St Malo. But constant adversity had made him despondent and resigned, while he saw facts as they really were with a sad lucidity. When he arrived in his kingdom the Whig clans of the north had daunted Seaforth's Mackenzies, while in the south Argyll, with his Dutch and other fresh reinforcements, had driven Mar's men out of Fife. Writing to Bolingbroke, James described the situation. Mar, with scarcely any ammunition, was facing Argyll with 11,000 men; the north was held in force by the Whig clans, Mackays, Rosses, Munroes, and Frazers; deep snow alone delayed the advance of Argyll, now stimulated by the hostile Cadogan, Marlborough's favourite, and it was perfectly plain that all was lost.

For the head of James £100,000 was offered by Hanoverian chivalry: he was suffering from fever and ague; the Spanish gold that had at last been sent to him was lost at sea off Dundee, and it is no wonder that James, never gay, presented to his troops a disconsolate and discouraging aspect.

On January 29 his army evacuated Perth; James wept at the order to burn the villages on Argyll's line of march, and made a futile effort to compensate the people injured. From Montrose (February 3-14) he wrote for aid to the French Regent, but next day, urged by Mar, and unknown to his army, he, with Mar, set sail for France. This evasion was doubtless caused by a circumstance unusual in warfare: there was a price of £100,000 on James's head, moreover his force had not one day's supply of powder. Marshal Keith (brother of the Earl Marischal who retreated to the isles) says that perhaps one day's supply of powder might be found at Aberdeen. Nevertheless the fighting clans were eager to meet Argyll, and would have sold their lives at a high price. They scattered to their western fastnesses. The main political result, apart from executions and the passing of forfeited estates into the management of that noted economist, Sir Richard Steele, and other commissioners, was—the disgrace of Argyll. He, who with a petty force had saved Scotland, was represented by Cadogan and by his political enemies as dilatory and disaffected! The Duke lost all his posts, and in 1716 (when James had hopes from Sweden) Islay, Argyll's brother, was negotiating with Jacobite agents. James was creating him a peer of England!

In Scotland much indignation was aroused by the sending of Scottish prisoners of war out of the kingdom for trial—namely, to

Carlisle—and by other severities. The Union had never been more unpopular: the country looked on itself as conquered, and had no means of resistance, for James, now residing at Avignon, was a Catholic, and any insults and injuries from England were more tolerable than a restored nationality with a Catholic king.

Into the Jacobite hopes and intrigues, the eternal web which from 1689 to 1763 was ever being woven and broken, it is impossible here to enter, though, in the now published Stuart Papers, the details are well known. James was driven from Avignon to Italy, to Spain, finally to live a pensioner at Rome. The luckless attempt of the Earl Marischal, Keith, his brother, and Lord George Murray, brother of the Duke of Atholl, to invade Scotland on the west with a small Spanish force, was crushed on June 10, 1719, in the pass of Glenshiel.

Two or three months later, James, returning from Spain, married the fair and hapless Princess Clementina Sobieska, whom Charles Wogan, in an enterprise truly romantic, had rescued from prison at Innspruck and conveyed across the Alps. From this wedding, made wretched by the disappointment of the bride with her melancholy lord,—always busied with political secrets from which she was excluded,—was born, on December 31, 1720, Charles Edward Stuart: from his infancy the hope of the Jacobite party; from his cradle surrounded by the intrigues, the jealousies, the adulations of an exiled Court, and the quarrels of Protestants and Catholics, Irish, Scottish, and English. Thus, among changes of tutors and ministers, as the discovery or suspicion of treachery, the bigotry of Clementina, and the pressure of other necessities might permit, was that child reared whose name, at least, has received the crown of Scottish affection and innumerable tributes of Scottish song.

CHAPTER XXXI

# The Argathelians *and the* Squadrone

eaving the fortunes of the Jacobite party at their lowest ebb, and turning to the domestic politics of Scotland, after 1719, we find that if it be happiness to have no history, Scotland had much reason to be content. There was but a dull personal strife between the faction of Argyll and his brother Islay (called the "Argathelians," from the Latinised *Argathelia*, or Argyll), and the other faction known, since the Union, as the *Squadrone volante*, or Flying Squadron, who professed to be patriotically independent. As to Argyll, he had done all that man might do for George I. But, as we saw, the reports of Cadogan and the jealousy of George (who is said to have deemed Argyll too friendly with his detested heir) caused the disgrace of the Duke in 1716, and the *Squadrone* held the spoils of office. But in February-April 1719 George reversed his policy, heaped Argyll with favours, made him, as Duke of Greenwich, a peer of England, and gave him the High Stewardship of the Household.

At this time all the sixteen representative peers of Scotland favoured, for various reasons of their own, a proposed Peerage Bill. The Prince of Wales might, when he came to the throne, swamp the Lords by large new creations in his own interest, and the Bill laid down that, henceforth, not more than six peers, exclusive of members of the Royal Family, should be created by any sovereign; while in place of sixteen *representative* Scotland should have twenty-five *permanent* peers. From his new hatred of the Prince of Wales, Argyll favoured the Bill, as did the others of the sixteen of the moment, because they would be among the permanencies. The Scottish Jacobite peers (not representatives) and the Commons of both countries opposed the Bill. The election of a Scottish representative peer at this juncture led to negotiations between Argyll and Lockhart as leader of the suffering Jacobites, but terms were not arrived at; the Government secured a large Whig majority in a general election (1722), and Walpole began his long tenure of office.

# Enclosure Riots

In 1724 there were some popular discontents. Enclosures, as we saw, had scarcely been known in Scotland; when they were made, men, women, and children took pleasure in destroying them under cloud of night. Enclosures might keep a man's cattle on his own ground, keep other men's off it, and secure for the farmer his own manure. That good Jacobite, Mackintosh of Borlum, who in 1715 led the Highlanders to Preston, in 1729 wrote a book recommending enclosures and plantations. But when, in 1724, the lairds of Galloway and Dumfriesshire anticipated and acted on his plan, which in this case involved evictions of very indolent and ruinous farmers, the tenants rose. Multitudes of "Levellers" destroyed the loose stone dykes and slaughtered cattle. They had already been passive resisters of rent; the military were called in; women were in the forefront of the brawls, which were not quieted till the middle of 1725, when Lord Stair made an effort to introduce manufactures.

# Malt Riots

Other disturbances began in a resolution of the House of Commons, at the end of 1724, *not* to impose a Malt Tax equal to that of England (this had been successfully resisted in 1713), but to levy an additional sixpence on every barrel of ale, and to remove the bounties on exported grain. At the Union Scotland had, for the time, been exempted from the Malt Tax, specially devised to meet the expenses of the French war of that date. Now, in 1724-1725, Scotland was up in arms to resist the attempt "to rob a poor man of his beer." But Walpole could put force on the Scottish Members of Parliament,—"a parcel of low people that could not subsist," says Lockhart, "without their board wages." Walpole threatened to withdraw the ten guineas hitherto paid weekly by Government to those legislators. He offered to drop the sixpence on beer and put threepence on every bushel of malt, a half of the English tax. On June 23, 1725, the tax was to be exacted. The consequence was an attack on the military by the mob of Glasgow, who wrecked the house of their Member in Parliament, Campbell of Shawfield. Some of the assailants were shot: General Wade and the Lord Advocate, Forbes of Culloden, marched a force on Glasgow, the magistrates of the town were imprisoned but released on bail, while in Edinburgh the master brewers, ordered by the Court of Session to raise the price of their ale, struck for a week; some were imprisoned, others were threatened or cajoled and deserted their Union. The one result was that the chief of the Squadrone, the Duke of Roxburgh, lost his Secretaryship for Scotland, and Argyll's brother, Islay, with the resolute Forbes of Culloden, became practically the governors of the country. The Secretaryship, indeed, was for a time abolished, but Islay practically wielded the power that had so long been in the hands of the Secretary as agent of the Court.

# The Highlands

The clans had not been disarmed after 1715, moreover 6000 muskets had been brought in during the affair that ended at Glenshiel in 1719. General Wade was commissioned in 1724 to examine and report on the Highlands: Lovat had already sent in a report. He pointed out that Lowlanders paid blackmail for protection to Highland raiders, and that independent companies of Highlanders, paid by Government, had been useful, but were broken up in 1717. What Lovat wanted was a company and pay for himself. Wade represented the force of the clans as about 22,000 claymores, half Whig (the extreme north and the Campbells), half Jacobite. The commandants of forts should have independent companies: cavalry should be quartered between Inverness and Perth, and Quarter Sessions should be held at Fort William and Ruthven in Badenoch. In 1725 Wade disarmed Seaforth's clan, the Mackenzies, easily, for Seaforth, then in exile, was on bad terms with James, and wished to come home with a pardon. Glengarry, Clanranald, Glencoe, Appin, Lochiel, Clan Vourich, and the Gordons affected submission—but only handed over two thousand rusty weapons of every sort. Lovat did obtain an independent company, later withdrawn—with results. The clans were by no means disarmed, but Wade did, from 1725 to 1736, construct his famous military roads and bridges, interconnecting the forts.

The death of George I (June 11, 1727) induced James to hurry to Lorraine and communicate with Lockhart. But there was nothing to be done. Clementina had discredited her husband, even in Scotland, much more in England, by her hysterical complaints, and her hatred of every man employed by James inflamed the petty jealousies and feuds among the exiles of his Court. No man whom he could select would have been approved of by the party.

To the bishops of the persecuted Episcopalian remnant, quarrelling over details of ritual called "the Usages," James vainly recommended "forbearance in love." Lockhart, disgusted with the clergy, and siding with Clementina against her husband, believed that some of the wrangling churchmen betrayed the channel of his communications with his king (1727). Islay gave Lockhart a hint to disappear, and he sailed from Scotland for Holland on April 8, 1727.

Since James dismissed Bolingbroke, every one of his Ministers was suspected, by one faction or another of the party, as a traitor. Atterbury denounced Mar, Lockhart denounced Hay (titular Earl of Inverness), Clementina told feminine tales for which even the angry Lockhart could find no evidence. James was the butt of every slanderous tongue; but absolutely nothing against his moral character, or his efforts to do his best, or his tolerance and lack of suspiciousness, can be wrung from documents.[37]

By 1734 the elder of James's two sons, Prince Charles, was old enough to show courage and to thrust himself under fire in the siege of Gaeta, where his cousin, the Duc de Liria, was besieging the Imperialists. He won golden opinions from the army, but was already too strong for his tutors—Murray and Sir Thomas Sheridan. He had both Protestant and Catholic governors; between them he learned to spell execrably in three languages, and sat loose to Catholic doctrines. In January 1735 died his mother, who had found refuge from her troubles in devotion. The grief of James and of the boys was acute.

In 1736 Lovat was looking towards the rising sun of Prince Charles; was accused by a witness of enabling John Roy Stewart, Jacobite and poet, to break prison at Inverness, and of sending by him a message of devotion to James, from whom he expected a dukedom. Lovat therefore lost his sheriffship and his independent company, and tried to attach himself to Argyll, when the affair of the Porteous Riot

---

[37] See 'The King over the Water,' by Alice Shield and A. Lang. Thackeray's King James, in 'Esmond,' is very amusing but absolutely false to history.

caused a coldness between Argyll and the English Government (1736-1737).

# The Porteous Riot

The affair of Porteous is so admirably well described in 'The Heart of Mid-Lothian,' and recent research[38] has thrown so little light on the mystery (if mystery there were), that a brief summary of the tale may suffice.

In the spring of 1736 two noted smugglers, Wilson and Robertson, were condemned to death. They had, while in prison, managed to widen the space between the window-bars of their cell, and would have escaped; but Wilson, a very stoutly built man, went first and stuck in the aperture, so that Robertson had no chance. The pair determined to attack their guards in church, where, as usual, they were to be paraded and preached at on the Sunday preceding their execution. Robertson leaped up and fled, with the full sympathy of a large and interested congregation, while Wilson grasped a guard with each hand and a third with his teeth. Thus Robertson got clean away—to Holland, it was said,—while Wilson was to be hanged on April 14. The acting lieutenant of the Town Guard—an unpopular body, mainly Highlanders—was John Porteous, famous as a golfer, but, by the account of his enemies, notorious as a brutal and callous ruffian. The crowd in the Grassmarket was great, but there was no attempt at a rescue. The mob, however, threw large stones at the Guard, who fired, killing or wounding, as usual, harmless spectators. The case for Porteous, as reported in 'The State Trials,' was that the attack was dangerous; that the plan was to cut down and resuscitate Wilson; that Porteous did not order, but tried to prevent, the firing; and that neither at first nor in a later skirmish at the West Bow did he fire himself. There was much "cross swearing" at the trial of Porteous (July 20); the jury found him guilty, and he was sentenced to be hanged on September 8. A petition from him to Queen Caroline (George II was abroad) drew attention to palpable discrepancies in the hostile evidence. Both parties in Parliament backed his application, and on August 28 a delay of justice for six weeks was granted.

Indignation was intense. An intended attack on the Tolbooth, where Porteous lay, had been matter of rumour three days earlier: the

---

[38] 'The Porteous Trial,' by Mr Roughead, W.S.

prisoner should have been placed in the Castle. At 10 P.M. on the night of September 7 the magistrates heard that boys were beating a drum, and ordered the Town Guard under arms; but the mob, who had already secured the town's gates, disarmed the veterans. Mr Lindsay, lately Provost, escaped by the Potter Row gate (near the old fatal Kirk-o'-Field), and warned General Moyle in the Castle. But Moyle could not introduce soldiers without a warrant. Before a warrant could arrive the mob had burned down the door of the Tolbooth, captured Porteous—who was hiding up the chimney,— carried him to the Grassmarket, and hanged him to a dyer's pole. The only apparent sign that persons of rank above that of the mob were concerned, was the leaving of a guinea in a shop whence they took the necessary rope. The magistrates had been guilty of gross negligence. The mob was merely a resolute mob; but Islay, in London, suspected that the political foes of the Government were engaged, or that the Cameronians, who had been renewing the Covenants, were concerned.

Islay hurried to Edinburgh, where no evidence could be extracted. "The High Flyers of our Scottish Church," he wrote, "have made this infamous murder a point of conscience... All the lower rank of the people who have distinguished themselves by the pretensions of superior sanctity speak of this murder as the hand of God doing justice." They went by the precedent of the murder of Archbishop Sharp, it appears. In the Lords (February 1737) a Bill was passed for disabling the Provost—one Wilson—for public employment, destroying the Town Charter, abolishing the Town Guard, and throwing down the gate of the Nether Bow. Argyll opposed the Bill; in the Commons all Scottish members were against it; Walpole gave way. Wilson was dismissed, and a fine of £2000 was levied and presented to the widow of Porteous. An Act commanding preachers to read monthly for a year, in church, a proclamation bidding their hearers aid the cause of justice against the murderers, was an insult to the Kirk, from an Assembly containing bishops. It is said that at least half of the ministers disobeyed with impunity. It was impossible, of course, to evict half of the preachers in the country.

Argyll now went into opposition against Walpole, and, at least, listened to Keith—later the great Field-Marshal of Frederick the Great, and brother of the exiled Earl Marischal.

In 1737 the Jacobites began to stir again: a committee of five Chiefs and Lords was formed to manage their affairs. John Murray of Broughton went to Rome, and lost his heart to Prince Charles—now a tall handsome lad of seventeen, with large brown eyes, and, when he pleased, a very attractive manner. To Murray, more than to any other man, was due the Rising of 1745.

Meanwhile, in secular affairs, Scotland showed nothing more remarkable than the increasing dislike, strengthened by Argyll, of Walpole's Government.

# CHAPTER XXXII

# The First Secession

For long we have heard little of the Kirk, which between 1720 and 1740 passed through a cycle of internal storms. She had been little vexed, either during her years of triumph or defeat, by heresy or schism. But now the doctrines of Antoinette Bourignon, a French lady mystic, reached Scotland, and won the sympathies of some students of divinity—including the Rev. John Simson, of an old clerical family which had been notorious since the Reformation for the turbulence of its members. In 1714, and again in 1717, Mr Simson was acquitted by the Assembly on the charges of being a Jesuit, a Socinian, and an Arminian, but was warned against "a tendency to attribute too much to natural reason." In 1726-29 he was accused of minimising the doctrines of the creed of St Athanasius, and tending to the Arian heresy,—"lately raked out of hell," said the Kirk-session of Portmoak (1725), addressing the sympathetic Presbytery of Kirkcaldy. At the Assembly of 1726 that Presbytery, with others, assailed Mr Simson, who was in bad health, and "could talk of nothing but the Council of Nice." A committee, including Mar's brother, Lord Grange (who took such strong measures with his wife, Lady Grange, forcibly translating her to the isle of St Kilda), inquired into the views of Mr Simson's own Presbytery—that of Glasgow. This Presbytery cross-examined Mr Simson's pupils, and Mr Simson observed that the proceedings were "an unfruitful work of darkness." Moreover, Mr Simson was of the party of the *Squadrone*, while his assailants were Argathelians. A large majority of the Assembly gave the verdict that Mr Simson was a heretic. Finally, though in 1728 his answers to questions would have satisfied good St Athanasius, Mr Simson found himself in the ideal position of being released from his academic duties but confirmed in his salary. The lenient good-nature of this decision, with some other grievances, set fire to a mine which blew the Kirk in twain.

The Presbytery of Auchterarder had set up a kind of "standard" of their own—"The Auchterarder Creed"—which included this formula: "It is not sound or orthodox to teach that we must forsake sin in order to our coming to Christ, and instating us in Covenant with God." The General Assembly condemned this part of the Creed of Auchterarder. The Rev. Mr Hog, looking for weapons in defence of Auchterarder, republished part of a forgotten book of 1646, 'The Marrow of Modern Divinity.' The work appears to have been written by a speculative hairdresser, an Independent. A copy of the Marrow was found by the famous Mr Boston of Ettrick in the cottage of a parishioner. From the Marrow he sucked much advantage: its doctrines were grateful to the sympathisers with Auchterarder, and the republication of the book rent the Kirk.

In 1720 a Committee of the General Assembly condemned a set of propositions in the Marrow as tending to Antinomianism (the doctrine that the saints cannot sin, professed by Trusty Tompkins in 'Woodstock'). But—as in the case of the five condemned propositions of Jansenius—the Auchterarder party denied that the heresies could be found in the Marrow.

It was the old quarrel between Faith and Works. The clerical petitioners in favour of the Marrow were rebuked by the Assembly (May 21, 1722); they protested: against a merely human majority in the Assembly they appealed to "The Word of God," to which the majority also appealed; and there was a period of passion, but schism had not yet arrived.

The five or six friends of the Marrow really disliked moral preaching, as opposed to weekly discourses on the legal technicalities of justification, sanctification, and adoption. They were also opposed to the working of the Act which, in 1712, restored lay patronage. If the Assembly enforced the law of the land in this matter (and it did), the Assembly sinned against the divine right of congregations to elect their own preachers. Men of this way of thinking were led by the Rev. Mr Ebenezer Erskine, a poet who, in 1714, addressed an Ode to George I. He therein denounced "subverting patronage" and

"the woful dubious Abjuration
Which gave the clergy ground for speculation."

But a Jacobite song struck the same note—

> "Let not the Abjuration
> Impose upon the nation!"

and George was deaf to the muse of Mr Erskine.

In 1732, 1733, Mr Erskine, in sermons concerning patronage, offended the Assembly; would not apologise, appeared (to a lay reader) to claim direct inspiration, and with three other brethren constituted himself and them into a Presbytery. Among their causes of separation (or rather of deciding that the Kirk had separated from them) was the salary of Emeritus Professor Simson. The new Presbytery declared that the Covenants were still and were eternally binding on Scotland; in fact, these preachers were "platonically" for going back to the old ecclesiastical claims, with the old war of Church and State. They naturally denounced the Act of 1736, which abolished the burning of witches. After a period of long-suffering patience and conciliatory efforts, in 1740 the Assembly deposed the Seceders.

In 1747 a party among the Seceders excommunicated Mr Erskine and his brother; one of those who handed Mr Erskine over to Satan (if the old formula were retained) was his son-in-law.

The feuds of Burghers and Antiburghers (persons who were ready to take or refused to take the Burgess oath), New Lights and Old Lights, lasted very long and had evil consequences. As the populace love the headiest doctrines, they preferred preachers in proportion as they leaned towards the Marrow, while lay patrons preferred candidates of the opposite views. The Assembly must either keep the law and back the patrons, or break the law and cease to be a State Church. The corruption of patronage was often notorious on one side; on the other the desirability of burning witches and the belief in the eternity of the Covenants were articles of faith; and such articles were not to the taste of the "Moderates," educated clergymen of the new school. Thus arose the war of "High Flyers" and "Moderates" within the Kirk,—a war conducing to the great Disruption of 1843, in which gallant little Auchterarder was again in the foremost line.

# CHAPTER XXXIII

# The Last Jacobite Rising

While the Kirk was vainly striving to assuage the tempers of Mr Erskine and his friends, the Jacobites were preparing to fish in troubled waters. In 1739 Walpole was forced to declare war against Spain, and Walpole had previously sounded James as to his own chances of being trusted by that exiled prince. James thought that Walpole was merely angling for information. Meanwhile Jacobite affairs were managed by two rivals, Macgregor (calling himself Drummond) of Balhaldy and Murray of Broughton. The sanguine Balhaldy induced France to suppose that the Jacobites in England and Scotland were much more united, powerful, and ready for action than they really were, when Argyll left office in 1742, while Walpole fell from power, Carteret and the Duke of Newcastle succeeding. In 1743 Murray found that France, though now at war with England over the Spanish Succession, was holding aloof from the Jacobite cause, though plied with flourishing and fabulous reports from Balhaldy and the Jacobite Lord Sempill. But, in December 1743, on the strength of alleged Jacobite energy in England, Balhaldy obtained leave from France to visit Rome and bring Prince Charles. The Prince had kept himself in training for war and was eager. Taking leave of his father for the last time, Charles drove out of Rome on January 9, 1744; evaded, in disguise, every trap that was set for him, and landed at Antibes, reaching Paris on February 10. Louis did not receive him openly, if he received him at all; the Prince lurked at Gravelines in disguise, with the Earl Marischal, while winds and waves half ruined, and the approach of a British fleet drove into port, a French fleet of invasion under Roqueville (March 6, 7, 1744).

The Prince wrote to Sempill that he was ready and willing to sail for Scotland in an open boat. In July 1744 he told Murray that he would come next summer "if he had no other companion than his valet." He nearly kept his word; nor did Murray resolutely oppose his will. At the end of May 1745 Murray's servant brought a letter from the Prince; "fall back, fall edge," he would land in the Highlands in July. Lochiel regretted the decision, but said that, as a man of honour, he would join his Prince if he arrived.

On July 2 the Prince left Nantes in the *Dutillet* (usually styled *La Doutelle*). He brought some money (he had pawned the Sobieski rubies), some arms, Tullibardine, his Governor Sheridan, Parson Kelly, the titular Duke of Atholl, Sir John Macdonald, a banker, Sullivan, and one Buchanan—the Seven Men of Moidart.

On July 20 his consort, *The Elizabeth*, fought *The Lion* (Captain Brett) off the Lizard; both antagonists were crippled. On [July 22/August 2] Charles passed the night on the little isle of Eriskay; appealed vainly to Macleod and Macdonald of Sleat; was urged, at Kinlochmoidart, by the Macdonalds, to return to France, but swept them off their feet by his resolution; and with Lochiel and the Macdonalds raised the standard at the head of Glenfinnan on August [19/30].

The English Government had already offered £30,000 for the Prince's head. The clans had nothing to gain; they held that they had honour to preserve; they remembered Montrose; they put it to the touch, and followed Prince Charlie.

The strength of the Prince's force was, first, the Macdonalds. On August 16 Keppoch had cut off two companies of the Royal Scots near Loch Lochy. But the chief of Glengarry was old and wavering; young Glengarry, captured on his way from France, could not be with his clan; his young brother Æneas led till his accidental death after the battle of Falkirk.

Of the Camerons it is enough to say that their leader was the gentle Lochiel, and that they were worthy of their chief. The Macphersons came in rather late, under Cluny. The Frazers were held back by the crafty Lovat, whose double-dealing, with the abstention of Macleod (who was sworn to the cause) and of Macdonald of Sleat, ruined the enterprise. Clan Chattan was headed by the beautiful Lady Mackintosh, whose husband adhered to King George. Of the dispossessed Macleans, some 250 were gathered (under Maclean of Drimnin), and of that resolute band some fifty survived Culloden. These western clans (including 220 Stewarts of Appin under Ardshiel) were the steel point of Charles's weapon; to them should be added the Macgregors under James Mor, son of Rob Roy, a shifty character but a hero in fight.

To resist these clans, the earliest to join, Sir John Cope, commanding in Scotland, had about an equal force of all arms, say 2500 to 3000 men, scattered in all quarters, and with very few field-pieces. Tweeddale, holding the revived office of Secretary for Scotland, was on the worst terms, as leader of the *Squadrone*, with his Argathelian rival, Islay, now (through the recent death of his brother, Red Ian of the Battles) Duke of Argyll. Scottish Whigs were not encouraged to arm.

The Prince marched south, while Cope, who had concentrated at Stirling, marched north to intercept him. At Dalnacardoch he learned that Charles was advancing to meet him in Corryarrick Pass (here came in Ardshiel, Glencoe, and a Glengarry reinforcement). At Dalwhinnie, Cope found that the clans held the pass, which is very defensible. He dared not face them, and moved by Ruthven in Badenoch to Inverness, where he vainly expected to be met by the great Whig clans of the north.

Joined now by Cluny, Charles moved on that old base of Montrose, the Castle of Blair of Atholl, where the exiled duke (commonly called Marquis of Tullibardine) was received with enthusiasm. In the mid-region between Highland and Lowland, the ladies, Lady Lude and the rest, simply forced their sons, brothers, and lovers into arms. While Charles danced and made friends, and tasted his first pine-apple at Blair, James Mor took the fort of Inversnaid. At Perth (September 4-10) Charles was joined by the Duke of Perth, the Ogilvys under Lord Ogilvy, some Drummonds under Lord Strathallan, the Oliphants of Gask, and 200 Robertsons of Struan. Lord George Murray, brother of the Duke of Atholl, who had been out in 1715, out in 1719, and later was *un reconcilié*, came in, and with him came Discord. He had dealt as a friend and ally with Cope at Crieff; his loyalty to either side was thus not unnaturally dubious; he was suspected by Murray of Broughton; envied by Sullivan, a soldier of some experience; and though he was loyal to the last,—the best organiser, and the most daring leader,—Charles never trusted him, and his temper was always crossing that of the Prince.

The race for Edinburgh now began, Cope bringing his troops by sea from Aberdeen, and Charles doing what Mar, in 1715, had never ventured. He crossed the Forth by the fords of Frew, six miles above Stirling, passed within gunshot of the castle, and now there was no force between him and Edinburgh save the demoralised dragoons of Colonel Gardiner. The sole use of the dragoons was, wherever they came, to let the world know that the clans were at their heels. On

September 16 Charles reached Corstorphine, and Gardiner's dragoons fell back on Coltbridge.

On the previous day the town had been terribly perturbed. The old walls, never sound, were dilapidated, and commanded by houses on the outside. Volunteers were scarce, and knew not how to load a musket. On Sunday, September 15, during sermon-time, "The bells were rung backwards, the drums they were beat," the volunteers, being told to march against the clans, listened to the voices of mothers and aunts and of their own hearts, and melted like a mist. Hamilton's dragoons and ninety of the late Porteous's Town Guard sallied forth, joining Gardiner's men at Coltbridge. A few of the mounted Jacobite gentry, such as Lord Elcho, eldest son of the Earl of Wemyss, trotted up to inspect the dragoons, who fled and drew bridle only at Musselburgh, six miles east of Edinburgh.

The magistrates treated through a caddie or street-messenger with the Prince. He demanded surrender, the bailies went and came, in a hackney coach, between Charles's quarters, Gray's Mill, and Edinburgh, but on their return about 3 A.M. Lochiel with the Camerons rushed in when the Nether Bow gate was opened to admit the cab of the magistrates. Murray had guided the clan round by Merchiston. At noon Charles entered "that unhappy palace of his race," Holyrood; and King James was proclaimed at Edinburgh Cross, while the beautiful Mrs Murray, mounted, distributed white cockades. Edinburgh provided but few volunteers, though the ladies tried to "force them out."

Meanwhile Cope was landing his men at Dunbar; from Mr John Home (author of 'Douglas, a Tragedy') he learnt that Charles's force was under 2000 strong. He himself had, counting the dragoons, an almost equal strength, with six field-pieces manned by sailors.

On September 20 Cope advanced from Haddington, while Charles, with all the carriages he could collect for ambulance duty, set forth from his camp at Duddingston Loch, under Arthur's Seat. Cope took the low road near the sea, while Charles took the high road, holding the ridge, till from Birsley brae he beheld Cope on the low level plain, between Seaton and Prestonpans. The manœuvres of the clans forced Cope to change his front, but wherever he went, his men were more or less cooped up and confined to the defensive, with the park wall on their rear.

Meanwhile Mr Anderson of Whitburgh, a local sportsman who had shot ducks in the morass on Cope's left, brought to Charles news of a practicable path through that marsh. Even so, the path was wet as high as the knee, says Ker of Graden, who had reconnoitred the British under fire. He was a Roxburghshire laird, and there was with the Prince no better officer.

In the grey dawn the clans waded through the marsh and leaped the ditch; Charles was forced to come with the second line fifty yards behind the first. The Macdonalds held the right, as they said they had done at Bannockburn; the Camerons and Macgregors were on the left they "cast their plaids, drew their blades," and, after enduring an irregular fire, swept the red-coat ranks away; "they ran like rabets," wrote Charles in a genuine letter to James. Gardiner was cut down, his entire troop having fled, while he was directing a small force of foot which stood its ground. Charles stated his losses at a hundred killed and wounded, all by gunshot. Only two of the six field-pieces were discharged, by Colonel Whitefoord, who was captured. Friends and foes agree in saying that the Prince devoted himself to the care of the wounded of both sides. Lord George Murray states Cope's losses, killed, wounded, and taken, at 3000, Murray, at under 1000.

The Prince would fain have marched on England, but his force was thinned by desertions, and English reinforcements would have been landed in his rear. For a month he had to hold court in Edinburgh, adored by the ladies to whom he behaved with a coldness of which Charles II would not have approved. "These are my beauties," he said, pointing to a burly-bearded Highland sentry. He "requisitioned" public money, and such horses and fodder as he could procure; but to spare the townsfolk from the guns of the castle he was obliged to withdraw his blockade. He sent messengers to France, asking for aid, but received little, though the Marquis Boyer d'Eguilles was granted as a kind of representative of Louis XV. His envoys to Sleat and Macleod sped ill, and Lovat only dallied, France only hesitated, while Dutch and English regiments landed in the Thames and marched to join General Wade at Newcastle. Charles himself received reinforcements amounting to some 1500 men, under Lord Ogilvy, old Lord Pitsligo, the Master of Strathallan (Drummond), the brave Lord Balmerino, and the Viscount Dundee. A treaty of alliance with France, made at Fontainebleau, neutralised, under the Treaty of Tournay, 6000 Dutch who might not, by that treaty, fight against the ally of France.

The Prince entertained no illusions. Without French forces, he told D'Eguilles, "I cannot resist English, Dutch, Hessians, and Swiss." On October [15/26] he wrote his last extant letter from Scotland to King James. He puts his force at 8000 (more truly 6000), with 300 horse.

"With these, as matters stand, I shal have one decisive stroke for't, but iff the French" (do not?) "land, perhaps none. ... As matters stand I must either conquer or perish in a little while."

Defeated in the heart of England, and with a prize of £30,000 offered for his head, he could not hope to escape. A victory for him would mean a landing of French troops, and his invasion of England had for its aim to force the hand of France. Her troops, with Prince Henry among them, dallied at Dunkirk till Christmas, and were then dispersed, while the Duke of Cumberland arrived in England from Flanders on October 19.

On October 30 the Prince held a council of war. French supplies and guns had been landed at Stonehaven, and news came that 6000 French were ready at Dunkirk: at Dunkirk they were, but they never were ready. The news probably decided Charles to cross the Border; while it appears that his men preferred to be content with simply making Scotland again an independent kingdom, with a Catholic king. But to do this, with French aid, was to return to the state of things under Mary of Guise!

The Prince, judging correctly, wished to deal his "decisive stroke" near home, at the old and now futile Wade in Northumberland. A victory would have disheartened England, and left Newcastle open to France. If Charles were defeated, his own escape by sea, in a country where he had many well-wishers, was possible, and the clans would have retreated through the Cheviots. Lord George Murray insisted on a march by the western road, Lancashire being expected to rise and join the Prince. But this plan left Wade, with a superior force, on Charles's flank! The one difficulty, that of holding a bridge, say Kelso Bridge, over Tweed, was not insuperable. Rivers could not stop the Highlanders. Macdonald of Morar thought Charles the best general in the army, and to the layman, considering the necessity for an *instant* stroke, and the advantages of the east, as regards France, the Prince's strategy appears better than Lord George's. But Lord George had his way.

On October 31, Charles, reinforced by Cluny with 400 Macphersons, concentrated at Dalkeith. On November 1, the less trusted part of his force, under Tullibardine, with the Atholl men, moved south by Peebles and Moffat to Lockerbie, menacing Carlisle; while the Prince, Lord George, and the fighting clans marched to Kelso—a feint to deceive Wade. The main body then moved by Jedburgh, up Rule Water and down through Liddesdale, joining hands with Tullibardine on November 9, and bivouacking within two miles of Carlisle. On the 10th the Atholl men went to work at the trenches; on the 11th the army moved seven miles towards Newcastle, hoping to discuss Wade at Brampton on hilly ground. But Wade did not gratify them by arriving.

On the 13th the Atholl men were kept at their spade-work, and Lord George in dudgeon resigned his command (November 14), but at night Carlisle surrendered, Murray and Perth negotiating. Lord George expressed his anger and jealousy to his brother, Tullibardine, but Perth resigned his command to pacify his rival. Wade feebly tried to cross country, failed, and went back to Newcastle. On November 10, with some 4500 men (there had been many desertions), the march through Lancashire was decreed. Save for Mr Townley and two Vaughans, the Catholics did not stir. Charles marched on foot in the van; he was a trained pedestrian; the townspeople stared at him and his Highlanders, but only at Manchester (November 29-30) had he a welcome, enlisting about 150 doomed men. On November 27 Cumberland took over command at Lichfield; his foot were distributed between Tamworth and Stafford; his cavalry was at Newcastle-under-Lyme. Lord George was moving on Derby, but learning Cumberland's dispositions he led a column to Congleton, inducing Cumberland to concentrate at Lichfield, while he himself, by way of Leek and Ashburn, joined the Prince at Derby.

The army was in the highest spirits. The Duke of Richmond on the other side wrote from Lichfield (December 5), "If the enemy please to cut us off from the main army, they may; and also, if they please to give us the slip and march to London, I fear they may, before even this *avant garde* can come up with them; . . . there is no pass to defend, . . . the camp at Finchley is confined to paper plans"—and Wales was ready to join the Prince! Lord George did not know what Richmond knew. Despite the entreaties of the Prince, his Council decided to retreat. On December 6 the clans, uttering cries of rage, were set with their faces to the north.

The Prince was now an altered man. Full of distrust, he marched not with Lord George in the rear, he rode in the van.

Meanwhile Lord John Drummond, who, on November 22, had landed at Montrose with 800 French soldiers, was ordered by Charles to advance with large Highland levies now collected and meet him as he moved north. Lord John disobeyed orders (received about December 18). Expecting his advance, Charles most unhappily left the Manchester men and others to hold Carlisle, to which he would return. Cumberland took them all,—many were hanged.

In the north, Lord Lewis Gordon routed Macleod at Inverurie (December 23), and defeated his effort to secure Aberdeen. Admirably commanded by Lord George, and behaving admirably for an irregular retreating force, the army reached Penrith on December 18, and at Clifton, Lord George and Cluny defeated Cumberland's dragoons in a rearguard action.

On December 19 Carlisle was reached, and, as we saw, a force was left to guard the castle; all were taken. On December 20 the army forded the flooded Esk; the ladies, of whom several had been with them, rode it on their horses: the men waded breast-high, as, had there been need, they would have forded Tweed if the eastern route had been chosen, and if retreat had been necessary. Cumberland returned to London on January 5, and Horace Walpole no longer dreaded "a rebellion that runs away." By different routes Charles and Lord George met (December 26) at Hamilton Palace. Charles stayed a night at Dumfries. Dumfries was hostile, and was fined; Glasgow was also disaffected, the ladies were unfriendly. At Glasgow, Charles heard that Seaforth, chief of the Mackenzies, was aiding the Hanoverians in the north, combining with the great Whig clans, with Macleod, the Munroes, Lord Loudoun commanding some 2000 men, and the Mackays of Sutherland and Caithness.

Meanwhile Lord John Drummond, Strathallan, and Lord Lewis Gordon, with Lord Macleod, were concentrating to meet the Prince at Stirling, the purpose being the hopeless one of capturing the castle, the key of the north. With weak artillery, and a futile and foolish French engineer officer to direct the siege, they had no chance of success. The Prince, in bad health, stayed (January 4-10) at Sir Hugh Paterson's place, Bannockburn House.

At Stirling, with his northern reinforcements, Charles may have had some seven or eight thousand men wherewith to meet General Hawley (a veteran of Sheriffmuir) advancing from Edinburgh. Hawley encamped at Falkirk, and while the Atholl men were deserting by scores, Lord George skilfully deceived him, arrived on the Falkirk moor unobserved, and held the ridge above Hawley's position, while the General was lunching with Lady Kilmarnock. In the first line of the Prince's force the Macdonalds held the right wing, the Camerons (whom the great Wolfe describes as the bravest of the brave) held the left; with Stewarts of Appin, Frazers, and Macphersons in the centre. In the second line were the Atholl men, Lord Lewis Gordon's levies, and Lord Ogilvy's. The Lowland horse and Drummond's French details were in the rear. The ground was made up of eminences and ravines, so that in the second line the various bodies were invisible to each other, as at Sheriffmuir—with similar results. When Hawley found that he had been surprised he arrayed his thirteen battalions of regulars and 1000 men of Argyll on the plain, with three regiments of dragoons, by whose charge he expected to sweep away Charles's right wing; behind his cavalry were the luckless militia of Glasgow and the Lothians. In all, he had from 10,000 to 12,000 men against, perhaps, 7000 at most, for 1200 of Charles's force were left to contain Blakeney in Stirling Castle. Both sides, on account of the heavy roads, failed to bring forward their guns.

Hawley then advanced his cavalry up hill: their left faced Keppoch's Macdonalds; their right faced the Frazers, under the Master of Lovat, in Charles's centre. Hawley then launched his cavalry, which were met at close range by the reserved fire of the Macdonalds and Frazers. Through the mist and rain the townsfolk, looking on, saw in five minutes "the break in the battle." Hamilton's and Ligonier's cavalry turned and fled, Cobham's wheeled and rode across the Highland left under fire, while the Macdonalds and Frazers pursuing the cavalry found themselves among the Glasgow militia, whom they followed, slaying. Lord George had no pipers to sound the recall; they had flung their pipes to their gillies and gone in with the claymore.

Thus the Prince's right, far beyond his front, were lost in the tempest; while his left had discharged their muskets at Cobham's Horse, and could not load again, their powder being drenched with rain. They received the fire of Hawley's right, and charged with the claymore, but were outflanked and enfiladed by some battalions drawn up *en potence*. Many of the second line had blindly followed the first: the rest shunned the action; Hawley's officers led away some regiments in an orderly retreat; night fell; no man knew what had really occurred till young Gask and young Strathallan, with the French and Atholl men, ventured into Falkirk, and found Hawley's camp deserted. The darkness, the rain, the nature of the ground, and the clans' want of discipline, prevented the annihilation of Hawley's army; while the behaviour of his cavalry showed that the Prince might have defeated Cumberland's advanced force beyond Derby with the greatest ease, as the Duke of Richmond had anticipated.

Perhaps the right course now was to advance on Edinburgh, but the hopeless siege of Stirling Castle was continued—Charles perhaps hoping much from Hawley's captured guns.

The accidental shooting of young Æneas Macdonnell, second son of Glengarry, by a Clanranald man, begat a kind of blood feud between the clans, and the unhappy cause of the accident had to be shot. Lochgarry, writing to young Glengarry after Culloden, says that "there was a general desertion in the whole army," and this was the view of the chiefs, who, on news of Cumberland's approach, told Charles (January 29) that the army was depleted and resistance impossible.

The chiefs were mistaken in point of fact: a review at Crieff later showed that even then only 1000 men were missing. As at Derby, and with right on his side, Charles insisted on meeting Cumberland. He did well, his men were flushed with victory, had sufficient supplies, were to encounter an army not yet encouraged by a refusal to face it, and, if defeated had the gates of the hills open behind them. In a very temperately written memorial Charles placed these ideas before the chiefs. "Having told you my thoughts, I am too sensible of what you have already ventured and done for me, not to yield to your unanimous resolution if you persist."

Lord George, Lovat, Lochgarry, Keppoch, Ardshiel, and Cluny did persist; the fatal die was cast; and the men who—well fed and confident—might have routed Cumberland, fled in confusion rather than retreated,—to be ruined later, when, starving, out-wearied, and with many of their best forces absent, they staggered his army at Culloden. Charles had told the chiefs, "I can see nothing but ruin and destruction to us in case we should retreat."[39]

This retreat embittered Charles's feelings against Lord George, who may have been mistaken—who, indeed, at Crieff, seems to have recognised his error (February 5); but he had taken his part, and during the campaign, henceforth, as at Culloden, distinguished himself by every virtue of a soldier.

After the retreat Lord George moved on Aberdeen; Charles to Blair in Atholl; thence to Moy, the house of Lady Mackintosh, where a blacksmith and four or five men ingeniously scattered Loudoun and the Macleods, advancing to take him by a night surprise. This was the famous Rout of Moy.

Charles next (February 20) took Inverness Castle, and Loudoun was driven into Sutherland, and cut off by Lord George's dispositions from any chance of joining hands with Cumberland. The Duke had

---

[39] See the author's 'History of Scotland,' iv. 446-500, where the evidence is examined.

now 5000 Hessian soldiers at his disposal: these he would not have commanded had the Prince's army met him near Stirling.

Charles was now at or near Inverness: he lost, through illness, the services of Murray, whose successor, Hay, was impotent as an officer of Commissariat. A gallant movement of Lord George into Atholl, where he surprised all Cumberland's posts, but was foiled by the resistance of his brother's castle, was interrupted by a recall to the north, and, on April 2, he retreated to the line of the Spey. Forbes of Culloden and Macleod had been driven to take refuge in Skye; but 1500 men of the Prince's best had been sent into Sutherland, when Cumberland arrived at Nairn (April 14), and Charles concentrated his starving forces on Culloden Moor. The Macphersons, the Frazers, the 1500 Macdonalds, and others in Sutherland were absent on various duties when "the wicked day of destiny" approached.

The men on Culloden Moor, a flat waste unsuited to the tactics of the clans, had but one biscuit apiece on the eve of the battle. Lord George "did not like the ground," and proposed to surprise by a night attack Cumberland's force at Nairn. The Prince eagerly agreed, and, according to him, Clanranald's advanced men were in touch with Cumberland's outposts before Lord George convinced the Prince that retreat was necessary. The advance was lagging; the way had been missed in the dark; dawn was at hand. There are other versions: in any case the hungry men were so outworn that many are said to have slept through next day's battle.

A great mistake was made next day, if Lochgarry, who commanded the Macdonalds of Glengarry, and Maxwell of Kirkconnel are correct in saying that Lord George insisted on placing his Atholl men on the right wing. The Macdonalds had an old claim to the right wing, but as far as research enlightens us, their failure on this fatal day was not due to jealous anger. The battle might have been avoided, but to retreat was to lose Inverness and all chance of supplies. On the Highland right was the water of Nairn, and they were guarded by a wall which the Campbells pulled down, enabling Cumberland's cavalry to take them in flank. Cumberland had about 9000 men, including the Campbells. Charles, according to his muster-master, had 5000; of horse he had but a handful.

The battle began with an artillery duel, during which the clans lost heavily, while their few guns were useless, and their right flank was exposed by the breaking down of the protecting wall. After some unexplained and dangerous delay, Lord George gave the word to charge, in face of a blinding tempest of sleet, and himself went in, as did Lochiel, claymore in hand. But though the order was conveyed by Ker of Graden first to the Macdonalds on the left, as they had to charge over a wider space of ground, the Camerons, Clan Chattan, and Macleans came first to the shock. "Nothing could be more desperate than their attack, or more properly received," says Whitefoord. The assailants were enfiladed by Wolfe's regiment, which moved up and took position at right angles, like the fifty-second on the flank of the last charge of the French Guard at Waterloo. The Highland right broke through Barrel's regiment, swept over the guns, and died on the bayonets of the second line. They had thrown down their muskets after one fire, and, says Cumberland, stood "and threw stones for at least a minute or two before their total rout began." Probably the fall of Lochiel, who was wounded and carried out of action, determined the flight. Meanwhile the left, the Macdonalds, menaced on the flank by cavalry, were plied at a hundred yards by grape. They saw their leaders, the gallant Keppoch and Macdonnell of Scothouse, with many others, fall under the grape-shot: they saw the right wing broken, and they did not come to the shock. If we may believe four sworn witnesses in a court of justice (July 24, 1752), whose testimony was accepted as the basis of a judicial decreet (January 10, 1756),[40] Keppoch was wounded while giving his orders to some of his men not to outrun the line in advancing, and was shot dead as a friend was supporting him. When all retreated they passed the dead body of Keppoch.

The tradition constantly given in various forms that Keppoch charged alone, "deserted by the children of his clan," is worthless if sworn evidence may be trusted.

As for the unhappy Charles, by the evidence of Sir Robert Strange, who was with him, he had "ridden along the line to the right animating the soldiers," and "endeavoured to rally the soldiers, who, annoyed by the enemy's fire, were beginning to quit the field." He "was got off the field when the men in general were betaking themselves precipitately to flight; nor was there any possibility of their being rallied." Yorke, an English officer, says that the Prince did not leave the field till after the retreat of the second line.

So far the Prince's conduct was honourable and worthy of his name. But presently, on the advice of his Irish entourage, Sullivan and Sheridan, who always suggested suspicions, and doubtless not forgetting the great price on his head, he took his own way towards

---

[40] 'Register of Decreets,' vol. 482.

the west coast in place of joining Lord George and the remnant with him at Ruthven in Badenoch. On April 26 he sailed from Borradale in a boat, and began that course of wanderings and hairbreadth escapes in which only the loyalty of Highland hearts enabled him at last to escape the ships that watched the isles and the troops that netted the hills.

Some years later General Wolfe, then residing at Inverness, reviewed the occurrences, and made up his mind that the battle had been a dangerous risk for Cumberland, while the pursuit (though ruthlessly cruel) was inefficient.

Despite Cumberland's insistent orders to give no quarter (orders justified by the absolutely false pretext that Prince Charles had set the example), Lochgarry reported that the army had not lost more than a thousand men. Fire and sword and torture, the destruction of tilled lands, and even of the shell-fish on the shore, did not break the spirit of the Highlanders. Many bands held out in arms, and Lochgarry was only prevented by the Prince's command from laying an ambush for Cumberland. The Campbells and the Macleods under their recreant chief, the Whig Macdonalds under Sir Alexander of Sleat, ravaged the lands of the Jacobite clansmen; but the spies of Albemarle, who now commanded in Scotland, reported the Macleans, the Grants of Glenmoriston, with the Macphersons, Glengarry's men, and Lochiel's Camerons, as all eager "to do it again" if France would only help.

But France was helpless, and when Lochiel sailed for France with the Prince only Cluny remained, hunted like a partridge in the mountains, to keep up the spirit of the Cause. Old Lovat met a long-deserved death by the executioner's axe, though it needed the evidence of Murray of Broughton, turned informer, to convict that fox. Kilmarnock and Balmerino also were executed; the good and brave Duke of Perth died on his way to France; the aged Tullibardine in the Tower; many gallant gentlemen were hanged; Lord George escaped, and is the ancestor of the present Duke of Atholl; many gentlemen took French service; others fought in other alien armies; three or four in the Highlands or abroad took the wages of spies upon the Prince. The £30,000 of French gold, buried near Loch Arkaig, caused endless feuds, kinsman denouncing kinsman. The secrets of the years 1746-1760 are to be sought in the Cumberland and Stuart MSS. in Windsor Castle and the Record Office.

Legislation, intended to scotch the snake of Jacobitism, began with religious persecution. The Episcopalian clergy had no reason to love triumphant Presbyterianism, and actively, or in sympathy, were favourers of the exiled dynasty. Episcopalian chapels, sometimes mere rooms in private houses, were burned, or their humble furniture was destroyed. All Episcopalian ministers were bidden to take the oath and pray for King George by September 1746, or suffer for the second offence transportation for life to the American colonies. Later, the orders conferred by Scottish bishops were made of no avail. Only with great difficulty and danger could parents obtain the rite of baptism for their children. Very little is said in our histories about the sufferings of the Episcopalians when it was their turn to be under the harrow. They were not violent, they murdered no Moderator of the General Assembly. Other measures were the Disarming Act, the prohibition to wear the Highland dress, and the abolition of "hereditable jurisdictions," and the chief's right to call out his clansmen in arms. Compensation in money was paid, from £21,000 to the Duke of Argyll to £13, 6s. 8d. to the clerks of the Registrar of Aberbrothock. The whole sum was £152,237, 15s. 4d.

In 1754 an Act "annexed the forfeited estates of the Jacobites who had been out (or many of them) inalienably to the Crown." The estates were restored in 1784; meanwhile the profits were to be used for the improvement of the Highlands. If submissive tenants received better terms and larger leases than of old, Jacobite tenants were evicted for not being punctual with rent. Therefore, on May 14, 1752, some person unknown shot Campbell of Glenure, who was about evicting the tenants on the lands of Lochiel and Stewart of Ardshiel in Appin. Campbell rode down from Fort William to Ballachulish ferry, and when he had crossed it said, "I am safe now I am out of my mother's country." But as he drove along the old road through the wood of Lettermore, perhaps a mile and a half south of Ballachulish House, the fatal shot was fired. For this crime James Stewart of the Glens was tried by a Campbell jury at Inveraray, with the Duke on the bench, and was, of course, convicted, and hanged on the top of a knoll above Ballachulish ferry. James was innocent, but Allan Breck Stewart was certainly an accomplice of the man with the gun, which, by the way, was the property neither of James Stewart nor of Stewart of Fasnacloich. The murderer was anxious to save James by avowing the deed, but his kinsfolk, saying, "They will only hang both James and you," bound him hand and foot and locked him up in the kitchen on the day of James's execution.[41] Allan lay for some weeks at the house of a kinsman in Rannoch, and escaped to France, where he had a fight

---

[41] Tradition in Glencoe.

with James Mor Macgregor, then a spy in the service of the Duke of Newcastle.

This murder of "the Red Fox" caused all the more excitement, and is all the better remembered in Lochaber and Glencoe, because agrarian violence in revenge for eviction has scarcely another example in the history of the Highlands.

# Conclusion

Space does not permit an account of the assimilation of Scotland to England in the years between the Forty-five and our own time: moreover, the history of this age cannot well be written without a dangerously close approach to many "burning questions" of our day. The History of the Highlands, from 1752 to the emigrations witnessed by Dr Johnson (1760-1780), and of the later evictions in the interests of sheep farms and deer forests, has never been studied as it ought to be in the rich manuscript materials which are easily accessible. The great literary Renaissance of Scotland, from 1745 to the death of Sir Walter Scott; the years of Hume, a pioneer in philosophy and in history, and of the Rev. Principal Robertson (with him and Hume, Gibbon professed, very modestly, that he did not rank); the times of Adam Smith, of Burns, and of Sir Walter, not to speak of the Rev. John Home, that foremost tragic poet, may be studied in many a history of literature. According to Voltaire, Scotland led the world in all studies, from metaphysics to gardening. We think of Watt, and add engineering.

The brief and inglorious administration of the Earl of Bute at once gave openings in the public service to Scots of ability, and excited that English hatred of these northern rivals which glows in Churchill's 'Satires,' while this English jealousy aroused that Scottish hatred of England which is the one passion that disturbs the placid letters of David Hume.

The later alliance of Pitt with Henry Dundas made Dundas far more powerful than any Secretary for Scotland had been since Lauderdale, and confirmed the connection of Scotland with the services in India. But, politically, Scotland, till the Reform Bill, had scarcely a recognisable existence. The electorate was tiny, and great landholders controlled the votes, whether genuine or created by legal fiction—"faggot votes." Municipal administration in the late eighteenth and early nineteenth centuries was terribly corrupt, and reform was demanded, but the French Revolution, producing associations of Friends of the People, who were prosecuted and grievously punished in trials for sedition, did not afford a fortunate moment for peaceful reforms.

But early in the nineteenth century Jeffrey, editor of 'The Edinburgh Review,' made it the organ of Liberalism, and no less potent in England than in Scotland; while Scott, on the Tory side, led a following of Scottish penmen across the Border in the service of 'The Quarterly Review.' With 'Blackwood's Magazine' and Wilson, Hogg, and Lockhart; with Jeffrey and 'The Edinburgh,' the Scottish metropolis almost rivalled London as the literary capital.

About 1818 Lockhart recognised the superiority of the Whig wits in literature; but against them all Scott is a more than sufficient set-off. The years of stress between Waterloo (1815) and the Reform Bill (1832) made Radicalism (fostered by economic causes, the enormous commercial and industrial growth, and the unequal distribution of its rewards) perhaps even more pronounced north than south of the Tweed. In 1820 "the Radical war" led to actual encounters between the yeomanry and the people. The ruffianism of the Tory paper 'The Beacon' caused one fatal duel, and was within an inch of leading to another, in which a person of the very highest consequence would have "gone on the sod." For the Reform Bill the mass of Scottish opinion, so long not really represented at all, was as eager as for the Covenant. So triumphant was the first Whig or Radical majority under the new system, that Jeffrey, the Whig pontiff, perceived that the real struggle was to be "between property and no property," between Capital and Socialism. This circumstance had always been perfectly clear to Scott and the Tories.

The watchword of the eighteenth century in literature, religion, and politics had been "no enthusiasm." But throughout the century, since 1740, "enthusiasm," "the return to nature," had gradually conquered till the rise of the Romantic school with Coleridge and Scott. In religion the enthusiastic movement of the Wesleys had altered the face of the Church in England, while in Scotland the "Moderates" had lost position, and "zeal" or enthusiasm pervaded the Kirk. The question of lay patronage of livings had passed through many phases since Knox wrote, "It pertaineth to the people, and to every several congregation, to elect their minister." In 1833, immediately after the passing of the Reform Bill, the return to the primitive Knoxian rule was advocated by the "Evangelical" or "High Flying" opponents of the Moderates. Dr Chalmers, a most eloquent person, whom Scott regarded as truly a man of genius, was the leader of the movement. The Veto Act, by which the votes of a majority of heads of families were to be fatal to the claims of a patron's presentee, had been passed by the General Assembly; it was contrary to Queen Anne's Patronage Act of 1711,—a measure carried, contrary to Harley's policy, by a coalition of English Churchmen and Scottish Jacobite members of Parliament. The rejection, under the Veto Act, of a presentee by the church of Auchterarder, was declared illegal by the Court of Session and the judges in the House of Lords (May 1839); the Strathbogie imbroglio, "with two Presbyteries, one taking its orders from the Court of Session, the other from the General Assembly" (1837-1841), brought the Assembly into direct conflict with the law of the land. Dr Chalmers would not allow the spiritual claims of the Kirk to be suppressed by the State. "King Christ's Crown Honours" were once more in question. On May 18, 1843, the followers of the principles of Knox and Andrew Melville marched out of the Assembly into Tanfield Hall, and made Dr Chalmers Moderator, and themselves "The Free Church of Scotland." In 1847 the hitherto separated synods of various dissenting bodies came together as United Presbyterians, and in 1902 they united with the Free Church as "the United Free Church," while a small minority, mainly Highland, of the former Free Church, now retains that title, and apparently represents Knoxian ideals. Thus the Knoxian ideals have modified, even to this day, the ecclesiastical life of Scotland, while the Church of James I, never by persecution extinguished (*nec tamen consumebatur*), has continued to exist and develop, perhaps more in consequence of love of the Liturgy than from any other cause.

Meanwhile, and not least in the United Free Church, extreme tenacity of dogma has yielded place to very advanced Biblical criticism; and Knox, could he revisit Scotland with all his old opinions, might not be wholly satisfied by the changes wrought in the course of more than three centuries. The Scottish universities, discouraged and almost destitute of pious benefactors since the end of the sixteenth century, have profited by the increase of wealth and a comparatively recent outburst of generosity. They always provided the cheapest, and now they provide the cheapest and most efficient education that is offered by any homes of learning of mediæval foundation.

CPSIA information can be obtained at www.ICGtesting.com
Printed in the USA
BVOW05s0929300914

368886BV00001B/213/P